In the eyes of the English Ro
but Italia, a place inhabited b
shaped by the eighteenth century, the age of
The people of Italy, divided by language, region, and culture, did
not share these artistic and historical ideals of Italia. After the
Napoleonic wars, however, all this was to change. Nationalism
began to replace local loyalties and the land 'where the lemon
trees blow' now attracted tourists, not just Grand Tourists.

What had seemed to Grand Tourists a museum of idealised
antiquity and Renaissance art became in the eyes of Byron,
Keats and Shelley and a host of other visitors a nation struggling
to assert itself but not quite able to do so. *Italia Romantica* is
a vivid history of the English Romantics' love affair with Italy
and of the changing attitudes in pre-unification Italy. Roderick
Cavaliero's compelling story is full of bandits, unreformed
Catholicism, poets and *improvvisatori,* shot through with
vignettes of timeless urban and pastoral life, remarkable
characters and anecdote.

Roderick Cavaliero is a writer and historian, author of *Admiral
Satan, Independence of Brazil, Strangers in the Land* and *The
Last of the Crusaders* (all I.B.Tauris).

Tauris Parke Paperbacks is an imprint of I.B.Tauris. It is dedicated to publishing books in accessible paperback editions for the serious general reader within a wide range of categories, including biography, history, travel and the ancient world. The list includes select, critically acclaimed works of top quality writing by distinguished authors that continue to challenge, to inform and to inspire. These are books that possess those subtle but intrinsic elements that mark them out as something exceptional.

The Colophon of Tauris Parke Paperbacks is a representation of the ancient Egyptian ibis, sacred to the god Thoth, who was himself often depicted in the form of this most elegant of birds. Thoth was credited in antiquity as the scribe of the ancient Egyptian gods and as the inventor of writing and was associated with many aspects of wisdom and learning.

ITALIA ROMANTICA

English Romantics and Italian Freedom

Roderick Cavaliero

TPP

TAURIS PARKE
PAPERBACKS

Published in 2007 by Tauris Parke Paperbacks
an imprint of I.B.Tauris and Co Ltd
6 Salem Road, London W2 4BU
175 Fifth Avenue, New York NY 10010
www.ibtauris.com

First published in hardback in 2005 by I.B.Tauris & Co Ltd
Copyright © 2005, Roderick Cavaliero

Cover image: *A Capriccio View of the Bay of Naples with Mount Vesuvius Erupting Behind* by Charles François Lacroix, 1777 © Christie's Images/CORBIS

ISBN: 978 1 84511 456 5

A full CIP record for this book is available from the British Library

Printed and bound in India by Replika Press Pvt. Ltd

To Sheba, Catherine and Harriet
Keepers of the Flame

CONTENTS

LIST OF ILLUSTRATIONS

�֍

PREFACE

This book started when, in retirement, I was persuaded to take over the management committee of the British School at Rome, and the financial affairs of the house in which John Keats died, in the same city. Management plans and budgets being poor fare for the imagination, I began to use the superlative resources of both institutions to explore the attitudes that the younger generation of British Romantic poets took towards Italy, and how these were reflected in the notions of other writers and through them of politicians. As soon as the Napoleonic wars were over Italy was open again for visits, but it was still the Italy of the Grand Tour, of ancient sites, monuments, paintings and sculptures. But into this vista the Italians themselves were beginning to push, hoping to further the unfinished liberalisation of Napoleon to the point that *Italia*, the land of ancient Rome and of the Renaissance, would become Italy, a free nation. Everyone who came to Italy agreed that it should, but did not think it ever would, until it produced a new race of heroes. Suddenly it did, and poetic despair started to turn to hope.

Some of the material has already appeared in published form in the *Keats–Shelley Review* and in the *Journal of Anglo-Italian Studies*. I am grateful to Professor Peter Vassallo, Director of the Institute of Anglo-Italian Studies at the University of Malta, Professors Richard Hodges and Andrew Wallace-Hadrill, successively directors of the British School at Rome, for academic and personal hospitality, to Mrs Sheba Abse Morabito and Miss Catherine Payling, successively curators of the Keats–Shelley Memorial House in Rome, for making the resources of its library available to me. My cousin, Dr Glen Cavaliero, made many suggestions to improve the text and helped me to avoid some crass errors. My wife, Mary, has supported my absence from the kitchen while writing it, with true Roman stoicism. My daughter, Louisa, put the illustrations onto a CD, which skill was beyond my capacity, and Jessica Cuthbert-Smith's editing was tactful, improving and thorough. To these, and to an unexpected legacy from my oldest friend, James Bazell, which helped to make this book possible, I am just amazedly grateful.

Roderick Cavaliero
Tunbridge Wells, 2004

INTRODUCTION

'The Land of Departed Fame'

Land of departed fame! whose classic plains
Have proudly echoed to immortal strains;
Whose hallow'd soil hath given the great and brave,
Daystars of life, a birth-place and a grave;
Home of the Arts! where glory's faded smile
Sheds lingering light o'er many a mouldering pile;
Proud wreck of vanish'd power, of splendour fled,
Majestic temple of the mighty dead!
Whose grandeur, yet contending with decay,
Gleams through the twilight of thy glorious day:
Though dimm'd thy brightness, riveted thy chain,
Yet, fallen Italy! rejoice again!
Lost, lovely realm! once more 'tis thine to gaze
On the rich relics of sublimer days.

Felicia Hemans, 'The Restoration of the Works of Art to Italy',
stanza 1.

And who are they that sing these strains
    That erst Torquato sang?
A race of slaves in all, save chains
    Not yet around them flung.
Degenerate children of the brave
    The virtuous and the free,
Too feeble now their land to save
    Too vicious and too cowardly ...

A poem in the *Dublin University Magazine* (1835).

In Italy is she really? with the grapes and figs growing everywhere
and lava necklaces and bracelets too that land of poetry with
burning mountains picturesque beyond belief ...

Flora Finching in Charles Dickens, *Little Dorrit*,
Book the Second, chapter ix.

At the dawn of the nineteenth century, Italy had been for 200 years the universal art gallery, *wunderkammer*, museum, classroom and repository of Europe's heritage. Scholars, statesmen, scientists, men and women of letters paid her the tribute of imitation, doing obeisance to her sacred sites and to the illustrious citizens of her glorious past. But of Italy as a nation there was no recognition. *Italia* remained a peninsula, recognised as a hearthland of civilisation, breeding ground of heroes, torch bearer of a new world religion and cradle of democracy. But for those two centuries, her political influence had almost vanished. Her states were tributaries to or allies of neighbouring world powers, playing for their survival in the territorial ambitions of Habsburg and Bourbon.

At this game they played well. From the middle of the sixteenth century, the peninsula enjoyed a prolonged period of peace and relative prosperity not enjoyed by the rest of Europe. It managed to keep out of the wars that convulsed lands north of the Alps, especially the Thirty Years War, and avoided being a tramping ground for foreign armies. Its states looked outwards to the perpetual war with Islam, fought by the republics of the Adriatic, by the Spanish overlords of Naples and Sicily, and by Tuscany and the papacy. Only towards the end of the seventeenth century was this era of peace disturbed, when Franco-Dutch-British naval rivalry extended into the Mediterranean and an international coalition was forged to prevent a union of the French and Spanish crowns. Two Italian kingdoms, Naples and Sardinia, came into existence. For his support to the cause of the Holy Roman Empire in the War of the Spanish Succession, the Duke of Savoy had, at the peace, been given Sicily to rule, but its Spanish sympathies being too strong and truculent, it was exchanged for Sardinia. The great powers in 1734 created a joint kingdom of Naples with Sicily and conferred it on Charles, the son of Philip V of Spain by his second marriage to Elizabeth Farnese; he was not expected to succeed to the Spanish throne. When in 1759, against all expectations, Charles IV of Naples became Charles III of Spain, rule of Naples and Sicily passed to his third son, Ferdinand I. Meanwhile, the King of Sardinia kept his court at Turin, not at Cagliari, and retained this title until 1861, when he exchanged it for that of Italy. The Kingdom of Naples, later of The Two Sicilies, kept its own Hispano-Italian dynasty, until overrun by that new kingdom in 1860.

In the north, the republics of Genoa and Venice clung to their ancient patrimony, shorn of nearly all their overseas possessions by the Turks, and the Milanese was an Austrian satrapy. The last Medici ruler of Tuscany dying childless in 1737, the grand duchy was assigned at the Treaty of Vienna to the husband of the Empress Maria Theresa. Their two children, the future emperors Leopold II (Grand Duke 1765–90, Emperor 1790–2) and Francis II (Grand Duke 1790–2, Emperor 1792–1835) ruled in Florence until summoned to the imperial throne by death. During the Napoleonic occupation of Italy, Elise Bonaparte ruled Tuscany with her husband as grand duke, but after the war the Habsburgs restored an Austrian archduke, Ferdinand III, Leopold's younger son. The Austrian archdukes were enlightened despots and ruled Tuscany with a liberality atypical of Austria's other allies. Even Shelley acknowledged that Florentines lived under only a nominal tyranny, administered according to the philosophic laws of Leopold.[1] The Papal State was still what Pope Julius II had carved out of Renaissance Italy: an oasis of relative calm under the rule of benign popes, not the least among the children of the Enlightenment, spared religious strife and political angst by charitable works and a blind eye to opinions not too fiercely held.[2]

From 1796 to 1815 the Italian peninsula was a battlefield for two European powers. As General Bonaparte, Napoleon broke the Austrian hold on Milan, traded the Venetian Republic to the Austrians in exchange, stripped the pope of his temporal domains, declared Genoa and Piedmont a Ligurian republic and himself President of the Republic of Italy. To complete the conquest of Italy by the new Rome, the French eagles chased King Ferdinand out of Naples to Sicily and, with the death of the French Republic, Napoleon made himself King of Italy and his brother Joseph King of Naples. Then, when he needed a king for Spain, he replaced Joseph with his brother-in-law, Joachim Murat and installed Joseph on the Spanish throne. Then in 1811, to establish his dynastic claim to Italy, he made his newborn half-Austrian son King of Rome. A Kingdom of Italy implied that there was an Italy of which to be king, but it only constituted the land between the Alps and the Volturno. Even under the Napoleonic dispensation there were to be two sovereign states, north and south, under Bonaparte dynasts. After his fall, the Holy Alliance restored *Italia* to her patchwork of *signorie* and determined to keep it that way. 'Italy from the Alps to the ocean', wrote Charlotte Eaton in 1820 with disgust, 'will once more be overrun by the Goth and sink under a tyranny the most galling and unenlightened that has disgraced modern times'.[3]

Italy and Italians could not help but be stirred by the infectious republicanism of revolutionary France. Milan welcomed her as the liberator when French troops first entered the city in 1796, and believed the Napoleonic rhetoric about freedom and liberty. Enthusiasm soon evaporated when Italy began to realise what French rule really meant. The rapacious spoliation of her treasures; the ruthless commandeering of supplies; high taxation; the cruel enlistment of her sons into armies to fight in central Europe, England (if they could ever get there), Spain and Russia; and the overthrow of their comfortable religion for mayfests and liberty caps, all depressed and ultimately suppressed popular aspirations for a free and sovereign Italy. With the end of the war, the old order was restored with almost grateful acquiescence. The Austrians returned to Milan and Ferdinand to Naples, having like a true Bourbon learned and forgotten nothing from his sojourn in Palermo. Napoleon's Austrian ex-empress ruled a pocket duchy in Parma, her brother ruled in Tuscany and Genoa was forced to return not to its old oligarchic style but to submit to Turin, where King Victor Emmanuel I of Sardinia ruled over great chunks of French Savoy, stretching as far as Nice, and over all Piedmont. To the disgust of its inhabitants the ancient and now extinct republic was handed over to a monarch whose prescription for his dominions was to restore everything to what it had been before the French invasion, to a rule so reactionary that it discouraged vaccination against smallpox on the grounds that it rendered the recipients languid. Unable to bear the fatigue of staying up late for entertainment, they went to bed early, a revolutionary habit![4] Italy was restored to its status as a geographical expression, an expression not actually coined until Metternich used it in a conversation with Lord Palmerston in 1847, a year before Europe was convulsed by nationalist insurrection.[5] But he was only expressing what had been fact for centuries.

During the war Great Britain had been obliged to play a major role in the Mediterranean. At a time when Europe was largely closed to British textiles, Italy provided a permeable market so that, by a curious irony, the Protestant nation found herself the (ineffective) partisan of the pope, whose refusal to confiscate British merchandise led to his dethronement by Bonaparte. British anxiety over India, twice apparently threatened by Napoleon – first when he took an army to Egypt, and secondly after Tilsit, when he sought to persuade Tsar Alexander to extend his Asian frontier to the Indian Ocean – dictated the retention of the Roman Catholic island of

Malta, whose citizens offered themselves to the British Empire. During the war, British troops had been garrisoned in Corsica, Sardinia and Sicily, and until the invasion of Spain and Portugal these were the only points from which they could prick the hide of the otherwise impregnable emperor, collaborating with Italian partisans (whom the French deemed bandits). Theirs was a new species of Italian bravado, thought to have died out with the extinction of the Renaissance *condottieri* by France and Spain.

Against advice, Lord William Bentinck, who was British commander-in-chief in Sicily, and thus, in effect, the uncrowned ruler of the island, had proposed in 1812 a constitution for Sicily. This had been taken as a hint that British policy after the war would be to offer constitutions to other states of Italy that had hitherto been despotisms, but when Bonaparte was finally consigned to St Helena, the Tory government in power proved to have other priorities. The need for stability in Europe, dictated by Wellington's anxieties over India, suggested support for the Holy Alliance, brokered by the Tsar of Russia with Metternich's enthusiastic support and that of the restored French Bourbons, who wished to be re-admitted to the councils of Europe. Britain thus forswore Bentinck's rhetoric, and those Frenchified Italians who had imbibed some of the principles of the French Revolution during the occupation went underground.

The war had denied mainland Italy to all those who believed, with Dr Johnson, that 'a man who has not been in Italy is always conscious of an inferiority'.[6] Access to her islands had been no compensation. Now the country was open to first-hand inspection of the effects of over 20 years of war. For most visitors, it was business as before. For those who had been reared on a vision of Italy that they were now actually seeing for the first time, there were no regrets about the passing of French rule. Most of the art treasures removed to Paris had been returned to their former owners. The restoration of rulers under the protection of Austria was generally accepted as being the best political solution for Italy, as there was no confidence that the Italians could be trusted with their own destiny. Only a few liberal voices in Britain's Parliament were raised against the government's uncritical support for Austria. For Wordsworth, who had in 1811 expostulated against the extinction of the Venetian Republic, Austria was a vile tyrant. He believed that if the constituent parts of Italy had only united, the French could have been driven out.[7] Instead, one tyrant had been replaced by another, and the extreme oppression of Austrian rule began to persuade other Britons that 'the former lords of humankind' could not have fallen so low as to deserve it.[8] Even the Tory government in London wished that the Austrians could be persuaded to rule less provocatively, while liberal sentiment, fired up by British poets led by Byron, protested that this treatment was both inhumane and unjust. Unhappily, failed revolutions and the cloak-and-dagger reputation of Carbonarism only succeeded in alienating that sympathy, so that people began to judge that the Italians were born losers. Their past was too daunting for them to live up to.[9]

Yet, within 60 years, the Metternichian system had crumbled, the kings of Sardinia and Naples were one with Nineveh and Tyre, the pope was a prisoner in the Vatican, and a King of Italy ruled from Rome over a unified state for the first time since the Antonines. The result was not solely due to Italy's own efforts, but the events were glorious enough to give Italians pride of nation and hopes of greatness. Italian unity was assisted by at least five powerful external factors: first there was the contrariness of an English parliament bent on suppression at home but liberalism abroad, which allowed Mazzini to propagandise tirelessly for the freedom of Italy from the safety of the British Isles. Second was the canny decision of Sardinia's prime minister to engage in a distant war in the Crimea and thus gain international credit from an Anglo-French alliance. Then there was Louis Napoleon's Bonapartist dream that sent French troops to slaughter Austrian on the fields of the Po valley in order to stop Mazzinian patriots from trying to assassinate emperors. A fourth factor was the studied neutrality of the British Mediterranean fleet, which looked the other way when 1,000 red-shirts under Garibaldi left Genoa; and fifth there was the cynical generosity of Bismarck in forcing the defeated Austrians to hand over Venice after the Seven Weeks War. The matter of Italy, moreover, had not left British statesmen indifferent. They had all had a classical education and two prime ministers, Benjamin Disraeli and William Ewart Gladstone, had studied Italian and Italy, while Lord John Russell and Lord Palmerston (who with Gladstone constituted 'the Italian Triumvirate') had visited Italy as young men on the Grand Tour.[10] Disraeli was the author of two Byronic Italian novels,[11] Gladstone denounced to the world the abuse of human rights in Neapolitan prisons, and both Russell and Palmerston saw a free Italy as a useful ally against both a prepotent Austria and a revived, Bonapartist France.

The entry of Italy into the political as well as the cultural bloodstream of England was eased in an unexpected way. If ever a country was to be liberated by poetry, Italy had that distinction. Alessandro Manzoni proclaimed that the mission of poetry was to prepare for the moral resurrection of a people, a sentiment he would have shared with Percy Bysshe Shelley.[12] The first generation of British Romantic poets, however – influenced by the post-Enlightenment pantheism of nature and by German illuminism – had turned to pedestrianism in the mountains, lakes, fells and valleys of pre-industrial Europe, wrapping themselves in a post-Christian gloom and mystery engendered by the storms and mists of high mountains, perched above the rococo wickedness, effeminacy and corruption of the cities of the plain. And the centres of Italian civilisation were in that plain. Napoleon's lightning campaigns in Italy, promising liberation from régimes based on inheritance, privilege and obscurantism, then brought the peninsula back into public interest, sharpened by the spice of being denied to visitors. The Mediterranean and Italian world was stirring: Greece was crying out against Turkish oppression, Spain was rising for liberty – the 'glorious events' that inspired Shelley's 'Ode to Liberty' took place in Madrid on 1 January 1820[13] – and Portugal was defying the greatest power in Europe by calling in a new world in Brazil to redress the balance of the old. Why should not the greatness that was Rome be revived in a united Italy? Her plight cried out to Britain's younger poets as they contemplated a world in revolutionary flux, and frightened a generation trying to turn the clock back to before 1789. Italy promised to be the laboratory of a new Europe. In 1804, Coleridge, acting as secretary to the British governor of Malta, travelled from Sicily to Rome, to be nearly arrested by the French as a spy. Ten years later, in 1814, Samuel Rogers tried to be the first to reach Italy after the war, only for Napoleon's flight from Elba to send all the tourists scuttling home; by 1817 Byron had settled in Venice, where he wrote Canto IV of *Childe Harold* and finished *Manfred*; in 1818 Percy Bysshe and Mary Shelley followed him to Italy. In 1821 John Keats died in Rome and, the following year, Shelley was drowned off the Tuscan coast, having sailed to Leghorn to welcome Leigh Hunt and his family to Italy, whither Hunt had come to edit an independent political and literary journal under Byron's patronage. In 1832 Disraeli produced *Contarini Fleming*, after a lightning tour of Europe. Even first generation Romantics like Walter Scott and William Wordsworth struggled in their old age to pay the statutory pilgrimage to a now stirring nation. But both Byron, who played a minor role in that stirring, and Shelley, who confined himself to hailing it, confessed to disappointment at what it achieved.

Somehow, whether it was the fragmentation of the country – but it had been fragmented since the fall of the Roman Empire – or the decadence of a people exposed for too long to autocratic regimes and intellectual tyranny – when had they not been? – the Italians seemed unable either to re-enact their past or to seize the promise of their future. For Shelley, Italy was an object lesson of what happened when a people accepted anything less than liberty. Her great achievements had been inspired by a strong spirit of liberty. Her decline followed when that spirit weakened. Let Britain beware! and learn the lesson from Italy, a 'lost Paradise of this divine and glorious world', a 'shrine / Where desolation, clothed with loveliness, / Worships the thing thou wert!' where 'beasts ... make their dens thy sacred palaces'.[14] When in 1848–9, Romantic heroes, worthy of the pen of Felicia Hemans (d. 1835), appeared at the defence of the Roman and Venetian republics by Giuseppe Garibaldi and Daniele Manin, both unsuccessfully, they quickly became the stuff of legend. England was ready to applaud.

Byron, once settled in Italy, abandoned the Romantic gloom of his 'heroic' poems for the sunlit wit and fantasy of his new masters, the Italian epic poets, and indulged his appetites in the more sexually liberal society of his adopted country. He also went in for a little *carbonarismo*, filling the lower apartment of his house with their 'bayonets, fusils, cartridges and what not'.[15] If that meant he was to be sacrificed as expendable, well, then, it would be for 'a grand object – the very *poetry of politics*. Only think – a free Italy!!!'[16] But it is doubtful whether he thought such a consummation was likely within his own expected three score years and ten. The cause was all, and worth fighting for, even if in vain.

> When a man hath no freedom to fight for at home,
> Let him combat for that of his neighbours;
> Let him think of the glories of Greece and of Rome,
> And get knocked on the head for his labours.[17]

But he was living in an Italy not actually fighting to be free, only talking about it. The failure of the Neapolitan revolution of 1821 and the impotent posturing of his *carbonaro* friends led to his defection to Greece, and another, perhaps more promising, fight for freedom.

Shelley, revelling in his freedom to write subversive and 'liberating' poetry in a land that was not capable of reading it, dived into Homer, Calderon, Aeschylus, Dante and Petrarch. Converted into Mediterranean man, he claimed the year before he died that 'We are all Greeks'.[18] Before he set foot in the Mediterranean, John Keats had plundered Greek myths and quarried Italian writers for poetic subjects. The shadowy hero Ossian, Scott's highland chiefs and Wordsworth's Lakeland peasants were threatened with displacement by the voices of a sun-washed, lively and oppressed people, crying to be heard.[19]

The conversion was not instant. The Gothic novelists had left a dark image of Italy that was never to be completely dispelled. Niccolò Machiavelli, Old Nick, had provided several good reasons for using a long spoon when supping with his pupils. And how could one tolerate a church that offered sanctuary for murderers, or respect convents that were prisons, Jesuits who were plotters, religious orders which were both mendicant and mendacious? The dexterous use of the stiletto (the weapon of the poor denied more gentlemanly weapons) suggested habits of treachery. Endemic banditry, the last refuge of poor peasants denied land, argued a breakdown of order, while the capacity of ordinary people to make the best of bad times indicated poverty of spirit. *Carbonarismo*, or networking secret societies, was a nursery for terrorism. Poor Italy was in the wrong on nearly every count. But Italians had once been great. If only they could recapture their past, might that greatness not return? To many Britons in the early years of the nineteenth century it seemed unlikely. Italy was, as a country, fatally flawed.

The term Romantic has become over time heavily endowed with definition, both cultural and semiotic. I use it as a chronological label, as defined at the time. The Classicists took their subjects from ancient Greece and Rome.

Romance arguments may be therefore taken from feudality, the chivalry of the Normans, the Crusades and religious wars, the atrocious punishments of the Inquisition, the nautical discoveries, the wars of the Portuguese, English and Dutch in the East, the conquest of America, the circumnavigation of the globe, the manners of the Native Indians, Negro slavery and that of the Europeans on the Barbary coast, the ecclesiastical governments of Rome and of Mecca, the transient civilisation under the Caliphs, the wars of the Turks, the commercial industry of the Italians etc. etc.[20]

A harmless half-hour's fun can be had matching a Romantic work to each of these subjects.

Italy, moreover, had become picturesque, as Flora Finching knew though she had never been there. It was no longer just a land of ancient memories, dusty sites and ruined buildings. Its religion was revealed as more than just a parody of solid Christianity, but as something almost inspirational, even if erroneous, and certainly 'picturesque'. It was, moreover, a suitable place for women to visit and, to their surprise, English women visitors found that their own sex was, in Italy, in many ways more liberated than at home. Italy inspired them with more romantic sentiments than it did their men, and women were to become some of the stoutest supporters of liberty and unification. But none so much as the Romantic poets, by virtue of their identification with liberty, exiles sometimes in their own lands, more often in that of others. Byron, Shelley, Leigh Hunt, Alfieri, Foscolo, William Rossetti almost exchanged habitats, while Leopardi and Keats laboured in the silence of the ignored.

This book attempts to chart the vision of Italy as it was developed by the second generation English Romantic poets, influenced as they were by the malign influence of the Gothic novelists. It examines the influence of Italian writers in new English translations at the end of the eighteenth and beginning of the nineteenth centuries, especially on Byron, perhaps the most influential authority on Italy in his day. It traces the awakening of a new historical awareness of an Italy apart from Rome and the Renaissance and the new use to which classical lore was put by poets as similar and yet so different as Keats and Leopardi. It examines the influence of new tourists, especially women, of landscape painting, of interests other than antiquarianism, it discusses social phenomena that influenced opinion, like lawlessness and the Roman Catholic Church. England greeted the Risorgimento with disbelief, given the poor opinion with which so many of her tourists returned from Italy, but with a sympathy born of the better knowledge of her situation that these same tourists had provided. Italy's transformation from geographical expression to nation and acceptance in her new role as a European power was certainly helped by this long process of familiarisation. Let Keats's short and fatal exile to Rome raise our curtain.

1

'This Wilderness of a Place for an Invalid'
Rome During the Exile of John Keats

It is impossible to live in a country which is continually under hatches. – Who would live in the region of Mists, Game Laws, Indemnity Bills etc., when there is such a place as Italy.

John Keats, to John Hamilton Reynolds,
Teignmouth, 10 April 1818.[1]

Dr Clark ... although there is no bounds to his attention, yet with little success 'can he administer to a mind diseased'. Yet all that can be done he does, while his Lady, like himself in refined feeling, prepares all that poor Keats takes, for in this wilderness of a place (for an invalid) there is no alternative.

Joseph Severn, 17 December 1820.

Go thou to Rome, – at once the Paradise
The grave, the city, and the wilderness;
And where its wrecks like shattered mountains rise,
And flowering weeds, and fragrant copses dress
The bones of Desolation's nakedness ...

Percy Bysshe Shelley, *Adonais,* stanza xlix.

John Keats and Joseph Severn entered Rome by the Lateran Gate on 15 November 1820, and within a few minutes had arrived at the Colosseum, a tumble-down ruin, covered in trees and creepers, open to all and sundry, a precious nature reserve in which, in 1855, a botanist recorded 420 different species.[2] Joseph Severn was later to risk his neck climbing the crumbling walls to pick a wallflower for Keats to enjoy the scent, and to exclaim that his eye was 'doubly charmed with the grandeur of antiquity and the freshness of nature exulting over it'.[3] The French, during their occupation of Rome in 1812, had tried to clean up the Colosseum inside, removing much of the shrubbery and general clutter but, by 1816, most of it had returned. Stendhal once observed an Englishman ride casually the length of the arena, watch the workmen engaged on desultory restoration, and then ride out again marvelling at the stupendous building they were constructing![4] Romans treated it with scant respect, but to travellers it was perhaps the one building that still gave an impression of Rome's mighty past:

> Arches on arches, as it were that Rome,
> Collecting the chief trophies of her line,
> Would build up all her triumph in one dome ...[5]

It was colossal, but the name, though descriptive (and applied later to theatres and cinemas which prided themselves on their size), did not belong to it. It referred to the colossal statue of Nero in bronze, topped by gold, which had once stood at the entrance to his equally colossal Golden House nearby. It should properly have been called the Amphitheatrum Flavium, as it was started by Vespasian and dedicated by Titus in AD 80. It had a sinister reputation after dark, being the haunt of footpads and beggars and a natural cauldron of the *mal aria*. Two Benedictine hermits kept vigil within the stadium at night, too poor to be of any interest to any lurking bandit. In 1819, Catherine Hinde and her party were truly alarmed when they thought they were about to be attacked by ruffians, when the two holy men appeared in order to accompany them safely out of the ruin.[6]

The two travellers, Keats and Severn, were coming north from Naples and the Lateran Gate was not the usual entry for foreigners into Rome. That was the Porta del Popolo on the far side of the city, where the Via Cassia brought travellers from Florence and the north. Here they could find lodgings or a hotel easily enough. All along the Via Babuino, with its tiny *vicoli*, were what we would now call self-catering apartments for foreigners and, in the Piazza di Spagna, they could park their great, high-sided travelling carriages. Lodging houses indicated by their names which clientele they favoured, so that most of them had their signs up in English or in French. There 'the *piano superiore* (which in England would be an inferior attic), [would be] stuffed with half a dozen children, and as many English nursery maids, tutors and governesses.'[7] The Piazza del Popolo was always busy. Most of the city's beggars congregated there in day-time, hoping for bounty from English milords for, no matter how modest their means, all English travellers to Rome, even Keats and Severn, were accounted rich. Would-be servants clambered onto the running-boards of newly arriving carriages, fighting for the attention of their passengers, hoping to be taken on. There was always someone offering a service in return for a tiny coin; everything and everyone could be hired in the piazza.[8] By night it was the principal haunt of the *donne curiali*, all displaying their special licences from the cardinal vicar, while in one of the nearby streets was the famous brothel that, when it was managed by the sisters Casenove, had been James Boswell's favourite haunt. The daughters of joy got their name from their licences, issued by the Curia. Prostitution was a recognised evil in papal Rome, and the tax that the 'curial ladies' paid was used for public works and the embellishment of the city.[9]

Being the tourist heart of Rome, the Piazza di Spagna was rather more select. Its elegant steps, dropping down from the Church of Santa Trinità dei Monti, like a cataract in stone contained by elegantly curving balustrades, delivered one to the bowl of the *barcaccia* fountain of Bernini *père*; a torrent of people flowed up and down the steps while men, women and children from the Abruzzi lounged in their colourful local dress, hoping to be hired as models for the innumerable amateur artists. In 1844 they were still there: the venerable and patriarchal model, the *dolce far niente* model, the assassin model, the haughty or scornful model along with Domestic Happiness and Holy Family groups, their faces all familiar from the walls of countless exhibition galleries.[10] The shops and *trattorie* in the piazza could provide all household services more cheaply than one could do them oneself. Strangers living in lodgings often had their meals sent in from one of the *trattorie* in the piazza. They usually consisted of one main dish, in a basket with a stove or heater to keep it warm, and it would be hauled up into the room. Meals were not cheap, costing as much as ten pauls or five shillings, and the cooks thought the English would eat anything. Only when Keats threw his dinner into the square did the service improve.[11] Anna Angeletti, aged 43 and recently widowed, had come from Venice with her daughters, both of whom looked scarcely younger than their mother, and converted No 26 into lodgings. She already had in residence a Mr Gibson on the ground floor. The third floor accommodated a 25-year-old Irishman called James O'Hara and a 27-year-old Italian army officer, Giuseppe d'Alia.

The Spanish embassy to the Holy See had given its name to the square and to the steps that led up to Santa Trinità dei Monti, which looked out over fields. The French Academy in the Villa Medici nearby was on the edge of woodlands. The Pincio gardens were just being laid out for perambulation on foot or on horseback, and riders could canter for miles up and down the hills of Parioli. A fit young man, like Keats in his walking days, could walk across Rome from wall to wall in two hours and would have seen very little to suggest that he was not living 100 years earlier. The city population within the Aurelian walls was about 135,000; the inhabited area was bounded on the south by the Capitol, on the west by the Tiber and on the east by the Pincian and Quirinal hills. The other hills of Rome, the Viminal, Esquiline, Caelian and Aventine, were silent and solitary. Among the vineyards on their slopes, fever lurked: for Sydney Morgan 'the Esquiline Hill is dreary and uninhabited. A monk hurrying home to his convent ... a wretch swollen and sallowed by the *mal-aria* begging on the road side – are all the traces of humanity or life which animate the desert ...'.[12] Many visitors took a morbid view of Rome. Dickens approached it through 'an undulating flat ... where, for mile and mile, there is nothing to relieve the terrible monotony and gloom ... the aptest and fittest burial ground for the Dead City'. When he eventually saw the innumerable towers, steeples and roofs, it looked like London.[13] Shelley called it 'a city as it were of the dead'; its population was thinly spread over a space within its walls nearly as large as London.[14]

Years of being the centre of tribute, first Roman and then Roman Catholic, had induced in the inhabitants a sense that the world owed them a living. A vast population lived on charity, and there was little commerce or industry. Cleaning up the city seemed to be no one's responsibility so that, despite the proliferation of fountains, the streets and squares were filthy; pretty well every receptacle, every nook and cranny, every fountain was used for human excrement. 'Indeed, of all its antiquities', Charlotte Eaton, the year before Keats arrived, imagined 'dirt to be the most indispensable'. Rome, she was inclined to think, had not been cleaned since it became a city.[15] The beggars were importunate in displaying their sores.[16] A quarter of the population, it seemed to the president of the Parlement of Burgundy, Charles de Brosses – who estimated the total population in 1740 at 150,000 – was in holy orders, a quarter worked as little as possible, a quarter did nothing at all, and the rest were statues.[17] One visitor preferred the statues. At least they did not cut throats.[18]

Rome had been a mecca for British travellers for over a century and, since the 1740s, was always full of English.[19] Since they had become rich they would do the Grand Tour, buy antiques (especially statuary), visit the places about which they had been taught (often at the end of a cane), and go home, satisfied that they had completed their education. Society revolved round the *conversazioni* held by Roman princes, where the indefatigable Boswell had found 'a great deal of formality and also a certain air of pleasing richness and grandeur'.[20] Sydney Morgan was less impressed: a gloomy evening would be passed in gossip until the opera started, but if there was no opera the people opened up their *rouge et noir* tables.[21] They took their tone from the two or three cardinals who could be persuaded to attend. The food, brought in from outside, was always cold, and most of it had been pilfered before it ever reached the guests. For a *conversazione* the palace servants were augmented by liveried ruffians who foraged their one square meal of the week by enrolling with a master who had never seen them before and who more often than not did not know how many servants he employed anyway. Conversation was not necessarily what happened at *conversazioni*; in Nice Smollett attended those at Government House where 'noble personages play at cards for farthings'.[22]

Public entertainments were usually religious. Tourists would be invited to attend the profession of nuns and the celebration of patronal feast-days in convents, accompanied by elaborate Masses and elegant music. The profession of a nun was considered almost an anthropological expedition for a northern Protestant. Catherine Hinde was able to overlook and to overhear a newly professed nun's conversation with her new companions. After the feathers, diamonds and every sort of finery, the young postulant looked far prettier in her new habit.[23] There were also the papal services, which were both splendid and long. Treating the events like theatre, the congregation behaved accordingly. When Joseph Severn was consul in Rome 40 years later (1861), he was required to translate for the British community the regulations governing the behaviour of foreign women in church, which Pio Nono had decided to enforce. On the first transgression, papal chamberlains were 'to use the most insinuating supplications, and in the sweetest and most imploring manner', but when this failed they must snatch away the offending lady 'without the hope of pardon, whoever she may be, and expel her from the holy place'. Any woman 'feeding, guzzling or laughing and screaming' during the most solemn moments of the Mass was to be dragged out of her place as soon as that moment was over, while at the end of the service she was to be prevented from climbing over the balcony to jump down and get away more quickly. Men, on the other hand, who insisted on chattering to the ladies during Mass, were only to be escorted out of the ladies' section.[24]

Why foreigners should behave so badly is hard to understand, except as a habitual reaction to something which went on too long and which they did not understand. They behaved as they did at the theatre, where most of what was on offer was of an insufferable dryness and piety. The one piece of theatre that was beginning to show signs of new life was the opera. The long reign of the *castrati* had at last come to an end. Women were still not allowed to sing in church but the stage was no longer banned to them. Until the papacy of Pius VII, opera performances had been rather like the Japanese *kabuki*, with androgynous males playing the soprano and contralto roles. Most of these had undergone a small operation, performed at booths which advertised the castration of the pope's chapel singers. Some were transvestites who made a second living lurking after the show in the cafés where they sold their services as catamites. Roman audiences tended to use the opera house as a club for conversation, and went to meet their friends and eat ice-creams, unless they had been hired as part of a claque, to cheer or hiss the singers. To Lady Blessington they were no worse than London audiences. 'The fine ladies come to see and be seen, ... and to flirt, and for the latter objects there are worse situations in the world, than an Opera box.'[25]

But now, five years after the final exile of Napoleon Bonaparte, a new conqueror was bestriding the world. Moscow, London and Vienna had already fallen, his name was on every tongue. 'There has been a splendid Opera lately', wrote Byron in May 1819 from Venice, 'by Rossini ... the people followed him about – crowned him – cut off his hair "for memory"; he was Shouted and Sonnetted and feasted – and immortalised much more than either of the Emperors.'[26] On 20 February 1816, the Teatro Argentina in Rome presented the world première of *Il Barbiere di Siviglia*. According to

Stendhal, the governor of Rome had been presented with the pretty libretto on a day when 'he was bored to tears with the very mention of morals and decency'.[27] The Roman public, who were only too well acquainted with people like Don Basilio, were delighted with it, and its success was followed on January 1817 by the first performance of *La Cenerentola* at the Teatro della Valle. If Keats and Severn had been minded to hear the music of Gioacchino Rossini, they could have done so better in Naples, where the future Signora Rossini ruled as diva over the Teatro San Carlo. The day after Keats died, Rossini's *Matilde di Shabran* was performed, at the Teatro Apollo, which the French had recently built. Little known though that opera is today, Lady Clarinda, daughter of Lord Foolincourt, was happy to sing excerpts to the assembled company at Crotchet Castle.[28] That first Roman performance was conducted by Paganini. The same year, Sydney Morgan was taken to see the Tarpeian Rock by a stable-boy whistling '*Fra tanti palpiti*' from *Tancredi*, premiered in Naples in 1813.[29]

For those whose appetite for religious ceremonies or for opera was soon sated and who found the antiques boring – and there were many such – Rome did not have a great deal to offer. There was Carnival, an orgy of horseplay behind the anonymity of masks and weird disguises. Its onset was signalled by the ringing of the bell on the Capitol which otherwise only rang for the death of a pope. English visitors were not much impressed by the horse-races, with riderless horses stimulated by crackers strapped to their girth or by nails driven into the harness, cantering down the Corso carrying the colours of the *rioni* or districts of the city. They enjoyed the usual torturing of animals, like bear-dancing and the *coccagna*, when young men tried to climb a greasy pole to win the live pig or goose tethered to the top. The wretched creature was usually torn to pieces before the end of the competition, which was followed by reckless drinking. And there were also the church *feste*, since scarcely a week passed outside Lent and Advent without a parish celebrating its onomastic saint with fireworks, brass bands and street circuses, all competing for splendour with the rival parish. But Rome being 'the great academy of the world',[30] most visitors had not come for the high or low life but for the art, buying pictures and statues for their houses and gardens, and recording the grandeur that was Rome, so that the landscape was filled with men and women on their stools, catching, in sketchbook and on canvas, the pictures that would adorn every polite drawing room back home.

Throughout the previous century, the English had made up the largest proportion of foreign tourists, having the money and the well-established ritual of the Grand Tour. They were also, like most rich and inarticulate tourists, monumentally unpopular among the Romans for their insolence and outrageous behaviour, and for their meanness. They were always afraid that they were being sold a forgery or being cheated in some incalculable way, so that they held on to their small change with a tight fist. Typical of their suspicions would be a Saint Manufactory, actually a painting by Thomas Uwins, who lived and painted in Italy from 1824 to 1830, which showed 'one of the most amusing things in the city' (Naples): the workshop of a craftsman who created antique statues of saints and angels for churches.[31] Of course, few of the 'new' tourists spoke any Italian – just English in a loud voice, or, worse, French. But with sublime lack of sensitivity they came in their hundreds, took apartments and stayed.

The English had returned to Italy in large numbers after the war because they were attracted by the climate, the cheap living (Shelley found that 'a crown here goes as far as a pound note in England in all affairs of eating and drinking'), the glamour of the Eternal City, and all the traditional *sehnsucht* for the land where the lemon trees bloom.[32] And, not least, by the reputation of the friendly pope, Pius VII. A sensitive, courteous old gentleman – he had been born in 1742 – he was, in 1821, within two years of his death. He had ascended the papal throne in 1800, elected by a conclave in Venice since the armies of Republican France had removed his predecessor and declared a Roman Republic under the protection of the French eagles. Gregorio Barnaba Chiaramonti could, in different circumstances, have made a very acceptable archbishop of Canterbury. He was urbane, gentle, no friend to fanaticism, cultivated and blessed with an ironic sense of humour; but he knew how to stand firm and suffer for his convictions. '*Sono sempre monaco*', he was reported as telling his lackey, '*posso fare tutto il mio bisogno, anchè vuotare il mio orinale*' ('I shall always be a monk, and do for myself, even empty my own chamber pot').[33] Though he signed the concordat with Napoleon and consecrated the emperor at his coronation, he was never a foe to England: indeed one of his first disputes with Napoleon was the permission he gave for non-Catholic foreigners to reside in Rome, considered by the arrogant French to be an unfriendly act, since the foreigners who took advantage of the indult were largely British. The pope had also demonstrated an unexpected independence when he refused to annul the marriage between Napoleon's younger brother, Jerome, and the American Miss Patterson, and thus free him to play his part in his brother's dynastic plans. And when in 1808 Napoleon declared the end to the rule of priests in Rome, the pope had solemnly signed the Bull of Excommunication before being carted off to France in a coach with only the equivalent of 22 sous in his pocket.

The ordeal of this saintly old man in the power of an increasingly megalomaniac emperor made an instant appeal to the English. According to the garrulous Chateaubriand, Napoleon had found 'a priest more powerful than he, who reigned over the spirit while he reigned only over matter. The pope kept the soul and threw him only the carcase.'[34] As Archbishop of Imola, Pius VII had allowed himself to be addressed as 'Citizen Cardinal' and he was sympathetic enough towards some of the ideas afloat at the time to carry the words Liberty and Equality on his writing paper. As with Pio Nono later in the century, his ideas of how to reconcile these two slogans with the traditional demands of episcopate and papacy were not advanced enough for him to be comfortable with them. He was not, however, required to worry about them when he returned to Rome in 1814, for there were few who regretted the end of French rule. Many of the younger members of the better families had slipped away to join the *banditti* in the campagna and escape conscription to the imperial armies, and the city's population had aged. The closure of the monastic houses and the end of their charitable works had nearly trebled the number of beggars in Rome to 30,000.[35] British troops, put ashore like commandos at Fiumicino to test the French presence in 1814, were besieged by starving women and children. When the returning pope paraded down the Corso, his carriage was drawn by those young nobles who had not joined the *banditti*. Rome and the Romans were eager to forget the French nightmare and the Liberty and Equality that went with it. The sack of the city that followed the declaration of the republic on 18 February 1798, had been 'worse than the sack of Brennus, Alaric, Genseric, Ricimer, and the (Constable of) Bourbon', the Papal State being robbed not only of valuable art treasures but also of 70 million scudi.[36]

What particularly pleased the British was that the pope appointed Cardinal Consalvi as proto-secretary of state. Sydney Morgan gave him credit for abolishing some of the 'horrible capital punishments of Rome', and believed that his religious tolerance had spared much suffering to Italy.[37] But Consalvi was less successful in his other aim, to modify the Roman bureaucracy on Napoleonic lines, and he was never able to repeat in the Eternal City the efficiency that had inspired the system in France. In Rome it was worked by men who had professed some of the degrees of priesthood, but not the last and most important one. Consalvi himself never advanced beyond the order of deacon. Others went as far as was consistent with being married, but promotion to the ruling class, or *prelatura*, normally went to the celibate who wore clerical garb. Like the *nomenklatura* of Communist states since the Second World War, the *prelatura* was chosen for its fidelity to ideology rather than for its competence. The administration of Rome did not, on the whole, improve as a result of Consalvi's reforms and it was soon to revert to being a byword for inefficiency.

When Pope Pius entered his palace on the Quirinale he found the rooms full of elegant Empire furniture and curtains, while the walls had been painted with scenes from Ovid. The more frivolous furniture and unsuitable paintings were removed, and the less lubricious deities on the walls were transformed, by the addition of a few chaste smocks, into saints and virgins. But at the same time he restrained the spiritual enthusiasm of those prelates who suspected that Rome had been the devil's playground for so long that it must be contaminated by heresy, freemasonry and the *carboneria*. Charcoal burners, who kept their fires going night and day and who sat around them chatting and smoking when ordinary mortals had gone to bed, must be up to no good. Nervous of the effect of any spark of dissent, the Austrian chancellor, Prince Metternich, tried but was never able to persuade the papal government to act with proper inquisitorial thoroughness. Had Keats been stronger, he might have dabbled, like Byron and Shelley, in the sort of liberty-loving bravado that could earn an Italian a mild prison sentence. Indeed, while Keats was coughing his lungs out in the Piazza di Spagna, Byron took part in an obscure drama in the Marches, which liberal papists like the father and brothers of his mistress, Teresa Guiccioli, played out before the well-meaning cardinal legate. Oppression in the Papal States there certainly was but, like ordinary justice, it was inefficient. Well-connected political conspirators and simple murderers usually got off scot-free.

This well-known feature of Italian life was a constant theme of the English who wrote with frissons of delighted distaste – coming from a nation where a child could be hanged for stealing a sheep – about the incidence of murder. Ann Radcliffe had opened her Gothic horror, *The Italian* (1797), with a tale within a tale. An Englishman visiting a church in south Italy is astounded to see that a known assassin enjoyed sanctuary there. He is even more astonished to hear that the man was kept and fed by public charity. It offends his sense of the rightness of things. But, says his companion: 'If we were to show no mercy to such unfortunate persons, assassinations are so frequent that our cities would be depopulated.' Tobias Smollett in 1766 was shocked to see a murderer sunning himself on the steps of the church in Nice where he had taken sanctuary after killing his wife.[38] Byron, who went constantly in anticipation of an attack from hired thugs, was contemptuous of writers of 'trash about Italy', who had never been there. 'They prate about assassination. What is it but the origin of duelling and "a wild justice" ... It is the fount of the modern part of honour – in what the laws can't or *won't* reach.' But he did agree that every man was open to it, more or less, like being mugged.[39]

So ubiquitous were the papal *sbirri*, or police, that murder was uncommon in Rome, so that Protestant Englishmen found it a sympathetic ambience in which to become acquainted with Mediterranean civilisation. Pius VII continued the papal tradition of patronage of the arts. Two years after Keats's death, the Braccio Nuovo in the Vatican was opened, where endless senatorial and imperial busts were displayed like a sculptural Debretts. Pius patronised both the Catholic Canova and the Protestant Thorwaldsen and John Gibson and also a school of German artists, known as the Nazarenes, who lived a self-imposed monastic life of dedication to the Muse, and produced a purer pre-Raphaelitish art than was later to appear in Britain. The architect and landscape gardener, Valadier, was still laying out the Pincio gardens where Keats took his exercise. The archaeologists, who had cleared a lot of the Campo Vaccino, or main Roman forum, under the French, continued under the patronage of the second wife of the fifth Duke of Devonshire; she was said to nourish a romantic passion for Cardinal Consalvi. This may have helped her in securing permits to dig and was currently 'remaking the gulf which [Marcus] Curtius closed' with the help of a team of manacled convicts.[40] The duchess was one of the exceptions to the general unpopularity of the

English, for she was open-handed and spoke Italian with a fine command of curses.[41] 'While Ciceroni dispute and Virtuosi stare', Sydney Morgan wrote, 'and Roman Princes and Cardinals boast of the past glories of the "eterna città", the Duchess of Devonshire is more effectually doing the honours of Rome, ancient and modern, by illustrating Horace, reprinting Virgil, making excavations, giving countenance and patronage to living talent and bringing forward modest professors into the distinguished circles of her own society.'[42] Altogether artists and their patrons felt comfortable and safe, since they could continue to disapprove of, but no longer suffer from, the pure zeal of reformed Roman Catholicism. Being for the most part propertied people, they liked to see firm government and plenty of police around. They found the papacy careful about the thing for which they had principally come, the Roman inheritance. Their money went a long way, and a large tip or bribe could influence the *prelatura* to cut through most labyrinths of bureaucracy, and those who were lucky enough to meet His Holiness felt better for the experience.

The warmest encomium on the Holy Father came, surprisingly, from Napoleon himself. 'He is a kind, gentle, excellent man – a lamb, an influence for good.'[43] On the fall of his persecutor, Pius immediately offered asylum to the distressed and more innocent members of the Bonaparte family: Napoleon's mother Letizia, and his uncle, Joseph Fesch, the son of the Swiss sailor in the Genoese navy who had married Letizia's widowed mother. Fesch had risen to be Cardinal Archbishop of Lyons and Primate of all the Gauls. Already resident in Rome was Letizia's second daughter, Pauline Borghese. Comfortably reconciled to, but separated from, her rich and indulgent husband, Prince Camillo, she was known to all Rome from her portrayal as *Venere Vincitrice*, All-Conquering Venus. Canova's famous statue had been completed in 1808 when her husband was governor-general of Piedmont and Genoa and it had been lodged, until recently, in the Palazzo Chablais in Turin. Asked how she could bear to pose in a state of nature before a man who was not her husband, Pauline is said to have remarked innocently that there had been a good fire. *Ben trovato*? Thomas Love Peacock puts the same story into the mouth of Mr Crotchet in *Crotchet Castle*, told there of an Italian countess sitting for Canova.[44] Northern visitors were shocked by the sheer exuberance of naked statuary in a holy city. The Scots seemed particularly wary (and weary) of nude statues. One rich traveller sent his valet to see whether there was anything worth seeing in the Capitoline museum; he returned to report that 'there's naething but a wheen naked men and women, sir, and I'm sure you've seen eneugh o' them lately; ye canna want to see ony mair'.[45]

John Keats did struggle as far as the Borghese casino where Canova's statue was on show. He thought it 'beautiful bad taste', like the Aeolian harp on which all breezes blew.[46] The princess, moreover, had aged. Catherine Hinde, who saw her on 12 March 1820, described her having 'the remains of great beauty, both of face and form though so reduced from a delicate state of health as to be a mere shadow'.[47] The dying poet so disapproved of her blatantly ogling his fellow consumptive, Lieutenant Isaac Marmaduke Elton, Royal Engineers, as she promenaded through the newly opened gardens, that he refused to take his exercise where he could be exposed to it. Such behaviour in Fanny Brawne would have killed him quicker than consumption, and he was scandalised that a mature woman of 40 should behave with such shameless indiscretion. So Dr Clark hired him a horse, for the rather princessly sum of £6 a month to ride elsewhere, actually at a snail's space for a few yards down the Corso.[48]

Madame Mère, Letizia Bonaparte, was, in 1820, living in the Rinuccini Palace in the Piazza di Venezia by the Corso. With her lived two of her grand-daughters, Lucien's two girls, the Princess Gabrielli and Madame la Comtesse de Posse. Their father, the youngest Bonaparte brother, had refused to renounce his love-bride for a royal princess, and now resided as Prince of Canino in the little town of that name north of Rome. Louis, the former King of Holland, lived a semi-invalid in the Palazzo Salviati opposite the Palazzo Doria, and Jerome, the former King of Westphalia, had installed himself in the palace of Keats's 'cold and tranquil banker', Alessandro Torlonia, Duke of Bracciano, who had at a critical moment refused the poet's drafts.[49] Torlonia was a self-made man whom Pius VII made Duke of Bracciano. Immensely rich and hospitable, he was a patron of Canova, the only Roman gentleman who could be bothered to collect contemporary art, and general banker to the foreign community. According to Stendhal, he made enormous profits from the exchange rate he offered,[50] though in fact he offered Keats a good rate but only if he cashed a large sum. When the two young men presented all they had, in one draft for £120 only to see it bounce, Severn was distracted with worry.[51]

2. Canova's presentation of Paulina Borghese as *Venere Vincitore*. Keats thought it 'beautiful bad taste', like the Aeolian harp on which all breezes blew.

Cardinal Fesch had his cardinalatial palace, in which he hung and re-hung his 30,000 paintings, while he fiercely contested the Bourbon attempt to remove him from his archiepiscopal see. He was the only member of the college of cardinals to be interested in paintings, which he claimed to be collecting to send to churches that had lost their treasures or never had any. Sydney Morgan, on being shown round by His Eminence, lighted on a range of apartments full of pictures stacked against the walls, intended for such presentations.[52] Fesch counted on and received the wholehearted support of the pope, largely for the exemplary show of piety he displayed, assiduously attending the papal chapels and carrying a cross barefoot in procession to the Colosseum. Just before Keats and Severn arrived in Rome, the cardinal and his half-sister had fallen into the hands of a religious charlatan, who claimed that Our Lady had told her that Napoleon was no longer in St Helena, having been air-lifted off by angels. Despite Pauline's efforts to dissuade her mother, the old lady paid highly for this intelligence and, shortly after Keats's death in 1821, a stranger was introduced into the Palazzo Rinuccini, with the news for Letizia that her son was free from his sufferings and that she would one day see him again, but not before there had been revolution, civil strife and much bloodshed in France. The King of Kings had decreed that the Emperor of Emperors would return to his people.

The unhappy woman clutched at this straw of hope, while Napoleon was actually sinking to his painful death in the middle of the Atlantic. Though the pope was glad to hear that Napoleon had died in sentiments of veneration for the Roman Catholic Church, the former emperor's mother had great difficulty in obtaining permission for a requiem Mass for the repose of his soul to be said in all the great Roman basilicas. After the pope, Madame Mère was the most famous person in Rome, and much visited, but after 1821 the old lady began to sink into obscurity. She refused, however, to remove the imperial eagles from her carriage. 'All Europe was prostrate before them for ten years and kings had got used to them. Why should I remove them?' She lived until 1836, long enough to hear that her son's remains had triumphantly returned to the Hôtel des Invalides in Paris.[53] While Napoleon was still alive, Pius never failed to stop if he met Letizia's carriage in the countryside to ask after 'our good Emperor'.[54] But even the pope could not go far off the beaten track before he ran a real risk of being waylaid by *banditti*. The flat *campagna* on the way to what is now Ciampino Airport was relatively safe. Keats and Severn on their way to Rome observed a cardinal there engaged in the national craze for shooting small birds, first attracting them to the ground by a small mirror attached to an owl tied loosely to a stick, a method frequently used as a decoy for skylarks, which would cluster round the tethered bird to bait it. His two liveried footmen stood by to load the fowling pieces and to see that the prelate did not shoot the owl.[55]

Keats had brought with him *Filippo*, a tragedy of Vittorio Alfieri, with which to expand his growing command of Italian. Keats was too ill to persevere with it and he probably never knew that the disturbingly healthy Alfieri, when he first came to Rome, had lived in the Piazza di Spagna, whence he pursued his athletic and adulterous love affair with the wife of the Young Pretender. Poets attract poets, and it is an intriguing possibility that Keats met the scatological poet and society doctor, Gioacchino Belli. It could have happened when Dr James Clark called in a second opinion. Belli was a *samizdat* author in papal Rome, and he struck new depths with the Petrarchan sonnet, each one a bitter and indecent satire in Roman dialect on the *prelatura* and its sanctimonious humbug. The dying English poet, Clark could have told him, also had a good line in bawdy verse.[56]

What is not conjecture is that Dr James Clark was not a very good doctor. But he was an exceedingly kind and considerate man, who made the dying Keats the subject of his special care, so that he was considerably out of pocket himself as a result. Clark had started in law, switched to medicine and been a ship's doctor, enrolling as an assistant surgeon on board a man-of-war after his preliminary training in Edinburgh. He sailed with the future Arctic explorer, William Parry, in search of the most northern influence of the Gulf Stream off the coasts of Norway and Scotland. As a result of this expedition, his doctoral thesis was on 'The Medical Effects of Cold'. In 1818 he accompanied a tubercular case to the south of France and Switzerland, liked the warm *midi* and, in 1819, settled in Rome. A year later this personable young man added to his laurels with a slim work on *The Climate, Diseases, Hospitals and Medical Schools in France, Italy and Switzerland*. Tuberculosis was to become his speciality. Yet he persisted in treating Keats's complaint as stemming from the bowels, and the medicine he prescribed – probably useless in any case – was more suitable for a constipative than a consumptive. But Keats appears to have been on a mercury regime for some time before that anyway, possibly since 1817 and probably for a venereal infection. Mercury in pill form (Potters Pills) was prescribed as a diuretic and for many stomach ailments. Indeed, if he was being treated with mercury (even in the form of calomel) it could only have exacerbated his tubercular condition. Because tuberculosis was such a dreaded disease and Anna Angeletti could have turned the two young men out if she had suspected that this was Keats's illness, Clark, realising there was nothing to be done, may have chosen to treat him for a bowel disorder out of kindness. As it was, Anna Angeletti was not taken in.[57]

Clark's subsequent career was to be a triumph of charm over skill. In 1834 he became physician to Leopold, King of the Belgians, and it was thus only a step to becoming physician to Queen Victoria's mother, the Duchess of Kent. In 1837 the new queen made him her physician-in-ordinary and a baronet. His reputation was dented when he misdiagnosed as pregnancy the tumour from which Lady Flora Hastings died, but the queen did not lose faith in him. His next victim was to be the Prince Consort himself, who died of typhoid fever caught from the drains of Windsor Castle, a danger Sir James failed entirely to detect. But ship's doctors had little experience of pregnant women or drains. It did not stop him from becoming a Fellow of the Royal Society and member of the Senate of London University. He died in 1870 loaded with honours, and would have disappeared down the oubliette of history had he not made, 50 years earlier, the first of the known misdiagnoses of his career.

There was not much any doctor could have done medically for John Keats but what Clark could, he did. He scoured the city for the right food; he found a nurse to relieve Severn; he arranged the funeral; he ordered the sexton to turf the grave over with daisies. In Imperial Rome only emperors could be buried within the city walls, and in papal Rome only Catholics. Non-Catholics had to rest without. Their cemetery was in the burial fields of ancient Rome, facing the little Monte Testaccio. It is certainly a place where one can fall in love with easeful death. The mount was a wholly artificial one, originally an in-fill site, the rubbish being composed of the broken *teste* or amphorae in which oil and corn were delivered in Roman times. It was, in fact, a giant bottle-bank, now a green mound, a riot of daisies and wild violets which raced down its sides into the cemetery. At one time, those slopes had been a place of medieval pilgrimage and the grandstand for the *Testaccio* games, mainly bull-baiting and pig-sticking. The romantic site, fixed by

3. Oscar Wilde, 'The Grave of Keats'. It is a late Romantic view to complement Shelley's description in *Adonais*. The manuscript is preserved in the Memorial House.

THE GRAVE OF KEATS

Rid of the world's injustice, and his pain,
He rests at last beneath God's veil of blue.
Taken from life when life and love were new
The youngest of the martyrs here is lain,
　Fair as Sebastian, and as early slain.
　No cypress shades his grave, no funeral yew,
　But gentle violets weeping with the dew
Weave on his bones an ever-blossoming chain.
O proudest heart that broke for misery!
　O sweetest lips since those of Mitylene!
　O poet-painter of our English Land!
Thy name was writ in water – it shall stand:
　And tears like mine will keep thy memory green,
As Isabella did her Basil-tree.

Shelley for all time as the 'slope of green access, / Where, like an infant's smile, over the dead, / A light of laughing flowers along the grass is spread',[58] is not today haunted by the ghosts of baited bulls or slaughtered pigs.

No one in those days knew whether consumption was contagious, but the Romans, who were too easily assailed by plagues of different kinds, and most of whom suffered from malaria, took no chances. Joseph Severn, who had seen his guineas vanish, was horrified by the bill he would have to face when the health authorities came in to sterilise a room where a patient had died of an ailment like Keats's. Even the wallpaper had to be steamed off the walls; the burning of the bedding and furniture was a matter of minutes. The costs were charged to the estate of the deceased. And the men employed to clean up after a death had no finer feelings. Most of them would probably die of one of the diseases they were seeking to prevent and, as they were held pariahs by their neighbours, the work was done with no respect for the dead, only for the pocket books of those who were paying. Severn had turned out his pockets to find only a guinea. No wonder the 'brutes' terrified him. Despite that dreadful experience, despite the indifference of the other English residents in No 26 Piazza di Spagna, despite their 'cursed lodging place', and 'the inhumanity, the barbarism of these Italians', the 'devils' who were going to present him with a bill for over £100, the 'funeral beasts', despite the last ignominious occasion when Anna Angeletti brought out all the crockery which she claimed the two young men had broken and which 'must have been the debris of the entire parish', which he then proceeded to smash to smithereens in so mad a rage that the prudent landlady forgot about the bill, despite all this, Joseph Severn did not take off for home when the daisies began to flower over the grave of his friend.[59] He had come out to Rome with Keats partly from friendship, but also to complete the picture that might give him the Royal Academy travelling pension.

Just as Clark was not a very good doctor, so Severn was not a very good painter. In 1818, however, he had won the Academy's gold medal for the best history painting by a student and he had a letter of recommendation from Sir Thomas Lawrence to Canova. The great sculptor had recently had a very successful visit to England, where he had been introduced to both the Prince Regent and the Elgin Marbles, and liked both.[60] Sir Thomas stood high in the admiration of the pope (whose portrait is perhaps Lawrence's best), but not very high in the admiration of the young Mr Severn, who thought the brilliant painting of George IV, then still in Lawrence's studio, 'unnatural'. Sir Thomas approved in general of Severn's proposal to paint a massive portrayal of *The Death of Alcibiades*. But nursing Keats made progress painfully slow. Canova not being in town, Dr Clark furnished Severn with an introduction to the sculptor who became known as the English Canova. John Gibson received Severn warmly in the presence of Lord Colchester, who was in the artist's studio looking for a bargain. Colchester was no insignificant lordling but Speaker of the House of Commons from 1802 to 1816, and from 1802 to 1807 he was a trustee of the British Museum, responsible for its purchasing policy and the inauguration of its library.[61] So, when Gibson treated Severn with no less care and attention than he did the nobleman, he did more than anything to reconcile the young man to being in Rome. If artists were treated like lords, and not like tradesmen, then Rome was the place for him.

Gibson, moreover, knew what it was like to come to Rome, hoping to conquer the artistic heights. He had once dreamed that he had been wafted there by an eagle and, on waking, vowed that he would walk there if necessary. It was not. He had arrived, three years before Severn, with letters to Canova from the Liverpool businessman and author of *The Life of Lorenzo de Medici*, William Roscoe, and Canova had greeted him with the words: 'I am rich. I am anxious to be useful to you in your art as long as you are in Rome.'[62] Immediately he gave him his first lessons in sculpture and, by the time Severn came to see him, Gibson was part of the Roman establishment with commissions from the sixth Duke of Devonshire and Sir George Beaumont, whose great coup was to buy the Michaelangelo *tondo* which is now in the Royal Academy of Arts in London. Gibson remained in Rome almost uninterruptedly to the moment of his death in 1866, when Joseph Severn was British consul. Had he returned to England, he told Elizabeth Eastlake, wife of the future President of the Royal Academy of Arts, 'my life would be spent in making busts and statues of great men in coats and neckties; here I am employed upon poetical subjects'.[63] From time to time he fell in love with his own statues, most seriously with his *Tinted Venus* who, with her blue eyes, salmon-pink flesh, blonde hair and golden snood, stood in like Galatea for Pygmalion, only no god was on hand to make her warm.

In 1821, Severn knew that he had to produce something by the spring or lose the chance of the scholarship but, when the finished work was sent to the Royal Academy, it was lost in the maze of rooms. The story ended happily when 'a tin case all bent double and without any direction or intimation as to whom it belonged' was found and opened, 'and lo, my dying Alcibiades'.[64] He was awarded the prize and the expenses of going to Rome in the first place were refunded. Severn was then set on the path to mediocre success. His friendship with Keats gave him a lustre that escaped his art and, as he considered the English in Rome 'not only the most polished society but the most Christian in the world – in the sense of humanity, cheerfulness, of living for others rather than ourselves', he did well from painting pastel portraits of its more attractive members.[65] He tried, without success, to interest the Royal Academy in setting up an English academy in Rome, on the model of the French at Villa Medicis. It was not, however, until 1912 that the British School at Rome was able to occupy the site of the British pavilion at the 1911 exhibition and, with funds from the Great Exhibition of 1851, admit artists for a stay in Rome, as part of their professional formation.[66]

Joseph Severn stayed on in Rome until 1841, obsessed by the memory of his friend and the desire to create a fitting memorial for him. In 1861 he returned as consul, to preside over the British community through the latter part of the reign of Pio Nono, and the annexation of papal lands by what Augustus Hare was always to call 'the Sardinians'. He retired in 1872, after Rome became the capital of Italy, and died in 1879. In addition to not being a very good painter, Severn was not a very good consul. He acquired the post through the good offices of Gladstone and the Prussian ambassador in Rome, Baron de Bunsen. To the professional diplomatists he was 'a good natured goose, utterly unfit and unqualified for the post'. He tried to mix diplomacy with art and had been reprimanded on several occasions for unprofessional conduct, but a lot of people liked him and many, both English and Italian, were grateful for his services on their behalf.[67] When he first arrived in 1820 the concept of Italy, as a sovereign state of all the lands between Sicily and the Alps, was unimaginable. Indeed she was not a country but 'Italia', a land with a past but not a future, a paradise of exiles.[68] 'Italy has had two lives!' wrote Samuel Rogers in his journal on approaching Rome on 22 November 1814. 'Can it be said of any other Country?' A third life, he implied, for the 'Niobe of Nations' would be too much to expect.[69]

2

'The Niobe of Nations'

A Romantic View of Italy

The Niobe of Nations! there she stands,
Childless and crownless, in her voiceless woe:
An empty urn within her withered hands,
Whose holy dust was scattered long ago;

Lord Byron, *Childe Harold*,
Canto IV, stanza lxxix.

And is there then no earthly place,
Where we can rest, in dream Elysian,
Without some curst, round English face,
Popping up near, to break the vision?

Thomas Moore, 'Rhymes on the Road' (1823).

There is a strange horror lying over [Rome] which I can neither describe nor account for; for it is a shadow of death, possessing and penetrating all things.

John Ruskin, letter to Rev. Thomas Dale, 31 December 1840.

*Ecco d'Italia i fatti
Tifo, Tedeschi e Frati*

[These are the plagues of Italy:
Typhus, Germans and friars]

An Italian proverb.

For 200 years, tourists had come to Italy to experience those two lives – the Roman and Renaissance pasts – at first hand, mostly as young men with their tutors to ensure that they understood what they saw and to help them spend their abundant money wisely. They had all been classically educated and their accounts duly noted the marvels of the ancient world, and the majestic panoramas of scenery or art. Apart from commenting on the vileness of the inns, they barely noticed the life around them. Only Laurence Sterne, whose *Sentimental Journey* took him as far as Savoy, then part of the Kingdom of Sardinia, recorded 'an adventure', when a mix-up over bedrooms led to a sentimental encounter with a Piedmontese lady and her Lyonnaise maid. The inhabitants of this land with no present and no future, when they obtruded on the tourists' notice, were treated dismissively, as if they had betrayed their 'two lives'.

By the end of the eighteenth century, the Grand Tour had acquired a bad name. John Polidori, like Dr James Clark an Edinburgh medical graduate, expert at the age of nineteen in somnambulism and mesmerism, damned it eloquently in the first pages of his Gothic horror tale, *The Vampyre*. Aubrey, wishing to

4. *Byron Contemplating Rome*, modelled on Tischbein's portrait of Goethe, was a popular print. The suggestion was that only the Colosseum matched the greatness of his genius, but in truth it was the only building in Rome everyone would instantly recognise.

accompany Lord Ruthven abroad, informs his guardians that 'it was time for him to perform the tour, which for many generations had been thought necessary to enable the young to take some rapid steps in the career of vice'. For Lord Ruthven, read Lord Byron. Polidori could only fulfil his desire for travel by attaching himself to the poet as his medical adviser, and his comment on the Grand Tour may have had a whiff of sour grapes. *The Vampyre*, the entertainment that started the competition in the Villa Diodati for a spine-chiller, the origin of *Frankenstein*, and which Byron disliked, as he did its author, was published in 1819.[1]

With the end of the Napoleonic wars the Grand Tour, as such, was over. Some believe it ended even sooner, in 1796.[2] Though privileged sons, rich collectors and idle bachelors tried to pick it up where the Napoleonic invasions of Italy had left it, the Grand Tour rapidly converted itself into ordinary tourism.[3] The shuffling of works of art from Rome, Milan and Florence to Paris at the hands of Bonaparte's cultural commissars had alerted governments to the value of their treasures. Napoleon Bonaparte, a latter-day Louis XIV, had tried to fulfil Colbert's wish that the French '*devons faire en sorte d'avoir ... tout ce qu'il y a de beau en Italie*'. The pillaging of Italian museums was so thorough that in 1798 a popular canzonetta assured the world that '*Rome n'est plus dans Rome / Elle est tout à Paris.*' The Louvre housed the bronze horses from St Mark's, Venice, the 'Venus de Medici' from Florence, Raphael's *Transfiguration*, the Belvedere *Apollo* and *Laocoon* from the Vatican, and the Caracci collection from Bologna.[4] Now they were all going home. Old Masters could no longer be picked up for a song and, if one hoped to furnish one's dwelling with relics from the classical past one might be lucky enough to pick up a shard, or buy a fake Roman artefact, but one did better to commission a classical copy from the spawn of Canova's studio, such as John Gibson.[5] With the first stirrings of the Hellenic resistance to Turkish rule, moreover, a whole new quarry of pure Greek sculpture, not decadent late Roman copies, began to divert serious collectors to Greece. The way had been shown by Lord Elgin who, while ambassador to the Porte from 1799 to 1803, had negotiated the purchase of the Parthenon figures which now bear his name, and which, after being acquitted of an abuse of diplomatic privilege, he sold to the nation in 1816. Canova admired them, and this, coming from the modern Phidias, was all that was needed to persuade Parliament to buy them. Being authentically the ancient (Greek) ideal of man, these figures replaced Michelangelo's, and it now became fashionable to admire ancient Greek rather than Renaissance sculpture.[6] But the shameless purchase of the marbles was an object lesson to European governments, and treasure-hunting in Italy was now frowned upon by the authorities.

The wars had provided occupation for those sprigs of landed families, who had undertaken the Grand Tour to learn how to convert their rolling acres in darkest Yorkshire into landscapes out of Poussin. From 1793, they had ruled the seas from Rio de Janeiro to Canton, cleared Egypt and Syria of the French, fought every inch of the way from Torres Vedras to Toulouse, subdued Mysoreans and Marathas, chased bandits round the heart of ancient India and carried the British flag beyond the capital of the Grand Mughal to the five rivers of the Panjab. They had even had a crack at the impossible task of providing Sicily with good government when the second son of the Duke of Portland and future governor-general of India, Lord William Bentinck, was appointed envoy to King Ferdinand of the Two Sicilies and commander-in-chief of British forces in Sicily, thus effectively governor of the island from 1811 to 1814. He was recalled by Castlereagh when, after the fall of Napoleon, Bentinck recommended liberal constitutions for the Genoese republic, Milan and Grand Duchy of Tuscany.[7] The Grand Tour, as a field trip to round off an education stuffed with study of Livy, Horace and Virgil, now seemed distinctly *vieux jeu*.

The tourists, too, had changed. Byron in 1817 described Rome as 'pestilent with English, – a parcel of staring boobies, who go about gaping and wishing to be at once cheap and magnificent'. In 1818 there could have been as many as 1,000 tourists in Rome,[8] and Mary Shelley found the English at Bagni di Lucca 'crowded here to the almost entire exclusion [of] Italians', adding, with a frisson of disgust, 'the walks are filled with English nursery maids'.[9] Grand Tourists had not taken their wives and children on the Grand Tour, much less their nursery maids. Twenty years later the tourists were still out in force. 'Rome is full of English', Macaulay complained to Lord Lansdowne on 19 December 1830. 'We could furnish exceedingly respectable Houses of Lords and Commons. There are at present twice as many coroneted carriages in Piazza di Spagna as in St James's Square.'[10] Post-bellum families, especially wives and sisters, now wished to share the experience of travel. Ned Williams, Shelley's sailing friend, knew a naval captain who spent £1,100 worth of prize money showing Italy to his two sisters '... a rough English sailor who, while the young ladies say – What a charming picture – really that statue if one knew what it meant would be very pretty – stands with one of them on each arm with his thumbs in his pockets, whistling and looking another way'.[11] The Italians had already spotted that not all the English were classical scholars. The remark that the Colosseum would be a fine building when it was finished had already become famous.[12]

In the preceding century most of the English residents in Italy, unless they were artists, scholars or diplomats, were fleeing from the debtors' prison or religious intolerance. Now they were fleeing more modern things. Byron was a refugee from scandal and the intolerable stuffiness of London society, the Shelleys were fleeing a devouring parent and poverty. Leigh Hunt fled penury, the Brownings the Barretts. More often families were escaping from the fogs and rain of an English winter, the terrible increase in pulmonary tuberculosis from industrialisation causing something like panic among the parents of delicate children.[13] High domestic costs at a time of depression in England also made Italy a cheaper place in which to live so that a prudent person could enjoy all the conveniences of life, 'except a carriage'; for £150 a year.[14] Percy Bysshe and Mary Shelley were able to live in Italy for four years on an exiguous income, with servants, dependants and, latterly, a boat. Byron could contemplate putting up the Hunts and their seven children in the ground floor of his Pisan palazzo without a dent in his expenditure.[15] Mass tourism may have begun, but the attraction was not just cheap hotels (or palazzi) in the sun, or still less the mindless browning of the legs that has vulgarised, when it has not ruined, the coastlines of the Mediterranean. The visitors continued to be drawn by *qu'est qu'il y a de beau en Italie*.

Changing attitudes of visitors to *Italia*, separated by decades from each other, had been slow to show themselves. In 1701, wherever Joseph Addison turned his ravished eyes

> Gay gilded scenes and shining prospects rise,
> Poetic fields still encompass me around
> And still I seem to tread on classic ground.[16]

Tobias Smollett, in Italy in 1764, published his travel journal, like his French contemporary, the President de Brosses, as a series of letters to prove that he had done all the right things and gone to all the right places. Some of his observations were unexpected. He did not bow down before the aura of great art, but lamented the emphasis on 'Peter writhing on the cross, Stephen battered with stones, Sebastian stuck full of arrows, Lawrence frying upon the coals, Bartholomew flayed alive'.[17] But for the most part his letters describe, not the people, but the antiquities. By 1780 William Beckford remembered his classical education enough to go, 'full of the spirit of Aeschylus, to the Olympic theatre [in Vicenza] and vent my evil temper in reciting some of the most tremendous verses of his furies'.[18] Having got the classics out of his system he returned to his journal where, for page after page, he described the passing countryside as if he were annotating Richard Wilson. Even for the urbane Samuel Rogers, breakfaster and poetaster, who first visited Italy in 1814, Italy was still the land of classic art and he had come to fulfil an education interrupted by 20 years of war. He was thrilled to look 'upon a lake [Garda] mentioned by Vergil & sailed upon [by] Catullus', while modern architecture (i.e. anything built since 400 BC) was 'but a jumble at best & as inferior to the Greek when in its purity as a Monkey to a Man'.[19]

By December 1823, checking up on the ancients was not the primary object of most English tourists. Marguerite Blessington was quite clear about her purpose in being in Italy. 'When one is basking in the warmth of this sunny clime ... it is impossible, even in despite of patriotism, not to admit that Italy is a preferable winter residence.'[20] Though an inveterate sightseer she was not there to improve herself. 'The besetting sin of this place has taken possession of me ... Oh, the *dolce far niente* of an Italian life! Who can resist its influence? Not I – at least.'[21]

Grand Touring had been serious business, whoring apart, and tutors tended to behave like tour guides before Thomas Cook invented them. There was a lot to fit in. Mostly, as for Addison, it was classical sites, but the opera was a draw and some made cautious anthropological forays into the Catholic Church by attending cardinalatial *conversazioni* in Rome. William Beckford joined the melancholy sinners prostrate before the sanctuary of St Anthony at Padua. In case his old drawing-master should fear for his faith, he said that it gave him a good opportunity to study the bas-reliefs by Sansovino on the saint's tomb. Samuel Rogers noticed the inhabitants when they were either pretty or quaint. 'Every peasant you meet is the same slouching sauntering figure you see in an Italian caricatura.'[22] More savagely Percy Bysshe Shelley formed an opinion shortly after his first arrival in Italy that he was not to change: 'The people here, though inoffensive enough, seem both in body and in soul a miserable race. The men are hardly men, they look like a tribe of stupid shrivelled slaves and I do not think I have seen a gleam of intelligence in the countenance of man since I passed the Alps.' He told his father-in-law that he found educated Italians polished on the outside, but lacking sensibility, imagination and understanding. 'It ends in nothing and produces nothing.'[23] The Blessingtons had come to enjoy themselves in their curious *ménage à trois*, and Marguerite was to comment on the Italians who inhabited her *Italia* in a similarly patronising way. Her letters home describe a feckless and self-indulgent people. 'To live is here [Naples] so positive an enjoyment that the usual motives and incentives to study and usefulness are forgotten, in the enervating and dreamy enjoyment to which the climate gives birth.' Goethe, 36 years earlier had called Naples a paradise. 'Everyone here lives in a state of lightheadedness, with a total lack of selfconsciousness', while Maria Gisborne, friend of the Shelleys, liked the Neapolitan 'sprightliness and semibarbarous naiveté' and 'boisterous mirth'.[24] *Italia* was now being visited for pleasure as well as for instruction. Mary Shelley, when she came to leave in 1823, was heart-broken to leave a country to which, despite the loss of her husband and two of her children, she was 'attached from a thousand reasons'. 'I love Italy – its sky canopies the tombs of my lost treasures – its sun – its vegetation – the solitude I here enjoy – the easy life one can lead – my habits now of five years growth – all and everything endears Italy to me beyond expression. The thought of leaving it fills me with powerful tumults.'[25] But not the people. Mary had never found the locals *simpatici*. 'The Italians [in Naples] are so very disagreeable ... there is no life here. They seem to act as if they had all died fifty years ago and now went about their work like the ghostly sailors of Coleridge's enchanted ship – except indeed when they cheat.'[26] 'The people [of Pisa] were wild and hateful', if not so hateful as their neighbours at Lerici who 'are like wild savages'.[27] Smollett at Lerici, 57 years earlier, had 'imbibed a strong prejudice against the common people of that country'. In 1765, he had delivered himself of the lapidary opinion that 'all the common people [of Nice] are thieves and beggars', admitting that it seemed always thus with 'people who are extremely indigent and miserable'.[28] In Mary Shelley's short Gothic romance, 'Eboli', set in the Naples of Joachim Murat (it appeared in *The Keepsake* in 1828) parades her customary epithets to describe the Italians generally: 'she was an Italian, with all the habitual quiescence and lassitude of her country women in the ordinary routine of life'; 'he had an Italian's subtle talents, swiftness of perception, and guileful arts'; in 'The Bride of Modern Italy', 'Italians, male and female, are not great patronizers of the truth'; and in 'The Pole', a tale probably written by Claire Clairmont but edited by Mary, 'brave as a Pole, and unprincipled as an Italian'; 'his life would not be safe in that land of assassins and traitors'.[29] Italy was *un paradiso abitato dai diavoli.*

Marguerite Blessington, being of more sanguine temperament, remarked that the Neapolitans 'abandoned themselves [to activity] with the gaiety of children broken loose from school'.[30] At least children were a step up from savages. The trouble was that the English, as they were universally known, did not mix much with the natives. In 1819 *The Gentleman's Magazine* reckoned that there might be as many as 1,500 young Britons being educated in Italy, 500 British residents in Rome, 400 families in Naples and 800 in Tuscany.[31] There were now so many of them that they were no longer dependent on the grand ducal *soirées* in Florence, on princely open houses in Naples, or even on *conversazioni* in Rome. They had not much enjoyed them. Claire Clairmont described one *conversazione* in Rome, 'where there is a Cardinal and many unfortunate Englishmen who, after having crossed their legs and said nothing the whole evening, rose all at once, made their bows and filed off'.[32] There were enough fellow visitors to form a society of their own. Moreover, 20 years of beating Boney, of conquering India, of ruling the seas, had converted the landowner who loved his acres, Palladianised his house and Capability Browned his estate, who rode to hounds in his farmer's rig and was a good fellow, into a remote, glacially superior proconsul with jacket too tight and neckband too high. Squire Weston had given way to Mr Darcy. Darcys were choosy about their friends. The Italian aristocracy was poor, monoglot and often strange, while ordinary foreigners in general were either comic or dishonest. Charlotte Eaton in 1820 summed up Italy's social disabilities trenchantly. 'I never met a race of people who had, generally speaking so remarkable a contempt for truth. ... In Italy there is nothing worthy of the name of society at all.'[33]

Italians, particularly, when they were neither servants nor peasants, were expected to conform to the average northerner's stock of fictional villains.. Now, however, in the spate of works that followed Gibbon's *Decline and Fall*, some real-life Italians began to be added to that stock: Though some of them are only known today to operamanes, they were at the time hot items from the pens of Leigh Hunt (Francesca from *Rimini*, 1816), Byron ('The Lament of Tasso', 1817,

Marino Faliero and *The Two Foscari*, 1821), Percy Bysshe Shelley (*The Cenci*, 1819), Edward Bulwer Lytton (*Rienzi*, 1835) and Walter Savage Landor (*Giovanna of Naples*, 1839).[34] Shelley also embarked upon but never persisted with a play about Tasso, as he seems to have been diverted by the more exciting colloquy between Julian and Maddalo.[35] They might not have been lovable human beings, but they had all been real people and lived in historical time. That their lives were surrounded by intrigue, jealousy, hatred and betrayal, all concoctions of the passions that lurked deep in the Italian psyche, only served to confirm some of the worst suspicions of Italy and the Italians.

After her unexpected success with *Frankenstein*, Mary Shelley decided to write her next novel about an historical Italian. The Shelleys crossed the Mont Cenis Pass into Italy on 30 March 1818. Mary was 21, already something of a celebrity. As they intended to stay in Italy for some time they embarked on a reading programme that would leave today's students gasping. To obtain command of the language, Mary started to read Richardson's *Pamela* in an Italian translation, following it with *Clarissa*. Those who have read both these prolix novels in English will recognise this as a Himalayan task. In addition, in the course of the year, she polished off Ariosto's *Orlando Furioso*, Tasso's *La Gerusalemme Liberata*, Alfieri's tragedies and autobiography, Dante's *Inferno*, the tragedies of Monti, not to mention *Tristram Shandy*, Gibbon's *Decline and Fall*, two volumes of Montaigne, Pope's Homer, the plays of Molière, Corneille and Ben Jonson in their original languages, and the *Aeneid* in Latin. In 1819, in addition to a punishing programme of English and European classics, she added *The Decameron*, the rest of the *Divine Comedy* and Sismondi's *Italian Republics*, It was the last that introduced her to Castruccio Castracane, Lord of Valperga.[36]

Everyone in 1818 knew that from the outset of the dark ages Italy had been trampled over by foreigners, Germans, Normans, Angevins, French and Spaniards, that its republics had fallen into the hands of despots, doges, popes and Bourbons. Now with the end of the French wars, the Germans, or rather Metternich's Austrians, were back in strength. Italy was a patchwork. The Italians were not the stuff of ancient Romans, and had dissipated their political and artistic genius since the Renaissance in the benighted and fussy frivolity of the baroque. But that year Canto IV of *Childe Harold* signalled a possible change of heart. 'My dear Hobhouse', Byron wrote on 2 January,

> that man must be wilfully blind or ignorantly heedless, who is not struck with the extraordinary capacity of this people, ... the facility of their acquisitions, the fire of their genius, their sense of beauty, and amidst all the disadvantages of repeated revolutions, the desolation of battles and the despair of ages, their still unquenched 'longing after immortality' – the immortality of independence.[37]

The diapason of that rolling sentence echoed Lord William Bentinck's clarion call to the Sicilians: 'Warriors of Italy, you are asked to assert your rights and your liberty.'[38] It recalled Wordsworth's unforgettable lament on the extinction of the Venetian Republic (1802) and it drowned Shelley's complaint to Thomas Love Peacock, eight months later, of the avarice, cowardice, superstition, ignorance, passionlessness of the Italians that he observed after a few days in the city from which Byron had launched his letter to Hobhouse.[39] Could the image of *Italia* – the land of art – yield to that of *Italy* – a united nation? In 1820, however, a revolution in Naples frightened King Ferdinand into giving the Neapolitans the liberal Spanish constitution that had enjoyed a brief life there in 1812. Shelley, writing as if from Pompeii, the 'city disinterred', symbol of resurrection, hailed this 'youngest giant birth, ... arrayed in Wisdom's mail' waving its lightning lance in mirth.

> Nor let thy high heart fail,
> Though from their hundred gates the leagued Oppressors
> With hurried legions move.[40]

Alas, the warning was in vain. The high heart of the young giant broke in terror before the disciplined legions of Austria, sent in by the Holy Alliance. In Turin, the same constitution, introduced by the regent Carlo Alberto, was snuffed out by Austrian mercenaries on the field of Novara. Lord John Russell, who had in 1819 deplored the fact that the country of Virgil and of Tasso should be whipped into obedience by Bohemian corporals, now saw those whips turned to scorpions.[41] It did look as if *Italia*, the Italy of the Shelleys, could never sustain the Italy of Byron and Bentinck. It was always going to be let down by the innate defects of a meridional people, dedicated to *dolce far niente*, when not dishonest, craven and superstitious, a subject people, very far from ready for constitutional rule. The two *grani* for their macaroni, iced water and a puppet show was their daily expenditure and the few yards of canvas for their shirt and trousers were either easily earned or acquired by ingenuity, and then it was 'delicious *far niente*'.[42] They were Europe's Indians, for in that faraway subcontinent, British officials, who expected India one day to replace the lost United States as the jewel of the imperial crown, believed that its inhabitants had been too deboshed by centuries of despotism and Brahmanism, to have the stamina or character for representative government. And Brahmanism was Macaulay's word to describe papal government.[43] As Sydney Morgan saw them, Italians 'were lost in voluptuous tranquillity and steeped in dull licentiousness: in religion bigots, in morals abandoned, in intellect infantine and in the scale of nations a nonentity'. She might have been writing about her native Ireland.[44]

The growing evangelical belief that calamity occurred to those who deserved it, and that poverty was a punishment for immorality or fecklessness, was quick to accept the defeat of constitutional zealots by advanced and disciplined armies as the deserved chastisement of moral depravity. Mary Shelley had no doubts about it. Italy's oppression was Italy's own fault, partly punishment for the sins of past generations, partly for the follies of the present. Mary Shelley put her contempt into the mouth of a Roman of the republic, miraculously revived to see to what his Rome had been reduced. 'The wretched Italians, who usurp the soil once trod by heroes, fill me with utter disdain. Dare they usurp the name of Romans – dare they imagine that they descend from the Lords and Governors of the World?'[45] Percy Bysshe did not dissent.

> There are two Italies, one composed of green earth and transparent sea and the mighty ruins of ancient times, and aerial mountains ... the other consists of the Italians of the present day, their works and ways. The one is the most sublime and lovely contemplation that can be conceived by the imagination of man; the other the most degraded disgusting and odious.[46]

Mary doubted whether the Italians could profit by their independence, even if they won it, 'being too demoralised and degenerate after years of petty tyranny'.[47] This opinion is unexpectedly repeated by one of characters in George Meredith's *Sandra Belloni*, 30 years later: 'These Italians are in bondage, and since heaven permits it, there has been guilt. By endurance they are strengthened, by suffering chastened; so let them endure and suffer.'[48] There were Italians who felt the same. For Massimo d'Azeglio, future prime minister of the Kingdom of Sardinia, the worst of Italy's enemies were not Teutons but Italians. 'The Italians have wanted to make a new Italy, but themselves remain the old Italians, with all the worthlessness and moral poverty that have been their undoing for ages past.'[49]

Yet, as Leigh Hunt admitted, 'we have the best part of Italy in books, and this we can enjoy in England.' But he could not inspire his countrymen to take advantage of it. Despite the presence of 200 English families in Florence, Tuscan censorship and English indifference both defeated his dream of producing a digest of the best English periodicals, to be a bridge between England and Italy.[50] And this failure coincided in the late 1830s with an unexpected shift of British interest away from Italy. The young queen married a German prince. Coleridge, who had helped to popularise Cary's version of Dante's *Divine Comedy* among his countrymen, had lost

5. Shelley in the ruins of the baths of Caracalla, Rome, by Joseph Severn. The Italy of the Shelleys tended to be of a splendid past which deserved, but was not likely to have, a splendid future.

himself in the byways of German philosophy, on which he now gave his weekly lectures, his early enthusiasm for Dante overtaken by the discovery of Schiller and Goethe. Byron and Shelley were dead. Leigh Hunt in the 1840s was in his anecdotage, writing his autobiography (published in 1850). Bulwer Lytton had blazed a Teutonic trail with his *Pilgrims of the Rhine* (1833), though he still had *The Last Days of Pompeii* and *Zanoni* to write. Even Mary Shelley was rambling round Germany. Thackeray's *Pumpernickel,* the Rhineland states and the German spas, began to prove more exciting (and cleaner) to tourists than the Tiber, the Papal States and Bagni di Lucca. Germany was every bit as much a patchwork of ancient *signories* as Italy, and each had its history too. Moreover, the Germans were a northern people whom, the latter-day prophets believed, God had chosen to rule the world. One could not say of Germany (though Thackeray tried) what Elizabeth Barrett Browning said of Italy, that 'the roots of thought here ... seem dead in the ground. It is as well that they have great memories – nothing else lives'.[51] (It was fortunate that she consented to live in Italy with Robert, so that the world was spared Bishop Wulfram ordering his Tomb in St Adalbert's Church, and the interior monologue of Eleazar of Worms.[52] *Paracelsus,* in real life Theophrastus Philip Aurelius Bompast von Horenheim, was warning enough.)

Italy had suddenly gone off the intellectual boil and the British cultural eye was shifting to northern Europe. From 1837 there was only one voice in England which ceaselessly tried to draw it back to the political present of Italy, and that belonged to Giuseppe Mazzini. As a boy in Genoa he had read every volume by Walter Scott, and copied out poems by Milton, Pope and Shelley. Burns and Wordsworth he saw as liberating influences, unshackling the mind from the tyranny of classicism. Byron and Foscolo were the angel voices of a Young Italy. He was shocked on arrival in London to find that the common image of his homeland was still that of Mrs Radcliffe and of his countrymen that of Casanova.[53] The image of *Italia* had hardly changed.

Taken up by the Carlyles, retained to choose Italian books for the new London Library which Carlyle and Dickens had just started and to which he could never afford to belong, Mazzini kept the cause alive in London. Even he had to recognise that by 1837 Italy was beginning to be neglected, that in politics as in literature, British attention had turned elsewhere and that the expectation of Italy's social and intellectual regeneration had died with the betrayed hopes of 1831.[54] Leigh Hunt, faithful to Byron, was still ready to profess that 'Italy is a wonderful nation, always at the head of the world in some respects, great and small, and equally full of life. Division among its children is its bane; and Mazzini's was the best note that has been struck in its favour in modern times'.[55]

In 1836 that future paladin of Italian freedom, Garibaldi, wrote to Mazzini from Brazil, suggesting he set up a government in exile and give him letters of marque to operate two privateers from Rio de Janeiro to prey on Austrian and Sardinian vessels in South American waters. Some 35 Sardinian and fourteen Austrian ships called at Rio de Janeiro every year. Soon three vessels, *Mazzini*, *Giovine Italia* and *Giovine Europa* were flying the Italian *tricolore* as they cruised in international waters.[56] In 1834, Camillo Cavour was leaning to appreciate constitutional liberty in London. When the triumvirate emerged from the shadows to lead their various bids for Italian liberty, they were able to pluck at that sympathetic chord, struck by Bentinck, Byron, the Shelleys, Leigh Hunt and Bulwer Lytton in the years after Waterloo. Italy was not peopled only by dastards or villains, but had heroes of her own. However, the impression given by dastards and villains could not be so easily erased.

3

'Behind the Black Veil'

Villains and Villainy

'Have you gone on with Udolpho?

'Yes, I have been reading it ever since I woke and I am got to the Black Veil.'

'Are you indeed? How delightful; Oh! I would not tell you what is behind the Black Veil for the world. Are you not wild to know?'

'Oh! yes, quite, what can it be? – But do not tell me – I would not be told on any account. I know it must be a skeleton.'

Jane Austen, Northanger Abbey (1803/1818).

She endeavoured to think it possible that Madame Montoni had not been taken to the turret, but, when she remembered his general character, the looks of the men who had forced Madame Montoni from her apartment, and the written traces on the stairs of the turret – she could not doubt that her aunt had been carried thither, and could scarcely hope, that she had not been carried to be murdered.

Ann Radcliffe, The Mysteries of Udolpho (1794),
chapter x.

His gigantic, shadowy form, clothed like the ghost in Hamlet, in complete armour, but with the beaver up, was seen at midnight, by the moon's fitful beams, to advance slowly along the gloomy avenue.

Mary Shelley, Frankenstein, Preface to the 1831 edition,
on The History of the Inconstant Lover.

Isabella Thorpe did not tell Catherine Morland what lay behind the black veil as it is one of the great anti-climaxes of literature. The revelation that what Emily St Aubert thought was the embalmed corpse of the murdered Lady Laurentini was only a wax-work *memento mori* adds little or nothing to the unravelling of one of the more bizarre and operatic plots of its time. Yet publishers were mad to have a good mystery and paid the author the unprecedented sum of £500 for the rights to *The Mysteries of Udolpho*. And 'tout Bath', according to the novel that earned Jane Austen £10, was talking about it as one might the latest episode of a television drama.

How much damage did Ann Radcliffe do to the image of Italy? In her lifetime she was compared to Shakespeare, her tales for their poetic power to *King Lear* and *Macbeth*. Coleridge in 1794 thought that *The Mysteries of Udolpho* was 'the most interesting novel in the English language' and in 1815 Henry Crabb Robinson thought Radcliffe's descriptive powers greater than Sir Walter Scott's.[1] Catherine Morland, a lively, well brought-up young woman of both sense and sensibility, was a typical reader, whose appetite for mysteries was, given the ordinariness of her life, unquenchable. Julia Mazzini, Emily St Aubert and Ellena Rosalba, heroines respectively of *A Sicilian Romance*, *Udolpho* and *The Italian* (the novel Catherine was going to read after she had finished *Udolpho*) were, in character, little different from Catherine Morland, bred to parental love and loyalty, sensible, biddable young women, fond of novels and poetry, happy in gardens, kind to inferiors, comfortable with equals and, above all, 'tremblingly jealous of propriety'.[2] Where they differed from Catherine Morland was that they lived in lands where they could be exposed to fearful mystery, to chilling danger, to threats against their moral and physical welfare and to apparently supernatural happenings. Catherine may have tingled with delicious excitement at the prospect of similar adventures at Northanger Abbey, but she was very glad that she did not experience them, and pretty certain, in early nineteenth-century England, that she would not.

Jane Austen started *Northanger Abbey* in 1798, only four years after the appearance of *The Mysteries of Udolpho* and one year after that of *The Italian*, but, though accepted by a publisher in 1803, it was only published posthumously in 1818. Ann Radcliffe's reputation was still high when it appeared, and though Jane remarked 'that it was not in her novels that human nature, at least in the midland counties of England, was to be looked for',[3] she still had a devoted readership. Her heroines had the most terrifying experiences but none of them was driven to compromise her virginal reputation. Each one was able to display the moral rigour and good sense that well brought-up young women always should. Emily might faint somewhat excessively in the face of shock but she was never violated. All of them were to survive the eighteenth-century equivalent of the Perils of Pauline with honour. It was to be the greatness of Jane Austen to show that the qualities Julia, Emily and Ellena were expected to show in the face of these perils could just as easily be tested in the furnace of family life.

Mrs Morland and Mrs Thorpe would never have allowed their daughters to read about Julia, Emily and Ellena had they not been sure that these heroines always behaved with the most perfect delicacy, despite having to flee persecutors, scramble round dangerous dungeons, and cross mountain passes on rough mules. Smollett described the Savoyard mules as almost a different species from others: 'they have such an aversion to horses, that they will attack them with incredible fury, so as even to tear them and their riders in pieces!'[4] The girls plunged through secret thickets, were tantalised by spectral music in moonlit ruins, and surrounded by *banditti*. Of course, none of them was English. One was French, the other two were Italians, for it was the fashion of the day to set novels of terror and mystery in terrifying and mysterious 'abroad'. Isabella Thorpe had a list of them ready for Catherine, all set in Germany: *The Castle of Wolfenbach* and *Mysterious Warnings*, both German Tales by Mrs Parsons, *The Necromancer of the Black Forest* by Peter Teuthold, *The Orphan of the Rhine* by Eleanor Sleath and *Horrid Mysteries*, a story from the German by the Marquis of Grosse, 'translated' by Peter Will. Ann Radcliffe, who never travelled further south than Holland, set three of her shockers in Italy, but they were no more 'Italian novels' than *Little Women*. One influence on her was Charlotte Smith, whose Gothic castles were English.[5] Like all well-educated women of her day, Ann Radcliffe knew enough Italian to read Tasso, but only one book has been identified as providing some local colour for *Udolpho* and that was a travel book, *New Observations of Italy and its Inhabitants* by one Grosley.[6] For all their spurious Italian authenticity, the action of *A Sicilian Romance*, *Udolpho* and *The Italian* could have been set in Charlotte Smith's Castle Mowbray. Notwithstanding the bogus nature of her expertise, however, Ann Radcliffe conveyed to many of her readers the authentic whiff of Italy, the Italy of cloaks and gondolas – 'there are two nice Radcliffe words for you', Byron told Augusta Leigh in 1816 – of *stiletti*, *ban-*

ditti, intrigue and inquisition.[7] The adroit use of the first was held to be the peculiar skill of the treacherous Italian, so that there was almost a 'stiletto-school' of tales about Italy. And there was good reason for alarm. Byron at Ravenna, according to Thomas Medwin, feared that, but for protection in high places, he would have been openly assassinated.[8] And Shelley was sure that Byron's Venetian servant, Tita, assigned to him as valet when he was staying at Ravenna, had stabbed two or three people to death.[9] Hired assassins were to be the stuff of drama and opera for decades: incompetent ones, like Giacomo and Beppo, in Auber's *Fra Diavolo* (Paris, 1830), comic ones, like Malvoglio and Barbarino in Friedrich Flotow's *Stradella* (Paris, 1837), and, of course, sinister ones like Sparafucile in Verdi's *Rigoletto* (Venice, 1851).

What lingered in the memories of Ann Radcliffe's readers were not so much her castles as her villains: the Marquis Mazzini (*A Sicilian Romance*), the Abbate Schedoni (*The Italian*) and Signor Montoni (*Udolpho*). Mazzini is an intemperate and inconsiderate father, obsessed by family pride, Schedoni, a priest whose wickedness is of antinomian proportions, is an amalgam of passion and will, ready to defy the most sacred prohibitions to achieve his purposes, while Montoni is a ruined and attainted Venetian voluptuary seeking, by murder, sacrilege and blackmail, to revenge his wrongs and re-enter the society from which he had been excluded. Italian villains were no strangers to English literature. Shakespeare and the seventeenth-century dramatists were very familiar with a certain stereotype, derived in part from Giordano Bruno, in part from Machiavelli and in part from Pope Pius V, the excommunicator of Queen Elizabeth. Christopher Marlowe invited Machiavel, an especially devilish character, to introduce *The Jew of Malta*, in which the faithful Florentine secretary and historian 'counted religion but a childish toy, / And held there is no sin but ignorance.' Webster's *Duchess of Malfi* has scarcely an honest character in it, apart from the unhappy duchess and her secret husband. And at the end of the eighteenth century there was a sudden revival of such Italian villains.

A real horror appeared in 1786, when the father of Sir John Moore – the son whose burial at Corunna was to become one of the iconic images of the long Napoleonic wars – produced *Zeluco*. Dr John Moore had already written a popular and generally sympathetic *View of Society and Manners in Italy*; and this history of a Sicilian brat, brought up without restraint, may have been intended as a warning to parents. Instead it was read as a warning against the Italian character. Zeluco starts his career of villainy by squeezing the life out of a pet sparrow and goes on to torment his wife, mother and mistresses, abuse his slaves and servants, strangle his baby son and die in a duel with the lover of his concubine. The egregious Dr Moore, with an eye to publicity, warned his readers not to peruse the story, 'which traced the windings of vice and delineated the disgusting feature of villainy'. It was a great hit. Byron in 1813, tongue in cheek, was pleased to suggest that had he continued with *Childe Harold*, he might have created 'perhaps, a poetical Zeluco'.[10]

Dr Moore, in his *View of Italy* actually admired the Italian character and its capacity to enjoy life and create happiness. Yet *Zeluco* was so removed from reality as to be perverse. It was to spawn a host of other works, some of greater literary worth and some of less, all equally false to the country in which they purported to be set. Ann Radcliffe's works were among them. She did not, fortunately, take *Zeluco* for her model, but the Elizabethan dramatists. In that sense the contemporary comparison with *Macbeth* is revealing; but what makes Radcliffe no rival to the Elizabethans is precisely her inability to make wickedness comprehensible rather than just wicked. She fails to do with the hellish cleric, Schedoni, what Shakespeare does with the Scottish tyrant. Schedoni and Macbeth are both interested in power, but Schedoni's lust for domination has no point. He cannot be pope, or prince, or potentate, or poet. He might have been born in the court of the Duchess of Malfi but all he can do is terrify young ladies – which is the terrorism of the prep school. Ann Radcliffe excels in weaving a tapestry of scenic splendour round the gratuitous unpleasantness her villains generate, surrounding them with an almost sympathetic natural environment in which to work wickedness. Forests and caves and mountains loom terrifyingly dark and menacing round their 'designer' castle, with its ivied turrets, crumbling ramparts, ruined keeps, suspected ghosts and labyrinths of deserted subterranean passages as illogical as the London Underground. It was enough to make Henry Tilney's hair stand on end throughout the two days in which he read *Udolpho*, but not enough to cause Julia or Emily or Ellena to wet their knickers. All the supernatural events, however, turn out to have material causes, and virtue and innocence are unfailingly triumphant. For all that, Ann Radcliffe remains what Walter Scott called her: the first poetess of Romantic fiction, and Italy was her inspiration.

What had the poor Italians done to re-enter English literature in this way? Shakespeare for his part never pretended that Italian

Renaissance villains were any different from English Renaissance villains; but a later readership was steeped in the literature of Greece and Rome, and knew that it was not burdened with a sense of sin or villainy. Accordingly, any writer looking for a model villain outside the Bible would turn to the Elizabethans. Italy, moreover, was the home of the papacy that, with Machiavelli and the Society of Jesus, made up a trinity of evil in the Protestant consciousness. That repository of virtue had, from Elizabethan times, 'habitually associated sensation and horror with an Italian setting and had created a most potent image of a country of incest and intrigue, violence and hypocrisy, whose Church was anti-Christ, whose Jews pursued the evil trade of usury and whose intellectuals were typified by the fiendish Machiavelli'.[11]

However kind, noble or brave individual monks, nuns or priests might be in the succour they gave to frightened innocence, whatever solemnity and beauty there might be in the service of religion, whatever feelings might have been comforted by religious art or music, readers of Radcliffe novels were never to forget that the Roman Catholic Church was not only in error, but intrinsically and fatally WICKED. Julia in *A Sicilian Romance* finds timely sanctuary in the Abbey of St Augustin, 'a large magnificent mass of Gothic architecture whose gloomy battlements and majestic towers rose in proud sublimity from amid the darkness of the surrounding shades'. Yet, as the author warns us, in a long aside: 'Here prejudice, not reason suspended the influence of the passions: and scholastic learning, mysterious philosophy, and crafty sanctity, supplied the place of wisdom, simplicity and pure devotion.'[12]

Such professions of immunity from ideological contamination were as mandatory at the time as at the height of the twentieth-century McCarthyite purge in the USA. Sydney Owenson, Lady Morgan, a young Irish author whose object was to present her country in as favourable a light as possible to the Wellingtonian establishment that was nerving itself for Catholic Emancipation, felt obliged in her novel, *The O'Briens and the O'Flahertys*, to attack the Society of Jesus, 'those once sovereign lords of the will and intellect of the human race, who did but follow the vocation that man has ever acknowledged, to rule and dupe his fellow man'.[13] Robert Southey, nose down in Lisbon, writing an immense *History of Brazil*, found himself unexpectedly engaged in an epic tribute to the Jesuits. No one else had attempted to protect the wretched natives from the rapacious and murderous white settlers. Yet Southey felt it necessary to stop, from time to time, to remind himself that the Society was, despite its heroic efforts in Brazil, a corrupt and dangerous assembly, one that used 'the same persuasion [on those for whom it was responsible] as that wherewith the enemy overcame man: ... ye shall be as Gods, knowing good and evil'.[14] The strange ideas about Jesuits are best epitomised in the confusion of Sir Walter Scott, normally sympathetic to Roman Catholics, if not to Roman Catholicism. The villain of *Rob Roy*, Rashleigh Osbaldistone, the aspirant to Diana Vernon's hand, having been educated at St Omers had 'the manners of an accomplished Jesuit', and is represented as either being one or being destined for one. He is also an informer for the Whig government – but then anything could be believed of a Jesuit.[15] The term Jesuit or Jesuitical was loosely applied indiscriminately to men and women whose religious practice smacked of hypocrisy or moral ambivalence. The Society had been re-established in 1814 by Pius VII, and in its early stages of reincarnation was strongly supportive of reaction, so that George Eliot, writing as late as 1857, could portray a staunch Church of England lawyer describing an evangelical curate as 'a fanatical, sectarian, double-faced, Jesuitical interloper'.[16] And in 1844 Dickens portrayed the Jesuits in Genoa as 'slinking noiselessly about in pairs like black cats', adding that he 'had no knowledge, elsewhere, of more repulsive countenances than are to be found among' the clergy of Italy.[17] The 'slinking' Jesuit remained a stereotype well into the twentieth century, reaching its apotheosis in Evelyn Waugh's Father Rothschild.[18] Monastic houses fared little better: Sydney Morgan spoke for the whole generation when she categorised all monasteries as repositories of 'disgraceful bigotry, filth and idleness'.[19] Even ordinary Catholics inspired contempt. In 1858 a domestic servant is amazed 'at the infatuation of gentlefolks in choosing to sojourn among "Papishes, in countries where there was no getting to air a bit o' linen, and where the people smelt o' garlic fit to knock you down"'.[20] Shelley, in the preface to *The Cenci*, articulates a common view of religious practice among Catholics as 'adoration, faith, submission, penitence, blind admiration; not a rule for moral conduct. ... The most atrocious villain may be rigidly devout.' Coleridge in Malta, having been told that all Sicilians hoped that the English would take over the government of the island, nurtured visions of being offered a vice-consul's post there and living contentedly on £100 a year.[21] He was put off by the conviction that 'the immorality, ignorance and vacancy, and utter absence of moral sense' he perceived in the island, 'derived from the

Roman Catholic religion'.[22] He even held that 'the passion of the Maltese for Noise ... is the sum of the indifferent part of the Religion'.[23]

There had been plenty of naughty nun stories to titillate the heroic prurience of Protestant Christians, the most notorious being *Santa Maria, or the Mysterious Pregnancy*, by Joseph Fox (1797), in which a priest drugs and violates nuns and then suffers them to be buried in a state of trance. So widely held among English readers was this fixation with the general delinquency of Italian Roman Catholics that one of the many writers for tourists was led to protest. John Chetwode Eustace, a Roman Catholic priest from Maynooth, who had quietly adapted himself to the Protestant ascendancy, wrote a four-volume *Classical Tour through Italy*, which appeared in 1815. 'Is a scene of lewdness or debauchery', he asked,

> to be introduced into Romance? It is placed in an Italian convent. Is an assassin wanted to frighten ladies in the country or to terrify a London mob on the stage? An Italian appears; a monk or friar probably, with a dose of poison in one hand and a dagger in the other. Is a crime too great for utterance to be presented dimly to the imagination? It is half disclosed in an Italian confessional. In short, is some inhuman plot to be executed, or is religion to be employed as the means or the instruments of lust or revenge? The scene is laid in Italy; the contrivers and perpetrators are Italians; and to give it a more diabolical effect, a convent or church is the stage, and clergymen of some description or other are the actors of the tragedy.[24]

Ann Radcliffe's attitude to Italy and the Roman Catholic religion did not derive from the enlightened perspectives of a seasoned traveller, a fact which disgusted Byron. Unlike him, who 'have lived among the Italians – not Florenced and Romed and Galleried and Conversationed it for a few months', none of the writers of English terror novels had any real knowledge of Italy.[25] That other great Gothic terrorist, 'Monk' Lewis, placed his monkish villains and villainies (modelled on Schedoni, then almost white-hot from the press) in Spain – a country he knew no more than Ann Radcliffe knew Italy. After a brief diplomatic career Lewis became a society lion and a member of Parliament. His 'Italian' novel, *The Bravo of Venice*, was written in 1805, before he had ever set foot in Italy, and was actually an adaptation from the German and not Italian at all.

Most tourists went to Italy, not to study the Italian character, but to collect marbles and contemporary paintings, fill a book of water-colours and dip a little into the Pierian spring. Popular imagination now began to follow the tourists over mountains and rivers, up volcanoes, past mansions pitched in dales and gloomy fortresses perched on crags. The principal inhabitants of the mountains became hermits with mysterious powers and a dark history; those of the mansions villainous and despotic members of the local aristocracy; while the crumbling fortresses, complete with oubliettes, secret passageways and dungeons, housed a mixed population of corpses, skeletons, spectres and *banditti* on the lookout for disoriented travellers, deceived by treacherous guides and seeking shelter from perpetual thunderstorms of tropical intensity. The landscapes so lovingly described by Ann Radcliffe, when not slightly drama-tised versions of the Chilterns or Weald of Kent, owed everything to the immensely popular etchings of the work of Salvator Rosa (1615–73).

Horace Walpole expressed that popularity, as he crossed the Alps on muleback in 1739. What he saw were all 'precipices, mountains, torrents, wolves, rumblings – Salvator Rosa!' It was unnecessary to say more than Salvator Rosa – as today we might say pure Fellini or pure Hitchcock. And what the eighteenth-century viewer looked for was Nature as the 'inevitable agent of human suffering, mingling all her great operations with the passions and interests of man, blasting him with her thunder-bolt! wrecking him in her storms! burying him in her avalanches! and whelming him in her tornadoes!'[26] One cannot help feeling sorry for poor Rosa. His reputation for *terribilità* was based on the famous self-portrait, which showed him unshaven and furtive, his black locks marred for lack of a comb, a sneer on his lips, his half face shadowed, and dark cloak clutched round him. Nearly everyone thought it portrayed him as the *banditto* he was popularly supposed to have been, kidnapped as a child and brought up by bandits to be cruel, violent, merciless and treacherous in an environment to match. A complete travesty! In fact the sardonic self-portrait was intended to represent the scorn of a contemporary intellectual for the follies of the seventeenth century!

The son of a prosperous Neapolitan builder, Rosa had a sound education and at one point considered taking holy orders. He also aspired to be a satirical poet but, as such a profession seldom paid good money, he entered his brother-in-law's studio and trained to be a painter. He was schooled in the prevailing style of Neapolitan

6. Salvator Rosa's self-portrait, which gave him his sinister reputation. Byron used to cultivate the 'Salvator Rosa scowl'.

painting, wallowing in its legacy from the Spanish Caravaggisti, so that his work had 'the dark, poisoned, morbid character' of that school to perfection.[27] His *figurine* look forward to Goya. While his great contemporary in Rome, Claude of Lorraine, peopled his Arcadian landscapes with dancing peasants and Grecian nymphs and shepherds, Rosa filled his with *banditti*, beggars and mendicant priests. His pupil, Alessandro Magnasco, bowing to the demand from Grand Tourists, took the fashion a few stages further, so that the Italian landscape began to demonstrate a violence which 'created a mood of psychological intensity – witches, magic, quack doctors, saints and monks in ecstasy'.[28] The legend that Rosa had been reared by bandits added to the seduction of his work. Sydney Morgan, though careful to say that it was conjecture, added considerable warrant for the myth in her life of Rosa, which appeared in 1823.[29]

Until well into the nineteenth century, Rosa's continued to be one of the paradigm images of Italy. An actual victim of bandits, William Moens, kidnapped near Paestum in 1865 and held for six weeks while his ransom was being raised, recorded:

> The men with their guns in their hands, their picturesque costumes and reclining postures, the lovely light and chequered shade of the trees, made a picture for Salvator Rosa. But I do not believe Salvator Rosa, or any other man, ever paid a second visit to brigands, however great his love of the picturesque might be, for no one would willingly endure brigand life after one experience of it, or place himself a second time, in such a peculiar situation.[30]

In Edward Bulwer Lytton's *Zanoni* (1842) – a mishmash of Rosicrucianism and Art for Art's Sake, set in the time of the French Revolution – the English artist, Clarence Glyndon, regularly goes to view the paintings of Rosa in a Naples gallery in order to delight in 'the majesty, not of the good, but of the savage, utterly free ... a sorcery, not of the starry magian but of the gloomy wizard'.[31] Four years later, however, Rosa was to be tumbled into the dustbin of taste by the magisterial judgement of Ruskin who, in the last volume of *Modern Painters*, condemned him for only seeing what was 'gross and terrible', and for possessing a temper 'confirmed in evil'.

Of all the artists whose work he had ever studied, *ce damné Salvator* gave Ruskin 'most distinctly the idea of a lost spirit'. But, in the novels of Italian terror, lost spirits are all the rage.[32] And there was another popular influence from Italy upon the visual imagination of the English – the mass-produced engravings of Piranesi, the *Capricci di Carceri* of 1745 and *Le Antichite Romane* of 1756, which travellers bought with great gusto. The landscapes of Horace Walpole's first trip to Italy may have reminded him of Rosa, but the gigantic helmet that descended to crush the unhappy son of Duke Manfred in *The Castle of Otranto* fell straight out of the eighth plate of the *Carceri*. And in doing so it started the cult of Gothic Italy.

Walpole and Thomas Gray on their 1734 visit had not gone south of Rome. Few travellers in the eighteenth century did. To take the locale of his novel out of the world of temples and amphitheatres, Walpole pretended that it was a translation from a medieval tale and set it in Otranto, about the nearest place to Greece, on the heel of Italy, a place about which he knew absolutely nothing, except that it had a castle. Naming his characters from the Guelphs whom he plucked from Dante, he wrote not only the first Gothic novel (set indeterminately in the thirteenth century), but the first tale of Terror, which so frightened Gray and his Cambridge friends that they could not go to bed at night unaccompanied. It was also the first novel in English with a medieval setting of any length and popularity and thus claimed direct ancestry of the work of Sir Walter Scott, who rescued that world from phantoms and populated it with real people.

The plot cannot, in fact, bear the weight of so many firsts, and Walpole teeters so often on the verge of farce that sometime he writes like Mervyn Peake or Ronald Firbank. Then, suddenly, he falls into passages worthy of *The Cenci*. The apparitions are neither frightening nor remotely plausible (and one wonders whether Thomas Gray was joking), but both Ann Radcliffe's Emily and Ellena have a common ancestress in Walpole's Isabella, who only escapes the malignant attentions of Manfred by penetrating the secret entrails of the Castle of Otranto. The novel appeared in 1764: that magic year in which Ann Radcliffe was born and Gibbon heard 'the barefooted fryers singing vespers in the temple of Jupiter'. That date is very significant, for in their turn Gibbon, Walpole and Radcliffe were to fix Italy in the centre of the Romantic renaissance in English letters. Their influence on Walter Scott was acknowledged by the great man himself. Though he had no intention of following him down his macabre path of terror, Scott accepted that Walpole had 'attained by the minute accuracy of a fable, sketched with singular attention to the costume of the period in which the scene was laid, that same association which might prepare his reader's mind for the reception of prodigies congenial to the creed and feelings of the actors'.[33] Radcliffe worked on Scott like a drug, 'of most blessed power in those moments of pain and of languor, when the whole head is sore and the whole heart sick'. He chose, however, to use the imaginative release she gave him in his own way. When James Ballantyne accused him of imitation over the supposed haunting of Woodstock Manor, Scott replied that his aim was not to scare the reader but to show the effects of supernatural terror upon the characters in his story.[34]

John Keats, too, was a Radcliffe fan. 'I am going into scenery', he wrote to Reynolds on 14 March 1818, 'whence I intend to tip you a damosel Radcliffe – I'll coven you and grotto you and waterfall you and wood you and immense-rock you, and tremendous sound you and solitude you.' He was drunk on her landscapes. Eleven months later, on 14 February 1819, he was writing to George and Georgina Keats, promising in his next packet 'the Pot of Basil, St Agnes Eve and, if I should have finished it, the Eve of St Mark. You see what fine Mother Radcliffe names I have – it is not my fault – I do not search for them'.[35] His venture into an Italy of visual and verbal splendour was a debt he, too, paid to Walpole. His final residence in Rome when Byron and Shelley were also in Italy, though he wrote nothing there, was a consummation of his Shakespearanisms and Radcliffisms.

Byron, who probably knew the Italians better than anybody, despised the 'Terrorists', and his lines on Matthew Lewis are worth repeating:

> Wonder-working Lewis, Monk or Bard,
>   Who fain would make Parnassus a churchyard; …
> Even Satan's self with thee might dread to dwell,
>   And in thy skull discern a deeper hell.[36]

Even so, it was popularly supposed that Byron himself had modelled his scowl on Schedoni, while the Corsair, Lara and the Giaour stepped straight from the portraits of that powerful monastic villain. A truer inheritance of Italy, however, is to be found in the rich tapestry of Browning's verse, where we trace a direct line from Shakespeare, Ann Radcliffe and John Keats, enriched by a solid and proper knowledge of the locale. Shelley, too, had tried his hand, when he was eighteen, at a terror drama (*Zastrozzi*, which he set in Germany, peopled with Italians and climaxing in Venice) and his passion for weird and wonderful tales worked so fiercely upon his imagination that he would wake at night, screaming. The fruit of these tales was probably ripest in his wife's first novel, *Frankenstein*, but his villains, Cenci and Castlereagh, both have the sombre features of Montoni and Mazzini. And in that first night meeting between Jane Eyre and Rochester, we can still discern the dark features of a hero of Terror, while Wilkie Collins's Count Fosco (*The Woman in White*, 1860) and his hint of *stiletti* has stepped straight from the penumbra of those midnight children, the *carbonari*. By 1847, the year of *Jane Eyre,* in the decade that saw Bulwer Lytton's *Zanoni* and Browning's 'The Bishop Orders his Tomb at St Praxed's Church', the fanciful terrors of Italy were waning. The dubious character of the nation still ruled, but the British were beginning to look on this imperfection in a kindlier light, as the fruit of the regimes by which the country had been ruled for two centuries. The negative image of the Gothic novelists had begun to be modified by equally powerful influences from within Italian literature itself, and Italy entered the bloodstream of English literature to become a central part of the English literary imagination.

4

'The Silence of the Living'

Dante, Tasso and Ariosto in England

The Colosseum, the obelisks, all the wonders which are collected here from the depth of Egypt and Greece ... from Romulus right up to Leo X, ... all these wonders are in honour of the dead. Our idle way of life is barely noticed; the silence of the living pays homage to the dead. They endure and we pass on.

> Germaine de Staël, *Corinne*, Book ii, chapter 3,
> Corinne's improvisation on the Capitol.

When I die I'll have Shakespeare placed on my heart, with Homer in my right hand and Ariosto in the other, Dante at my head, Tasso at my feet and Corneille under my arse.

> Benjamin Robert Haydon to Keats, 8 April 1818.[1]

I am for Ariosto against Tasso.

> Samuel Taylor Coleridge, *Table Talk*, 12 July 1817.

In 1807 Italy was the subject of a literary bestseller when Germaine de Staël published *Corinne*. *Italy* was the novel's subtitle, and her hero was a dull prig, a conscientious Scottish nobleman, Oswald, Lord Nelvil, suffering a crisis of self-doubt following the death of his father, for whom he had had an exaggerated respect. Its heroine was a bluestocking Roman with the gifts of an *improvvisatrice*, who was actually the daughter of another English nobleman and an Italian mother. Thus de Staël was assured of a readership which her enemy, Napoleon, might have wished to deny her. The dialogue between Oswald and Corinne for half the novel is little more than an extended seminar on Italy clad, rather diaphanously, in the garments of a love affair.

Goethe, another master spirit of the age visited Italy in 1786–7, but his diary of that visit in the form of letters home only appeared as *Reise in Italien* thirty years later. Even longer than the thirty years it took Goethe to publish his notes on Italy, it was 173 years before John Evelyn's diary was published in 1818. All three works, despite the years that separated Evelyn from the German poet and the French novelist, described an Italy of the dead. Evelyn, a staunch Anglican and personal friend of Roman Catholics, having witnessed the execution of Thomas Wentworth, Earl of Strafford, and with civil war brewing in England, deemed it prudent in 1644 to take himself abroad. By 1645 he had reached the comparative peace of Italy. His diary was an exact account of the tourist sites that were to become a mandatory part of the Grand Tour. But it lay unread. Its appearance shortly after de Staël's novel and Goethe's letters confirmed that a well-organised system of tour guides had existed even in the mid-seventeenth century and lived happily off travellers ever since. Whether these travellers were English, French or German, their main interest was in the classical inheritance, and in High Renaissance art, which stretched from Raphael (1483–1520) to the Bolognese School, which culminated in Guercino (1590–1666), and which formed the bulk of the burgeoning collections at the courts of northern Europe. When Germaine de Staël decided to unwrap Italy for her world, she followed the same curriculum that had served for Evelyn and Goethe and the President de Brosses, and hundreds of other journalists and letter writers, but linked it to a Romantic tale of blue-blooded boy meets talented girl. Her object was to transform Italy, from the destination of everyone who wished to avoid feeling inferior, to an education in sensibility. British and, for that matter, French taste was yet to embrace the 'pre-Raphaelite' schools of Siena and Florence, the discovery of which still lay in the future, but the story of medieval Italy (not Walpole's travesty of it) had begun slowly to unfold during the eighteenth century, progressively exposed by the pen of Gibbon as a quarrelsome and distracting threat to the seamless eternity of Byzantium. It acquired colour from learned antiquarians, and was given substance by a Swiss banker and acolyte of Germaine de Staël. This man's magisterial work on the Italian republics proved, furthermore, to be the key to Dante's *Divine Comedy*, which Gothic and tantalising poem had proved impenetrable to ordinary readers. The Grand Tour, moreover, had exposed the ignorance on the part of northern visitors of what had happened to Italy between the fall of Rome and her miraculous renaissance.

The writer filling this gap was Jean Charles Leonard de Sismondi (the family name was actually Sismonde), who had been a banker's clerk in Lyons, until the execution of Louis XVI and the outbreak of war. His Genevan birth and Swiss nationality providing only uncertain protection in a France in embattled mood, he prudently took himself off to London where he spent the winter of 1794 so lugubriously that he decided to risk all and go home. But the eighteenth-century certainties of the city of his birth had been overturned, and the Sismondes' fortunes so much reduced by political turbulence that the family sold what was left of their property and bought a small farm near Lucca. Sismondi threw himself into being a farmer, but an intellectual rather than successful farmer, even writing a *Treatise on Tuscan Agriculture*. Italian provincial life, however, and its exclusive Roman Catholic culture did not suit the Protestant mind of a Genevan Calvinist, and by 1801 he was back in Geneva, forsaking the cultivation of his garden for that of his mind, determined to become a political economist. But one with a difference. Economists, he believed, had overmuch concentrated on the acquisition of wealth and ignored what was to be done with it, once acquired, to improve human happiness.

Germaine de Staël turned Sismondi from a boring Swiss political economist into one of the seminal influences on the Romantic movement. The daughter of Louis XVI's director-general of finance – Jacques Necker, whose dismissal had sparked off the sack of the Bastille – all her life believed that, but for the machinations of his enemies, her father's prescription for the economic and miraculous regeneration of France would have worked and thus avoided revolution. Now she swept the 28-year-old economist into her entourage at Coppet. There he fell in love with her, but not she with him – the Sismondes were just good bourgeois, and Germaine preferred to share her bed with men of aristocratic pretensions. He was commanded to join her caravan on its journey into Italy, where he was to be one of the midwives of *Corinne*. De Staël loved history more than political economy, on which she had rather staid physiocratic views, and with her encouragement Sismondi was able in 1807 to launch the first of the sixteen volumes that constituted *The History of the Italian Republics of the Middle Ages* and which occupied him until 1817. Without de Staël's 'orders' to some of her literary friends to review the volumes as they appeared, they might have passed straight into oblivion. With her support, and long before the work was finished, Sismondi had become a literary personality, returning for his research to Geneva, where he acted as secretary to the chamber of commerce, and gave public lectures on the literature of southern Europe. With the history of the Italian republics rivalling in length, if not in literary power, Gibbon's *Decline and Fall of the Roman Empire*, he then turned to a *History of France* which occupied him for 23 years and ran to 29 volumes. 'Formerly I hated history', Ruskin, travelling to Italy in 1845 with three volumes of the *Italian Republics*, told his father, 'now I am always after Sismondi. I had not the slightest interest in political science, now I am studying the constitutions of Italy with great interest.'[2]

The Italian republics attracted both Sismondi and de Staël as an early demonstration of man's desire for political freedom, from the challenge of the cities of the Lombard plain to the overweening ambitions of Frederick Barbarossa, to the rise and fall of Florence as the avatar of republicanism. The republics had successfully challenged the largest feudal conglomerate, the Holy Roman Empire, to which they often acted as bankers, and engendered prodigal wealth, much of which was spent on art and works for the public good. Florence, a second Athens, provided Sismondi with a study of the popular benefits to be derived from the accretion of private riches, which always absorbed him.[3] He, as a result, provided Italians with a roll call of hard, successful men to offset the popular image of either effete or unscrupulous successors to the Romans, fated to be ruled by foreigners. He recognised that *Italia*'s prodigal wealth and fertility had always attracted the envy and acquisitiveness of her larger neighbours, whose ruling dynasties were attracted to the idea of the Roman purple, and the most successful of his tyrants were those republican leaders who used political rivalries to carve out economically viable satrapies of their own. Though the history was a long catalogue of cruelty and failure, which branded Italians with a image they have never wholly succeeded in shaking off, Sismondi's work also provided evidence that they could manage democratic freedoms and might do so again. Mary Shelley was an early student of Sismondi, who introduced her to Niccolò Tegrini's *Life of Castruccio Castracano*, written in 1496, the mine from which she hewed her second novel, *Valperga*.[4] Castruccio Castracano was a native of Lucca, one of those ambitious adventurers who kept the Guelph–Ghibelline wars alive in the fourteenth century. Tegrini describes the rise of a warlord, a consummate field commander as unprincipled as he was skilful, who invited the Bavarian elector, Lewis, to collect his iron crown from Milan and then have himself, despite papal anathemas, crowned by schismatic bishops as Holy Roman Emperor in the Vatican. Castracano's reward for this bit of imperial meddling was to become, with imperial help, the tyrant of Tuscany. But in 1328 he suddenly died, and Florence was saved.

Mary Shelley's Castruccio rejects the prospect of simple happiness as Lord of Valperga, in consort with the suggestively named Euthanasia, for the lure of power. His character so deteriorates as the novel develops that even the besotted Euthanasia renounces him and joins in a conspiracy to have him removed. The plot is betrayed, Euthanasia is sent into exile and drowned en route. No happy ending here. Mary had suffered too much in the writing of it, for she had lost everything but her husband and one surviving son. Some compare *Valperga* favourably with George Eliot's *Romola*.[5] *Castruccio Castracano* was also the source of a short story that she wrote at the same time as *Valperga*. 'The Tale of the Passions' appeared in the second number of *The Liberal*, the journal that Leigh Hunt had been summoned to Pisa to produce at the initiative of Percy Bysshe and with Byron's money. Set at the time of the death of Manfred's son Corradino, which she had been researching in her usual intensive way, it describes in chilling detail the fate of a young woman who appealed for the life of the young emperor, then a prisoner in the hands of her former lover. She may have banked on his former feelings for her, but her appeal only resulted in her own and Corradino's death at his hands, reflecting the ruthlessness of the times, which Sismondi made no effort to conceal.

Though both stories have many of the features of a Radcliffean Gothic novel, Mary's *Valperga* does recognise that Italy is peopled by Italians who have an agenda for their own future. Euthanasia's 'young thoughts darted into futurity, to the hopes of freedom or Italy, of revived learning and the right of peace for all the world'.[6] On another occasion, one of her characters despises the Florentines, whose 'watchword is that echo of fools and laughing stock of the wise – liberty'.[7] Liberty, freedom, two words that only occur in a Radcliffe novel as the object of a distressed maiden escaping her persecutors, were to become in Mary's lifetime the watchwords of a new Italy, an Italy reduced to servitude by its fatal gift of beauty, unable to 'awe the robbers back, who press / To shed [her] blood, and drink the tears of [her] distress'.[8]

De Staël/Corinne's long seminar on Italy incorporates philosophical studies of the country's history, literature and art, in all of
which Italy was far richer than superficial tourists gave her credit
for. Even the opinions of so knowledgeable a pupil as her Scottish
lover, Oswald Nelvil, have to be corrected. Dante, Petrarch, Guarini,
Tasso and Metastasio were not the sum, Corinne informed her small
circle of rapt admirers, of Italian literature. There were Chiabrera,
Guidi, Filicaia and Parini, not to mention Sannazaro and Politian
who wrote in Latin. Like most of de Staël's readers, they bow their
heads in agreement and, indeed, within eleven years of the publication of *Corinne*, Byron had loosely woven Filicaia's *Italia, Italia ! Oh
tu cui die la sorte / Dono infelice di bellezza*[9] into *Childe Harold*, and a
few years later still Felicia Hemans used his lines as the epigraph to
her 'Lines on the Restoration of the Works of Art to Italy'.

Not to be silenced, however, Lord Nelvil attacks the emptiness of
Italian prose, to which Corinne in turn bows her head. 'Being
deprived of their independence over the last few centuries by unfortunate circumstance, Italians have lost all interest in truth and often
even the possibility of expressing it.' Italians are afraid of new
thoughts, but through laziness. Moreover, she ends lamely, 'the
peoples of the South are inhibited by prose and depict their true
feelings only in verse.'[10] The Italians had no theatre to compare with
England or France, for in Italy there were only 'violent passions or
idle pleasures'; that was not their fault, but 'violent passions produce such highly coloured crimes and vices that they make all
distinctions of character disappear'.[11] For Corinne, the observation
of the human heart was an inexhaustible source for literature 'but
the nations which are more suited to poetry than to reflection
indulge more in the intoxication of joy than in philosophical irony'.
Machiavelli had caused Italians to recoil from the terrible truth he
revealed about the human heart, so they had taken refuge in poetic
exaggeration. James Forsyth in 1813 found every Pisan bookshop
and social circle swarming with poets but, in speculating how so
many made a living, reckoned it was not from sales but from dedication fees.[12] Walter Savage Landor appeared to speak from his own
experience when he stated, in the mouth of his fictional secretary
companion, J. J. Stivers, 'here in Italy the poets are as troublesome as
flies, and pretty nearly as plentiful. At every inn as you alight, they
bring you a copy of verses ... [an] *Epitalamio* or *Lode*, in which every
prince is Tito, every green-grocer *Mecenate*'.[13] There was hardly a
town of any size without its theatre, exhausting the little stock of

classical drama, translations and comedies of manners. The Italians had failed to inspire a great dramatic tradition, not because there were no great dramatic actors, but because there was no great drama to enact. If a central authority could fight against the indolence natural to the climate and give life to the whole nation which was currently satisfied with a dream, then, Corinne/de Staël believed, a great tradition would be born.[14]

Corinne, partly because of de Staël's international reputation as Necker's daughter and Napoleon's one unsilenced critic, became one of the most widely read books in Europe. Not least among its achievements was the promotion of Italy, not as the supine figure of *Italia*, over whom tourists, grand or otherwise, crawled and poked and dug, but a sleeping giant that would shortly find its voice and astonish the world. If that voice, when it became heard, was to belong not to a new Alfieri but to Giuseppe Verdi, no matter. By unveiling the names of Italy's literary paladins, de Staël inspired a wish to read them. By 1821 and the death of John Keats, the English were able to do so in their own tongue.

A knowledge of Italian literature, often read in Italian, was a property of many English readers who never travelled abroad, especially women whose education had not been in Latin and Greek.[15] Most of the works listed by de Staël were part of every decent library. Giovanni Battista Guarini's *Pastor Fido* (1589), known to lovers of Handel and Mozart, had been much translated, while Machiavelli's *Prince* as well as his *History of Florence* and *Art of War* had been available in English before the end of the sixteenth century. Constitutional lawyers and religious knew the works of Cesare Beccaria, which were to find their English clothing in the work of Jeremy Bentham. Alfieri, despite being the lover of Bonnie Prince Charles's widow, had not been translated into English but his plays were often also written in French and had a European réclame. Keats took one of them to read in Rome. There was, however, one big exception. Until 1817, the three parts of the *Divine Comedy* of Dante Alighieri were almost universally unread in Britain. Extracts from the *Inferno* had been translated into English, mainly the story of Ugolino, who was forced to watch his children die of starvation in prison and whose teeth were fixed permanently into the skull of his persecutor.[16] These translations, including Thomas Gray's, which referred to 'clotted blood with hair' and 'shuddering lips', had made Ugolino into a Gothic hero, and the image of Dante himself began to

be associated with the gaunt and horrid semblance of his own creation. Macaulay thought that portraits of Dante could give Chantrey
hints for his projected head of Satan![17] It was hardly surprising then
that, while young women sighed over Tasso and artists toyed with
Rinaldo and the besotted sorceress Armida, Dante was considered
too Gothic, medieval and Roman Catholic for their impressionable
and tender minds. According to Thomas Medwin, Byron found
most of the *Divine Comedy* a great bore: 'Who can read with
patience, fourteen thousand lines, made up of prayers, dialogues
and questions, without sticking fast in the bogs and quicksands, and
losing his way in the thousand turns and windings of the inextrica-
ble labyrinth of his three-times nine circles?' Shelley, on the other
hand, 'the more he read Dante, the more [he] admired him'.[18] Sismondi had given Dante a heroic accolade as a prophet of liberty,[19]
but Shelley was attracted by his dedication to love and 'Intellectual
Beauty', being the greatest exponent of spiritual love for women, to
which Shelley aspired in his passion for Emila Viviani, 'the only Italian for whom I ever felt any interest'.[20] Shelley's great accolade to
Dante as understanding the secret properties of love even more than
Petrarch, the first epic poet after Homer, a bridge over the stream of
time which unites the ancient to the modern world, may have been
written in 1821 but it was not available to the ordinary reader until
1840.[21] His words were therefore more prophetic than a contribution
to the rediscovery of the *Divine Comedy*.

Dante was also very difficult to read. Benjamin Robert Haydon
might have him 'at his head'[22] but, as Napoleon once jested sourly,
Dante's fame was increasing and would continue to increase only
because no one ever read him. Henry Boyd, Church of Ireland
incumbent of Killeigh near Tullamore in County Offaly, produced
the first English translation of the whole of the *Inferno* in 1785, dedicated to the Italophile Frederick Augustus Hervey, later Earl of
Bristol, then Bishop of Derry. A second clergyman, Henry Francis
Cary, became interested in Dante at Oxford and began to translate
him when he secured his first living, completing the *Inferno* in 1805.
He had it printed at his own expense and, enjoying only a modest
stipend, did not think he could afford to complete the trilogy. He
went on, however, to translate the *Purgatorio* and *Paradiso*, printing
both in 1812 from his private purse, and the total work would have
remained as unnoticed as had been Boyd's *Inferno* were it not for a
chance encounter with one of the master spirits of the age. Cary and
Samuel Taylor Coleridge were each separately pacing the beach at

Littlehampton when the philosopher poet was attracted by hearing the clergyman recite Homer to his little son in Greek. This was too unusual an occurrence to be allowed to pass unremarked. Coleridge introduced himself and took away a copy of the newly translated *Divine Comedy*. He read it at once and was so impressed that, during his winter lectures, he gave it much-needed publicity. A second edition in 1817 started to sell well.

In Cary's translation, vivid and robust like the original, Dante burst upon the English consciousness like a meteor. Critics might complain of Cary's simple, almost vulgar style – for they were used to religious epics being set in rolling Miltonic stanzas – but it was Cary who provoked the artist's eye of William Blake, between 1824–7, to produce the stunning watercolours of the *Divine Comedy*, now in the Tate Gallery. Blake confessed to using Cary as his crib, for he had a copy of the poem in Italian. And, through Blake, Cary hopped over the Channel to inspire Delacroix and Gustave Doré. By that unexpected transference, the *Divine Comedy* was romanticised, for Dante's 'conceptions most monstrous and horrible' were antipathetic to the classical spirit. Crabb Robinson, for one, was amazed at how his friend Blake threw 'grace and interest' over them.[23]

Dante was an almost exclusive discovery of the Romantic poets. Wordsworth thought Dante might have been 'extolled above measure', but in the speech patterns of his own poetry, Wordsworth came closest to Dante's direct and economic dialogues. Hazlitt hailed the *Divine Comedy* as 'the first great step from Gothic darkness and barbarism',[24] while Carlyle saw the three sections of the poem as 'a great supernatural world cathedral'. For him Dante 'speaks to the noble, the pure and great, in all times and places', a 'world voice' to compare with Shakespeare's, and while he apostrophised Italy as 'dismembered, scattered asunder', 'yet the noble Italy is actually one; Italy produced its Dante; Italy can speak!'[25] Obstinately, readers seldom progressed beyond the *Inferno*, finding in *Purgatorio* and *Paradiso* a spirituality which was either objectionable or obscure to Victorian Calvinism and, while Dante remained a hero in Carlyle's terms, his public was to prove Napoleon right. With the deaths of the Romantics Dante slipped back into limbo, but his place as spokesman for a revived and independent Italy remained implanted in every educated Briton's mind.

Torquato Tasso was quite another thing. *La Gerusalemme Liberata* was an epic poem in 20 books, written in *ottava rima*, and first published in 1580, describing the first crusade of Godfrey de Bouillon and his fellow paladins to liberate Jerusalem. Interleaved with the marches, sieges and battles are fairy tales of sorcerers, enchant-resses, *belles dames sans merci*, paynim knights, who turn out to be lovely Amazons for whom their Christian foes sustain an invincible passion. Rinaldo and Armida, Tancredi and Clorinda, Olindo and Sofronia, and Erminia live in its pages with a vividness that for 200 years inspired work by Monteverdi, Handel, Gluck, Poussin, Tiepolo, Spenser and Milton, not to mention a host of lesser artists. No epic work since the *Aeneid* had so great a cultural impact on Europe as *La Gerusalemme Liberata*, not even *Paradise Lost*, which was known only to English-speaking readers. *La Gerusalemme Liberata* had appeared in English in 1600, 20 years after its first publication in Italy, translated by Edward Fairfax, the natural son of Sir Thomas Fairfax, and dedicated to Queen Elizabeth. It was dubbed *Godfrey of Bulloigne or the Recovery of Jerusalem*, and was an instant success. King James I valued it above all poetry; his unhappy son Charles I read it during his confinement before execution. Milton learned Ital-ian to read it. More than any other work, it brought Italian literature to northern readers, and when people said they had read Tasso, they usually meant that they had read Fairfax.

Tasso, either in the original or in Fairfax's translation, was cer-tainly on every educated person's reading list in the eighteenth century. Even Ann Radcliffe had enough Italian to read *La Gerusa-lemme Liberata*. Some readers were almost as familiar with it as with Horace or Catullus. Leigh Hunt had started to learn Italian with a friend in 1799, shouting out in antiphon Metastasio's 'Ode to Venus' as loudly as they could over Hornsey Fields.[26] While in prison Hunt read through the 56 volumes of *Parnaso Italiano* and found it truly 'a lump of sunshine' on his shelves,[27] so that by 1821 Shelley was ask-ing him to correct his Italian.[28] Leigh Hunt tells the story of an usher in a country school who, identifying an exhausted young foreigner with a guitar as an Italian, addressed her in Latin, Italian being in his view but a bastard of the Latin.

'*Non dubito quin tu lectitas poetam illum celeberrimum Tassonem. Taxum,* I should say properly, but the departure from the Italian name is considerable.' The stranger did not understand a word.

'I speak of Tasso,' said the usher, 'of Tasso.'

'*Tasso! Tasso!* ...' repeated the fair minstrel, '*oh, conosco Tas-so!*' and she hung with an accent of beautiful languor upon the first syllable.

'Yes,' returned the worthy scholar, 'doubtless your accent may be better. Then of course you know the classical lines:

> *Intanto Erminia infra l'ombrosy pianty*
> *D'Antica selva del cavallo* – what is it?'

The stranger repeated the words in a tone of fondness, like those of an old friend:

> '*Intanto Erminia infra l'ombrose piante*
> *D'antica selva del cavallo è scorta;*
> *Nè più governa il fren la man tremante*
> *E mezza quasi par tra viva e morta.'*[29]

['Meanwhile Erminia, borne by her steed deeper into the shades and shadows of an ancient wood, could no more guide it with her shaking hand, half dead, half live she seemed upon its back.']

This was the passage of *La Gerusalemme Liberata* that its readers knew best. In 1785 Mrs Piozzi imagined that she heard the gondoliers singing it outside her window in Venice, while Corinne and Oswald heard them swapping stanzas from one end of the Grand Canal to the other.[30] Tasso's martyrdom as a madman, confined for seven years for his supposed love of the Duchess of Ferrara (unlike Dante's spiritual love of Beatrice), and his death before his final apotheosis on the Capitol in Rome, combined to make his houses in Ferrara and Rome places of pilgrimage as sacred in their time as the house at the foot of the Spanish Steps, in which John Keats died, is in ours. So many English visited Tasso's supposed birth house in Naples that the *lazzaroni* assumed he was a great warrior to whom they felt impelled to pay respects.[31] Byron, who had probably read *La Gerusalemme Liberata* as early as 1811, only wrote his 'Lament of Tasso' after visiting Ferrara in 1817. Shelley, too, visited Ferrara to see the manuscript of the great poem, and his fragment of 'Tasso', written in 1818, in which there was a character called Maddalo, was to be devoted to the madness that resulted from Tasso's love for Leonora d'Este. Diverted by his meetings with Byron, Shelley used Maddalo instead, in *Julian and Maddalo*, as Julian's fellow-visitor to the madhouse in the Venetian lagoon, in which was confined a man driven mad for love. Tasso was, for most of his admirers, a symbol of Italy deprived, capriciously, of liberty. He was, also, the author of words to which Shelley was passionately attached: '*Non merita il nome di creatore, se non Iddio ed il Poeta*' ['God and the Poet alone merit the name of creator'].[32]

The third member of the great trinity was Ludovico Ariosto. His *chef d'oeuvre, Orlando Furioso,* was part heroic epic and part burlesque, set in the chivalric wars of Charlemagne against the Moors. It was partly a tribute to the ancestors of one of the princely houses which found itself impotent in the contest between French and Spanish power in Italy, partly a court diversion, even satire, of a culture that flourished almost on suffrance. Ariosto was not seeking to write a new *Iliad* or *Aeneid*. The romance was spiced with pantomime. John Harington's 1591 translation – which inspired Spenser's allegoric tribute to Queen Elizabeth I in the Arthurian *Faerie Queene* – remained unrivalled for two centuries and may still claim the primacy today.[33] But *Orlando* was rediscovered in the mid-eighteenth century, not by anyone wishing to find a model for the paladins of the new British empire, but by two under-employed enthusiasts for the Italian language. The first was the keeper of the wardrobe at Hampton Court and the second an accountant in the service of the East India Company. The first, William Huggins (1696–1761), was the son of the warden of the Fleet prison who, after studying at Magdalen College, Oxford, refused a fellowship as he did not wish to take holy orders, and entered royal service. His position in royal pay being almost a sinecure, he set himself, over 20 years, to translate *Orlando Furioso.* In 1755 it appeared in two volumes under both his name and that of an Irish cleric and chaplain to the Earl of Hillsborough, Temple Henry Croker (1730?–90). Croker, who wrote the dedication to George III, at first claimed a greater part than he deserved in the translation and in a second edition credit was returned to Huggins, who went on to attempt a translation of Dante, of which an extract appeared in *The British Magazine* in 1780. Huggins had no way with words: Boswell reports him arguing with Thomas Warton on Ariosto's influence on Spenser, resorting to incoherence – 'I will militate no longer against his nescience'.[34] But he was an enthusiast, even erecting on his estate a small hexagonal *tempietto* dedicated to the poet, on which he had carved the following lines:

> Per me se'n va l'incerto Viandante
> Qui non s'albergha un oribil Gigante,
> Né della fata Alcina il bel sembiante;
> Castello non son io del Mago Atlante;
> Ma benché rozzo un Cumulo, son posto
> Pegno d'Amore verso il Divino Ariosto

[The puzzled wayfarer may walk through me. Here does not live a horrible giant, nor the witch Alcina with her lovely face. I am not the castle of the Magus Atlante. Though only a rough pile, I am here as a pledge of love for the Divine Ariosto].

A very Romantic thing to do.[35]

Like Huggins, the other translator, John Hoole, was one of Johnson's circle. The son of a watchmaker, he was educated, he told Johnson, in Grub Street.[36] Unable to follow his father's avocation because of poor sight, Hoole was admitted to India House as an accounts clerk. He was a good accounts clerk, rising slowly by degrees to be the chief accountant of the East India Company. In 1772 he presented to Parliament a state of East India Affairs that precipitated the Regulating Act of 1773, which overhauled the government of India and made Warren Hastings governor-general.

In what must have been the leisurely tenor of life in Leadenhall Street – despatches took from three to six months to reach London from Calcutta – Hoole set about learning Italian and translating Tasso and Ariosto. His version of *Jerusalem Liberated* appeared in 1763 and ran to seven editions, the last appearing in 1819. The first ten books of *Orlando Furioso* came out in 1767, and the whole poem 'reduced' to 24 books in 1791, with all the passages that might bring a blush to a maiden's cheek omitted. Dr Johnson was persuaded to write the dedication to Queen Charlotte, an unlikely descendant of Tasso's patroness, for the d'Este family of Ferrara was related to both branches of the British royal family. One branch of the d'Estes had married into the ruling house of Brunswick-Lüneburg from whom the electors of Hanover, later kings of England, were directly descended. And when James II married as his second wife Maria Beatrice (Mary of Modena), the daughter of Alfonso d'Este IV (1634–62), she became ancestor to both the Old and Young Pretenders. Lamenting that it had not been the poet's good fortune to live under a British queen, where 'he might, among the descendants of that illustrious family have found a more liberal and potent patronage',[37] Johnson also begged his friend, Warren Hastings, to become a patron. In gratitude, Hoole got up a city club for Johnson, while he went on to write three dramas based on plays by Metastasio, some of whose work he had published in translation in 1767.[38]

Johnson did not think much of the Fairfax version of *La Gerusalemme Liberata*. In his essay on Waller, he reproduced a long passage of Fairfax to show how much Waller had improved on the master from whom he claimed to have learned the art of versification.[39] He hoped that, with Hoole's translation, neither needed reprinting. Charles Lamb, on the other hand, a very junior colleague of Hoole's at India House, though he hailed him 'the great boast and ornament of India House', was not impressed by Hoole's new version. Without having read either Tasso or Ariosto, Lamb had imagined that Southey's *Joan of Arc* ('I had not expected to presume any thing of such excellence from Southey') had been written, for its 'exquisite combination of the ludicrous and the terrible', in the manner of both poets. But now he had read Hoole's Tasso, he found it more vapid than smallest small beer 'sun-vinegared'.[40] Southey, however, who had read Hoole's version when he was ten (1784) claimed that it created the first of 'his epic dreams'. By 1805 Wordsworth had translated two books of *Orlando Furioso*, and Leigh Hunt rendered 65 stanzas in 1820.[41] The Shelleys both read *Orlando Furioso* when they entered Italy in 1818, Percy Bysshe Shelley finding Ariosto 'entertaining, graceful and *sometimes* a poet. ...[but] ... Where is the gentle seriousness, the delicate sensibility, the calm and sustained energy without which greatness cannot be?' There was too much revenge, cruelty and superstition – give him Petrarch every time, or Tasso. Even with this lukewarm endorsement and despite his 'assumed and artificial style'[42] Ariosto engaged the enthusiasm of Byron and, through him, entered the British bloodstream.[43]

Of all the Romantics the poet who seemed most invaded by the ghosts of Italy was John Keats. He did not go to Italy, like Byron and Shelley before him, to escape northern prigs, only northern weather. He had hoped to improve his knowledge of Italian by reading the plays of Alfieri with the help of a dictionary but, in the event, he barely got beyond the first. For the play was *Filippo*, and Severn says that he was discouraged by the first two lines he read: '*Misera me! sollievo a me non resta / Altro che'l pianto, ed il pianto è delitto.*' ('Wretched me. My only solace is from tears and weeping is a crime.') It was too depressing.[44] His enthusiasm for the Italian language, which had fired him three years before, had faded with disease. But in 1817, in a letter to his sister Fanny, he had wished that Italian would supersede French in every school throughout the country. Italian, Fanny read, 'is full of real Poetry and Romance of a kind more fitted for the Pleasure of Ladies than perhaps our own'.[45] By September 1819 Keats was boasting to his brother and sister-in-law in America that 'in the course of a few months I shall be as good an Italian scholar as I am a French one'.[46] His pathway to linguistic competence was to be six or eight stanzas a day of *Orlando Furioso*. After a relentless diet of Italian classics taken in this way, Keats would then 'get complete in Latin', particularly medieval and the Renaissance Latin 'of Aretino, Sannazaro and Machiavelli'. Apart from the pleasure of a constant immersion in great poetry, he found intellectual satisfaction in being acquainted with foreign languages. Just as Macaulay, who knew long passages of the Authorised Version of the Bible by heart, owed his proficiency in foreign tongues to his reading those passages in whatever foreign version was available to him, so Keats acquired his French, and what Italian he was able to learn, from reading great poetry. Given the immense length of *Orlando Furioso* – too diffuse, he told John Taylor,[47] – Keats made little progress with the language at the pace he was going, and by November he was tired of it: 'I would rather read Chaucer than Ariosto.'[48]

If he had made only modest progress with Italian he had learned how to adopt the Ariostan style, and in 1820 produced a poem in the manner of the master. 'The Cap and Bells' was not published until 1848, as he never finished it. It is a fantastic tale, about the ill-starred loves of a fairy, Prince Elfinan, betrothed to a fairy princess, Bellanaine, but in love with a mortal. As the intended fiancée's father is also besotted with a mortal, the tale is about how, with the aid of a drunken magician, they are to spirit off and enjoy their mortals. There the similarity with Ariosto ends, as Keats develops the satire to include fairies compositely drawn from the literary establishment of the day – Wordsworth, Coleridge, Southey, Hazlitt, Hunt – to represent schools of poetry. George Reynolds was going to provide the poem with mock-learned footnotes, making the project closer to *Iolanthe* than *Orlando Furioso*.

Orlando Furioso impressed Voltaire as being the *Iliad*, *Odyssey* and *Don Quixote* rolled into one, and the sage of Ferney admired the way Ariosto treated his heroes, Ruggiero and Bradamant, 'with a gay badinage'. But Keats tired of 'The Cap and Bells', as he tired of the jokey style that Byron did better. He preferred the more serious Tasso who, according to Severn, had been Keats's favourite reading as a boy. He was certainly acquainted with Armida the Fair and Rinaldo the Bold, as he demonstrated in his poem 'On Receiving a Curious Shell and a Copy of Verses'. And Keats, in his more lubricious moments, might have wished he could freely write the sort of verse that Tasso/Fairfax had been able to give their readers. Here is Armida the Fair setting out to 'undo the crusaders':

> Her breasts, two hills o're spred with purest snow,
> Sweet, smooth and supple, soft and gently swelling,
> Betweene them lies a milken dale below,
> Where love, youths gladness, whitenes make their dwelling,
> Her brests halfe hid, and halfe were laid to show;
> Her envius vesture greedie sight repelling
> So was the wanton clad, as if thus much
> Should please the eie, the rest unseen, the tuch.
>
> As when the sun-beames dive through Tagus wave,
> To spie the store-house of his springing gold,
> Love pearsing thought so through her mantle drave,
> And in her gentle bosom wandred bold:
> It view'd the wondrous beautie virgins have,
> And all to find desire (with vantage) told
> Alas what hope is left, to quench his fire
> That kindled is, by sight; blowne, by desire.[49]

No wonder he included Tasso in his 'Ode to Apollo' with those other bards who stood 'in fealty' to the god – Homer, Virgil, Milton, Shakespeare and Spenser. Had he been less ill and depressed during those last weeks in Rome he might have made the pilgrimage to Tasso's burial place at Sant'Onofrio on the Janiculum hill. But he could not face it. He had already decided that he had no chance of becoming a poet like Tasso, and 'bewailed his cruel fate that he was about to be cut off before he had completed anything great'.[50]

Keats owed much to the Italian enthusiasms of his friends Leigh Hunt, Benjamin Robert Haydon and Benjamin Bailey. James Leigh Hunt, who poured out verse with the industry but not the skill of an Ariosto, considered himself a universal man, familiar with world literature. He too had read Tasso and in 1816 delivered himself of an immense poem in four cantos. The Tale of Rimini was dedicated to Byron and to the mutual love of Paolo Malatesta and Francesca da Rimini. Hunt wrote on and on, imagining that he was recreating in English the colour and cadences of the great Italian bard. Keats's unerring ear, however, told him that Hunt spoiled his verses by too pernickety an attempt to reproduce Italian rhythms. Indeed, Hunt has 'damned ... Masks and Sonnets and Italian tales'.[51]

Hunt's example made Keats want to do better and to this sense of friendly rivalry we owe 'Isabella', 'The Eve of St Agnes' and 'The

Eve of St Mark'. Each was inspired more by international Gothic than by Tasso or Ariosto, and 'Isabella', taken from a tale by 'Boccace', suggests that Keats read the original story in French. The *ottava rima* he used for 'Isabella' he took from Fairfax, but the lush language and the occasional archaisms he borrowed from Leigh Hunt's *Rimini* and, more profoundly, from his own reading of Chaucer. Indeed he apologises to the author in stanzas 19 and 20:

> O eloquent and famed Boccaccio
>   Of thee we now should ask forgiving boon,
> Grant then a pardon here, and then the tale
>   Shall move on soberly, as it is meet;
> There is no other crime, no mad assail
>   To make old prose in modern rhyme more sweet:
> But it is done – succeed the verse or fail –
>   To honour thee, and thy gone spirit greet;
> To stead thee as a verse in English tongue
> An echo of thee in the north-wind sung.

He is spinning the story out with simile and images, unlike Boccaccio himself, who wrote (for his time) with commendable brevity and wit. Transmuted by Keats's genius for words these poems become tapestries of incomparable richness. Like the 41st Symphony of Mozart and the great C Major Symphony of Schubert, they were the prelude to a glory untimely thwarted by death. 'Isabella' and 'St Agnes' were to have been part of an anthology of poems taken from *The Decameron*, entitled *The Garden of Florence*, composed jointly with his Enfield friend, George Reynolds, who actually wrote two of them, but who then decided that his vocation was not to be a poet and returned to the law. *The Garden of Florence* appeared in 1821, shortly after Keats's death, without 'Isabella'.

Benjamin Bailey had urged Keats to read Cary's translation of the *Divine Comedy*, so he took the three-volume edition with him on his walking tour of Scotland.[52] Had Keats read it when it first appeared he must surely have included Dante among the bards who stood in fealty to Apollo, where his absence is, to contemporary ears, strange. The terse account in the *Inferno* of the loves of Paolo Malatesta and Francesca da Rimini, which formed the burden of Hunt's *Rimini*, made Keats, when he read it, dream that he was in the region of hell. He was deep into Cary's *Inferno* and Milton's *Paradise Lost* when he wrote 'The Fall of Hyperion', and its infernal and Miltonic echoes can be detected:

> But horrors, portioned to a giant nerve,
> Oft made Hyperion ache. His palace bright
> Bastion'd with pyramids of glowing gold,
> And touched with shade of bronzed obelisks
> Glared a blood-red through all its thousand courts,
> Arches and domes and fiery galleries.

(ll. 175–80)

Indeed, 'Hyperion' is studded with echoes of the two infernal poets: the defeated Saturn's grove in Book 1 reeks of the mournful wood of cantos 14 and 15 of the *Inferno*, trod by the restless souls of homosexuals.

Cary may have taught Keats the poetic effect of the short, sharp line that ends each stanza of 'La Belle Dame Sans Merci':– 'And no birds sing'; 'And made sweet moan'; 'So kiss'd to sleep' – it was with these that Cary sharpened the blank verse of his translation, for he made no attempt to use the *terza rima* style. But the Dantean image that haunted Keats was that of the two lovers, condemned for their immortal and immoral kiss. Compare Cary's style:

> When of that smile we read,
> The wished smile, so rapturously kissed
> By one so deep in love, then he, who ne'er
> From me shall separate, at once my lips
> All trembling kissed.

With Keats's:

> Pale were the sweet lips I saw
> Pale were the lips I kiss'd and fair the form
> I floated with, about that melancholy storm.[53]

The image of Fanny Brawne, interminably separated by the divine decree of his ill-health, returned again and again to haunt him. Italy was to be not the consummated visit of a poet to the land which was poetry, but a place of separation, exile, disappointment and death. Keats's experience of the country was too short and too late for it to inspire raw poetry, like Shelley's and Byron's, who lived there for several years and whose lines are filled with their Italian experience. His experience had come from books.

Shelley's subjects that are specifically Italian were encountered at first hand. His West Wind is an Italian wind, the *aziola* is an Italian owl, 'Lines Written among the Euganean Hills' are a lament for Venice, Prometheus is unbound from an Apennine landscape. Shelley's

– 77 –

last unfinished poem, 'The Triumph of Life', was written in part on the balcony at Casa Magni in Lerici as he looked out upon the Gulf of Spezia. His work is drenched with a sense of place and, in *Adonais*, that sense of place is transmuted into the supreme elegy in a Roman (but non-Catholic) graveyard. If *The Cenci* could have been written in a library in London, *Julian and Maddalo* could not.[54] As for Byron, *Childe Harold* was an early *apologia pro vita italiana sua*: 'She walked in beauty like the [Italian] night'. *Beppo* and *Don Juan* were Ariostan poems. Keats's last sonnet – written on a blank page of Shakespeare's poems – in which he allowed himself the luxury of one last illusion, that 'pillow'd upon my fair love's ripening breast' he 'might live for ever – or else swoon to death', was a pathetic *vale* to his love and life in words that Dante's Paolo Malatesta could have used, written in a Hampstead garden.[55] Poetry was now to bathe in a beaker of the warm Italian south.

5

'A Full-Grown Oak'

The Romantic Hero

He stood out like a full-grown oak in a grove of saplings. There was boredom and contempt written in every line of his strong dark face.

> Alan Boon of Mills & Boon,
> describing the sort of hero his firm liked in its romantic fiction.

> There was a laughing devil in his sneer,
> That raised emotions both of rage and fear;
> And where his frown of hatred darkly fell,
> Hope withering fled, and Mercy sighed farewell.

> Lord Byron, *The Corsair*, Canto I, stanza 8.

> What is the end of fame? 'tis but to fill
> A certain portion of uncertain paper;
> Some liken it to climbing up a hill,
> Whose summit, like all hills, is lost in vapour:
> For this men write, speak, preach and heroes kill,
> And bards burn what they call their 'midnight taper'.

> Lord Byron, *Don Juan*, Canto I, stanza 213.

Keats was open to any literary influence he could express in his own sharply personal voice, but his fame was slow to develop. His experience of Italy, moreover, came too late to be more than second-hand. It was only with the sedulous care of Joseph Severn, ready to meet any visitors to Rome and give them a personal tour of their short sojourn there, that the association of Keats with Italy became part of a Romantic legend. For Byron, however, Italy was where, assisted by its climate, food and indulgent habits of lust and love, he sloughed off the heroic skin that had made him, even before he left England for good in 1816, a Romantic icon.

The eighteenth century had witnessed a revival of interest in heroism among Britons, partly inspired by the speed with which their country had become a world power, conqueror of huge expanses of the new world and overlords of the subcontinent of India. A 'British' hero had first appeared in the last year of the Seven Years War, especially welcome to the Scots who had done so much to win the colonial wars, and created a climate of welcome for new translations of the Renaissance epics. James Macpherson (1736–96) wrote his first 'Ossianic' fragment in 1759, and proceeded a year later to produce *Fingal*, being his 'translation' of an ancient Scottish epic by Ossian, the son of Finn. The attribution was accepted enthusiastically by his contemporaries, and Schiller and Goethe admired the poems enough to quote extensively from them, so that 'Ossian' was, with *Werther*, among the the favourite reading of Napoleon Bonaparte. Dr Johnson, however, remained always a sceptic. The new paladins carried Ossian along with Tasso and Ariosto in their knapsacks, as conquered India provided paynims, moors, giants, serpents and witches galore, the very stuff of heroic romance. Thackeray's Clive Newcome was as entranced by Orme's *History of Indostan* as any Renaissance princeling by *Orlando Furioso*.[1] But the historic heroes produced in the course of Great Britain's rise to world power status between 1756 and 1815 – Cook, Clive, Wolfe, Nelson, Wellington – did not appeal to the British Romantics, whose radicalism rejected the political establishment of which they had become the pillars. Their sympathies were with the rebellious American colonists and the revolutionary French, throwing off centuries of tyranny, and with the common soldiers and sailors by whose efforts the generals and admirals achieved their victories while treating them little differently from slaves. Their supreme hero, Napoleon Bonaparte, retained his allure as champion of liberty and begetter of change until he aspired to be superman, but then, as he sailed towards a lonely exile in the mid-Atlantic, he was crowned with a different Romantic halo, and became an object of pity, like the titan Prometheus, sharing the suffering of all men who had the effrontery to challenge destiny.

Today, historic heroes are dismissed as puppets of economic and racial forces, while Tasso's crusaders and Ariosto's paladins are real puppets, which still perform on tiny stages in Sicily and the south of Italy, where *La Gerusalemme Liberata*, known as *Rinaldo* to the

Neapolitans, had long been the required listening of the people. Sydney Morgan would never forget the grotesque figure, with an immense wig, a torn cocked hat, the fragments of a jacket and a pair of bright buskin small-clothes from the cast-off wardrobe of an English groom, wearing no shoes or stockings, who read through immense spectacles from a tattered Tasso, every Sunday on the Mole near her lodging in Naples, conducting himself in stately measure with a stick, and improvising a commentary of his own between the stanzas.[2] The Romantic hero was a Byronic invention. Even Stendhal was forced to acknowledge that and, unable to compete, he made his Fabrice del Dongo and Julien Sorel anti-heroes.

It was Sismondi who indirectly gave Byron his image of a Romantic hero The corsair Conrad stepped straight off the page on which Henri Füssli (Fuseli) had drawn a crusader repudiating his wife.[3] The pencil sketch of a heroic, seated nude spurning with his right foot his thinly clad wife represented, according to the painter, a certain Ezzelino Bracciaferro, who returned from the crusades to find that there had been 'a hitch in her constancy during his absence'.[4] For that he killed her. Füssli had, in fact, no historical person in mind; he had simply invented him. But it was enough to start Byron on a wild goose chase through Italian histories of the time, until he found the Ezzelin he wanted in Sismondi's writings. In that gallery of ruthless heroes, Eccelino (Ezzelino) IV of Romano stands out as ambitious, intrepid and entirely devoted to the cause of the Emperor Frederick II, '*Stupor Mundi*'. He combined great military talents with a complete absence of any pity or remorse. Just as Mary Shelley's later choice of ruffian, Castruccio Castracano, established his power base in Florence, Eccelino established his in the cities of Verona, Vicenza and Padua where, after being elected captain of the people, he consolidated his authority by the use of terror. Anyone who threatened his position or so much as criticised him was incarcerated and tortured. As the executioner emptied the prisons, so they were filled by new victims denounced under torture.

> By day and night in the cities under his sway, the air rang with the agonising shrieks of the wretched sufferers who were expiring under the dreadful variety of torture. All that was distinguished ... for public virtue, or birth, station or wealth, even for the qualities of personal beauty, fell under the suspicion and hatred of the gloomy tyrant.[5]

This was what the English expected to read about Italian tyrants. Indeed, for Oscar Wilde's Dorian Gray, the tyrant 'whose melancholy could be cured only by the spectacle of death, and who had a passion for red blood as other men have for red wine' had a horrible fascination.[6] In 1256 the pope declared Eccelino an infidel and licensed a crusade against him, in which many of the *popolani* enrolled, hopeful of the benefits of the crusade indult, and of some cheap plunder. Most of them succumbed to the tyrant's sword. In 1259, Eccelino, 'unequalled in Italy for bravery and military talent, always an enemy to luxury and proof against the seductions of women, making the boldest tremble with a look, and preserving in his diminutive person ... all the vigour of a soldier', advanced on Milan, but he overreached himself, was wounded and taken prisoner. At the age of 65, rather than endure captivity, he tore off his bandages, refused medical help and died.[7]

Romantic heroism is all in the looks. Size was not at issue. Napoleon was short, so was Byron. And Eccelino, too, was *'d'une petite taille'*, but *'par son seul regard, il faisoit trembler les plus hautes'*.[8] It helped for a romantic hero to

> ... have a laughing Devil in his sneer,
> That raised emotions both of rage and fear;
> And where his frown of hatred darkly fell,
> Hope withering fled – and Mercy sighed farewell.[9]

The early Byronic hero had the will of a Bonaparte, despised blind fate, suppressed timid fear and crushed deterrent scruple, being ruled only by his existential destiny. The Corsair knew himself a villain, but no worse than those who called him so; 'he stood alike exempt / From all affection and from all contempt.'[10] Great wickedness had its own kind of grandeur; in its very loneliness and despair it achieved a heroic quality. 'His deeds had driven him forth to war with man and forfeit heaven', like Milton's Satan, and da Ponte's (and Mozart's) Don Giovanni.[11] For the first it was better to reign in Hell, than serve in Heaven. To be weak was miserable and the antidote to weakness was 'unconquerable will, / and study of revenge, immortal hate, / and courage never to submit or yield'.[12] The second, for whom the pursuit of women was more necessary than the bread he ate or the air he breathed, was quite ready to meet his doom at the stony hand of the Commendatore, that *vecchio infatuato* whose summons to repent he dismissed with scorn.[13]

7. Lord Byron, by an unknown artist.
This shows the more feminine Byron, more Don Juan than the Corsair.

Byron, however much he may have admired Miltonic, or Mozartian models, was uncomfortably aware that what passed for heroism could also pass for criminality. Had he lived in the twentieth century he would have recognised, in Satan's defiance, Hitler's mad despair when he knew the war was lost and, in Don Giovanni's appetite for women, Mussolini's *machismo* that reduced Il Duce to a serial rapist, a sexual hooligan. His own heroic narratives, *The Giaour* (1813), *The Corsair* and its unsatisfactory sequel *Lara* (1814), *The Siege of Corinth* (1816) and *Manfred* (1817), while immensely popular and providing dramatic stories for Verdi, Rossini and Schumann to set to music, were little more, as Jane Austen recognised, than adolescent posturing, 'the misfortune of poetry to be seldom safely enjoyed by those who enjoyed it completely'.[14] Manfred's Byronic passion for his sister Astarte, whose shade he tries to raise through his influence on infernal spirits, his melodramatic failed suicide, his longing for death and his conviction of the vanity of human knowledge makes him, to practical sensibility, ridiculous, as does his mordant view of life from an Alpine crag:

> In all the days of past and future, for
> In life there is no present, we can number
> How few – how less than few – wherein the soul
> Forbears to pant for death, and yet draws back
> As from a stream in winter, though the chill
> Be but a moment's.[15]

Faustian spirits whose only contacts are chamois hunters and cenobitic abbots were hardly representative of the scientific confidence of the new century. Indeed the final scene of the drama reads remarkably like the last act of da Ponte's *opera buffa, Don Giovanni*. In *Manfred* a demon spirit demands his soul, while a holy man calls for repentance, to which his simple response, before 'expiring' is: 'I do defy – deny – / Spurn back and scorn ye!'[16] In *Don Giovanni*, the funerary statue of his first and only victim in the opera calls for his repentance or he will be dragged down to hell. The answer is a simple No.

However much these brooding and disenchanted heroes might appeal to the romantic imagination, their avatar in real life, Napoleon, espoused political programmes too disturbing to those who, however disenchanted with the human condition, were not quite ready to embrace social equality and the distribution of wealth. Manfred, moreover, is an ineffectual hero. So, clearly, thought John

Hookham Frere, the former diplomatist whose career had come to an end when, as ambassador in Madrid, he advised Sir John Moore to retire before Napoleon's advance via Corunna instead of Portugal, thus nearly causing the loss of the entire expeditionary force. Having retired to live in 'liberated' (British) Malta, Frere produced in 1817 an epic, in *ottava rima* in the style of Pulci, entitled *Prospectus and Specimen of an intended National Work by William and Robert Whistlecraft, of Stowmarket in Suffolk, Harness and Collar Makers, intended to comprise the most interesting particulars relating to King Arthur and his Round Table*. 'Whistlecraft' was an elaborate joke; if a wood engraver (William Blake) could be a poet why not a harness and horse-collar maker? Its fanciful style appealed so much to Byron that he decided to cap it with a Venetian romance called *Beppo*. Byron had now decided where he wanted to be and his recipe for being Italian had become, not 'Florencing and Roming and Gallerying and Conversationing' but 'belong(ing) to their families and friendships and feuds', by becoming a *cavaliere servente*, an institution which he extolled as a civilised way for Italian wives to escape the restrictions of monogamy.[17] To capture the magic of his new environment, he produced, in dazzling puns and excruciating rhymes, a travel brochure for an exotic and colourful land, *Italia*, in which there were, mercifully, no heroes. In poetic terms it fulfilled the same aims as a 1980s television advertisement entitled *un bel cornetto* (in which a villainous speedboat driver snatches the ice-cream out of the hand of a pretty girl, idling in a gondola, whose *gondoliere* sings a *canzone* in praise of the ice-cream cornet she is about to lose). 'England', Byron averred, 'with all thy faults I love thee still', listing all the things he disliked about England, her politics, her oppression, her food, her beer, her weather. For,

> ... with all its sinful doings, I must say
> That Italy's a pleasant place to me,
> Who love to see the sun shine every day
> And vines (not nailed to walls) from tree to tree.

He likes to be able to ride out without a cloak in case it rains and

> ... know, too, that if stopped upon my route
> Where the green alleys windingly allure,
> Reeling with grapes red wagons choke the way, –
> In England, 'twould be dung, dust or a dray.[18]

And so on: bright skies, and *becaficas*, small finches, like ortolans much esteemed as a gastronomic delight, for dinner. *Beppo* trips along, a slight and wilful morality tale, in which the absent husband (after being kidnapped and Mussulmanned by Turks) returns unexpectedly to find his wife enjoying carnival with her *cavalier servente*. Being rich on stolen Turkish goods, Beppo settles down to a delightful *ménage à trois* and they all live happily ever after. Not exactly heroic, but Byron had become entranced by anti-heroics in the Italian mode. While he cultivated the Salvator Rosa scowl, showed off to advantage on horseback or in the water and claimed an exemption from the usual laws of sexual behaviour, he was too lame and too plump to be either a Giaour, a Conrad/Lara or a Manfred. Anyhow, Italy had cured him of the peevishness which produced them; he was even surprised that anyone should have taken them seriously.[19] His authentic hero, henceforward, was to be himself. Don Juan but not a Don Giovanni; he was too self-mocking to allow a manservant to catalogue his conquests. He neither raped nor seduced – women fell to him like the figs devoured by *becaficas* – and, when finally heart-snared, he played out the role of *cavalier servente* with a rueful countenance, more like Don Quixote than Don Juan Tenorio. The heroic attributes of Conrad and Ezzelin had found, to his disgust, their epitome in the glacial *superbia* of his own countrymen, the proconsuls who now had an empire to rule: Lord William Bentinck, King Ferdinand's virtual viceroy in Sicily; 'Hibernian' Strangford, ambassador in Rio de Janeiro and the puppet master of the Portuguese and Brazilian monarch; Sir Richard Church, the Anglo-Irish hammer of banditry in Puglia; and that arch Anglo-Irishman, the soldier who, after helping to conquer India, had finally defeated Napoleon. Of Wellington or 'Villainton', Byron wrote

> You have obtain'd great pensions and much praises:
> Glory like yours should any dare gainsay,
> Humanity would rise and thunder 'Nay!'[20]

Their international characteristic, as Madame de Staël's Corinne remarked to Lord Nelvil, was pride in themselves.[21] There were now 'no accomplished blackguards, like Tom Jones, / But gentlemen in stays, as stiff as stones.'[22] Byron no longer wanted them as heroes. He repudiated the England of the Iron Duke. The rhetoric of heroism had become as absurd to him as it had been to Pulci and Ariosto, and the voice that now appealed to him, above that of the great Tasso, who 'sang of dreadful arms and the Captain [Godfrey de Bouillon, a medieval Arthur Wellesley, Duke of Wellington] who liberated the great sepulchre of Christ',[23] was that of an ex-cleric, Giovanni Battista Casti.

Casti, like Mozart's librettist, da Ponte, was a priest who had turned from storming heaven to an attempt on the heights of Parnassus. He was born in Montefiascone and rose to be a canon of its cathedral church. (Montefiascone was the home of the wine dubbed 'Est. Est. Est' by the cellarer of an earlier prelate, and immortalised in Rossini's *Cenerentola/Cinderella* as the cellar of which Cenerentola's stepfather is created baron.) The prebendary stall proving too confined, Casti set off to travel Europe as a kind of jongleur, visiting the court of Catherine the Great, about which he wrote *Poema Tartaro*, a mock-heroic satire on the pretensions of that unusual sovereign; Catherine also figures in Canto IX of *Don Juan*. Thence he moved to Vienna where, at the age of 60, he was appointed to succeed Metastasio as *poeta cesario*, or court poet. Unlike his predecessor, whom Leopardi thought the greatest poet of his age, Casti toyed with libretti for comic opera, before retiring in 1776 to live the life of a lay gentleman in Paris, where he died in 1803. Undisturbed by the Revolution through which he lived, he wrote a long poetical treatise, *Gli Animali Parlanti*, which in Orwellian fashion, exploded the pretensions of political systems.[24]

Lorenzo da Ponte, 'a real profligate of genius', tried to convince posterity that, but for Casti, he would have become court poet in Vienna. When he published a savage review of Casti's first libretto for an *opera buffa*, he made an enemy who poured his poison into the ear of the court theatre director who poisoned in turn that of the Emperor Joseph II. It was, da Ponte claimed, his disappointment at not becoming court poet that made him accept an engagement to adapt Beaumarchais's *Le Marriage de Figaro* for Mozart.[25] If true, the world has much for which to be grateful. It may also be grateful for da Ponte's edition of *Gli Animali Parlanti*, which he produced in London in 1803. Whatever their differences, da Ponte was always ready to give the poet's crown to his old rival and he believed that his new, carefully bowdlerised, edition of *Gli Animali Parlanti* would encourage teachers of Italian and their pupils to read a poem which covered the recent years of revolution with such wit and erudition. When Casti objected strongly to alterations to the text, da Ponte replied that he would 'alter' (i.e. expurgate) Ariosto, Tasso, even

Dante, if it removed any inhibitions to modest young people from reading the classics of Italian literature. Casti, before he could reply, 'died of indigestion in the house of Jerome Bonaparte', and da Ponte's version, translated by William Stewart Rose as *The Court of Beasts*, was finally produced by John Murray in 1819.[26]

Rose (1775–1843) was the son of one of William Pitt's chancellors of the exchequer, 'reading clerk' to the House of Lords, and a friend of Sir Walter Scott. After producing one volume of the naval history of the Seven Years War, he retired in boredom, and concentrated on medieval romances. His translation of *Amadis de Gaul* (the tale which had turned Don Quixote's head) was favourably reviewed by Scott and, after visiting Italy and Istanbul in 1814, he settled down near Venice to produce, five years later, a free reading of *Gli Animali Parlanti*. John Murray also persuaded him to produce a version of *Orlando Furioso* which, with Scott's encouragement, was published in two volumes between 1823 and 1831. Scott may have regretted his encouragement. At one of Samuel Rogers's breakfasts it was 'proposed that the Italian should be printed for the sake of assisting the indolent reader to understand the English'.[27] The copy of Rose's Casti rendering, sent to Byron in Venice, was confiscated by the customs, but Byron was already acquainted with Casti's poem in the original.[28] Byron also managed to obtain a copy of Casti's *Novelle Galanti*, a reworking of ancient legends into a series of mordant, even scatological sermons, told in *ottava rima*, in the Ariostan mode. There he found an authentic Italianate voice in which he could speak in the idiom of Whistlecraft. As for Italy herself, he had become disillusioned with her sons. The 'Germans' were at the River Po, like the barbarians at the gate, but carnival was on, so the Italians danced and sang and made merry![29]

Byron possessed two Italian editions of *Orlando Furioso*[30] and recognised the true father of both Casti and Whistlecraft and, according to Thomas Medwin, of *Don Juan* too. Medwin claimed that Byron borrowed not only the name of his hero, but plagiarised some of the scenes directly from Casti's *Diavolessa*, a picaresque poem about two Spanish scapegraces. In Casti's poem, Don Juan ends in hell; where Byron intended his hero to end is not known; he soon left his model far behind.[31] The ironic style of Ariosto's romance, at once courtly, voluptuous, self-indulgent and comic, finds strong echoes in *Don Juan*. Its eponymous hero is neither an Orlando nor a Ruggiero, much less a Don Giovanni but, like Ariosto's heroes, Don Juan inhabits a saga in which experience triumphs over innocence, and success is almost accidental. The Renaissance epic poets, Tasso as well as Ariosto, Boiardo and Pulci, all conformed to the convention that, in between battling with pagans, giants, dragons and Muslims, the heroes should enjoy rest and recuperation, often in dalliance with sorceresses in a 'false Eden', thus providing a restful, faintly lubricious respite for the reader. Byron's Don Juan, too, enjoyed his 'false Edens', and Cherubino-like fantasies in between being tossed on the waves of a brutal and licentious world.

For his own epic poem, Byron sought

> ... a hero; an uncommon want,
> When every year and month sends forth a new one,
> Till, after cloying the gazettes with cant,
> The age discovers he is not the true one.

Having dismissed all Britain's and France's recent military and naval commanders, including the Duke of Wellington, Bonaparte and Nelson, he

> ... takes our ancient friend. Don Juan –
> We all have seen him in the pantomime,
> Sent to the Devil somewhat ere his time.[32]

But this Don Juan is not the unsuccessful lover of da Ponte's libretto, who fails to score a single seduction throughout the drama, thus casting real doubt on the veracity of Leporello's 'catalogue'; nor is he Molière's seedy gentleman, but a Cherubino, the lovesick page of *Le Nozze di Figaro*. Byron almost certainly did not have either Beaumarchais's Chérubin or da Ponte's Cherubino in mind. If anyone, his disenchanted image of a hero is Don Quixote. But the Don of the dolorous countenance had no sexual encounters and Don Juan had many. His first conquest is Julia, an older woman who has not been sexually awakened by her much older husband and, possibly, her maid Antonia – three in a bed seems very much the implication of Canto I. (On the other hand, since ladies of quality could not get dressed or undressed without assistance, and men of all ages were ignorant of the arcana of hooks and eyes, a maid was an essential assistant to any bed sequence. By and large, bodice-ripping went on below stairs only.[33]) Juan 'is the sudden victim of an attack of romanticism' – I should prefer to call it romanticitis – 'taking long walks in the woods and pondering the universe during those moments in which he can distract himself from the image of Julia'.[34] The scene in which the adolescent Lothario is caught by the cuckolded husband *in medias res* has strong echoes of Cherubino's adventures in the Countess's closet in Act 2 of the Mozart opera, even to Julia's reproach to her 50-year-old husband for ever doubting her virtue.

On that auspicious beginning, no doubt a wishfully reconstructed scene from Byron's own wishful adolescence, his hero is launched on a career of erotic adventure. Haidee, the Greek beauty who finds Don Juan's shipwrecked body on her private beach and revives him (with the help of Zoë, her maid, whose role on this occasion is less ambivalent, being mainly to prepare eggs for breakfast) is his next conquest. Together they enjoy an idyll worthy of *The Blue Lagoon* (1908), an immensely popular, because doubtfully moral, novel of two children marooned on a deserted island, who grow up, have a baby, and are drowned at sea. *The Blue Lagoon* was remarkable for the complete lack of any account of sexual awakening, to conform with the moral standard of the day, and for the lush romanticism that informs advertisements for holidays in the tropics today.[35] But in *Don Juan*, Haidee's inconsiderate papa returns unexpectedly and has Juan shipped off to the slave market of Constantinople. Disguised as a maidservant he is introduced to Gulbeyaz, the sultan's consort, who attempts to get him into bed, only to be pre-empted by another of her slaves, Dudu, who discovers Don Juan's unexpected attributes; but her lust is then thwarted by the sudden arrival of her husband. By what seems like a sleight of hand, Juan escapes both castration and crucifixion to find himself in Russian service, where he helps to console the Semiramis of the North for her loss of youth and beauty. The rest of his story is the getting of wisdom, accompanied by worldly wise banter from the author. Don Juan ends (where Chérubin also ended in the Beaumarchais trilogy), faced with an ageing but still voluptuous duchess in an English country house, masquerading as a ghost but hoping to be ravished. Juan had expected someone more in the mould of Julia or Haidee or Dudu, but you cannot win every time.

There was no reason for *Don Juan* to end before Don Juan's own death, and Byron may have seen it as a *roman fleuve*, long enough to displace Wordsworth's *The Excursion* as the contemporary epic, 'gaily substituting a sexual ethic for Wordsworth's solemn asceticism'.[36] He told Marguerite Blessington in Genoa in 1822 that he was writing a continuation of the poem at the end of which Don Juan would turn Methodist.[37] The poem was too brilliant to inspire imitations, only impostures – 'Impostors have published *two* new *third*

Cantos of Don Juan', Byron complained[38] – piracies and parodies, and also a curious Byronic tale from the pen of Benjamin Disraeli, who visited Italy in 1826. He had hired Byron's former boatman, Maurice, to take him out at night on Lake Leman and tell him about his employer. Disraeli's visit was a Byronic adventure, as he followed his idol round Milan and Venice, where he did not attempt to swim in the Grand Canal. He visited Tasso's cell at Ferrara as much to see Byron's signature scratched on the wall as to empathise with the sufferings of the Italian poet. Florence, Pisa, Lucca, Turin, Genoa followed. Everywhere Disraeli went his dandified manners and sprightly conversation won him friends as a Byronic surrogate.

Contarini Fleming (1832) is a *Don Juan* poem in novel form. Baron Fleming, a Saxon nobleman, had while idling in Venice married a daughter of the noble house of Contarini, which name he gave to the only child of their union. He subsequently becomes an international civil servant, the power behind an unnamed Scandinavian throne (Denmark). Contarini's mother having died, he is brought up by a stepmother who is fair if not loving. His father is too busy to take much notice of him, so Contarini, who is nothing if not a coxcomb, runs wild, leading his fellow collegians into the forest to become *banditti*, flunking out of university and falling in love with unattainable beauties. His father, with astonishing forbearance, secures him a post in the government, in which he proves to be his father's effective assistant, until he publishes, anonymously, a satirical novel which pillories everyone in the court. He is then sent off with a faithful Swiss servant to train for the diplomatic service in Paris, absconds again and goes to Venice. There he falls in love with the last unmarried Contarini, who is betrothed to a fellow Venetian nobleman. They elope and find refuge in Crete, where, after another *Blue Lagoon*ish rhapsody of perfect connubial bliss equal to Juan's with Haidee, Alcesté dies in childbirth, taking their stillborn son with her to the grave. Contarini falls into a suicidal despair which only continued travel can assuage. He goes to Florence and writes a great Romantic poem, and then to Andalucia, Albania, Greece, Turkey and Egypt before settling, with the fortunes inherited from both his parents, near Naples, there to build a villa modelled on Hadrian's at Tivoli and to wonder whether he will participate in 'the political regeneration of the country to which I am devoted': virtually the last words of the book. Contarini's friend, a distinguished artist, diagnoses his condition as Romanticitis: 'a case of complete exhaustion. If there be anything more exhausting than love, it is sorrow; and if there be anything more exhausting than sorrow, it is poetry. You have tried all three.'[39]

Italy was merely a staging post in the quest for a cure for Contarini's *cafard*. Apart from descriptions of Venetian high life and the masked balls – the standard Venetian stereotype – his sole reference to other Italians is to observe, 'with curious admiration, the black eyes and picturesque forms that were flashing and glancing about me in all directions'.[40] *Contarini Fleming* was published by John Murray, but it made neither the author nor the publisher any money. Though Disraeli was pleased with it, being 'the secret history of my feelings', it was received no more warmly than his first novel, *Vivian Grey*, and its relentless travelogue becomes wearisome as Contarini merely repeats other travellers who had been everywhere before him, particularly Byron. It tells us a lot about Disraeli himself, with some of the self-mockery that redeems *Don Juan*, but very little that was new about Italy.

Contarini makes one other comment on Italy's political future, which was to wish that she could return to the days of city states. 'Italy might then revive and England may regret that she has lost the heptarchy.'[41] Somewhere that idea stayed in Disraeli's mind, so that he was deeply suspicious of Napoleon III's plans to unite Italy under French protection. This was not entirely due to a cynical calculation that war between France and Austria could upset the domestic budget he was preparing, and thus interfere with a British general election, from which that notorious Whig Italophile, Palmerston, could only profit. In fact, the war started on the same day that the election campaign was launched and the Tories were defeated. Disraeli really did believe that Italy would be happier as a federation of independent states. He distrusted Garibaldi's republican and anti-clerical views, resolutely refused to meet him during Garibaldi's triumphant visit to London in 1864 and likened Pio Nono to 'an old man on a Semitic throne baffling the modern Attila'.[42] England may, at the outset of the twenty-first century, be in the process of reviving the heptarchy, and some Italians are playing with the idea of separating north from south, but Disraeli was out of his time. He never had cause, however, to repudiate another of Contarini's apothegms, that 'it was enchanting to be acquainted with the secrets of European cabinets, and to control or influence their fortunes'.[43]

The romantic hero, a full-grown oak in a grove of saplings, with boredom and contempt written in every line of his strong dark face, the creation of popular trash for nannies who now accompanied their employers on visits to Italy, was not the creation of the Romantics. Their hero, despite the laughing devil in his sneer and his frown of hatred that raised emotions both of rage and fear, was essentially an introspective, self-questioning paradigm, seeking self-knowledge rather than sexual triumph, fighting a battle against the uneven odds of destiny and perverse fate. Byron saw the ludicrousness of this engagement in a world that was neither tragic nor comic, but essentially ironic and disordered. The Romantic hero who had emerged from the Italian middle ages finally disappeared into opera, and was still wandering the world as Siegfried and Parsifal 50 years after the deaths of Napoleon I and Byron. Manzoni, when he wrote *I Promessi Sposi* borrowed his hero, a simple young *contadino* caught up in the toils of his social and economic but not moral betters, from the world of Sir Walter Scott.

Though Contarini Fleming thought it 'a bitter jest that the most civilised portion of the globe should be considered incapable of self-government',[44] the images of the *cavaliere servente*, of Beppo, of the Byronic Don Juan, of Gambas dancing with the barbarian at the gates, of failed risings and muddling *carbonari*, of a playground for more serious nations, all made nonsense of the idea of Italy as a land of independent people. Like India, she was better governed by northern nations, which were blessed by God with the capacity to rule lesser breeds.

6

'Yet Fallen Italy, Rejoice Again'

The Awakeners

❧

> But hark, what solemn strains from Arno's vales
> Breathe raptures wafted on the Tuscan gales!
> LORENZO rears again his awful head,
> And feels his ancient glories round him spread,
> The Muses, starting from their trance, revive,
> And at their ROSCOE's bidding wake and live.
>
> Bishop Hervey, second Earl of Bristol,
> 'Memoir of the Author', *Life of Lorenzo de Medici*, p. 30.

> Though dimm'd thy brightness, riveted thy chain,
> Yet, fallen Italy! rejoice again!
> Lost, lovely realm! once more 'tis thine to gaze
> On the rich relics of sublimer days.
>
> Felicia Hemans, 'The Restoration of the Works of Art to Italy',
> ll. 11–14.

> Awake, Mother of Heroes, from thy death-like sleep.
>
> William Wordsworth, 'On Leaving Italy',
> *Memorials of a Tour in Italy*, stanza 25, ll. 13–14.

Sismondi may have been the great evoker of the Italian middle ages, of the birth of republics and of the glory of city states, but the man who called up the genius of Renaissance Florence for a British readership was a self-educated citizen of Liverpool, who seldom left his native city, much less his native land. With no more than the most perfunctory education, leaving school at twelve and thereafter helping his father, a small-time market gardener, with lumping the season's new potatoes to market, William Roscoe was in 1768, at the age of at fifteen, lodged with a retired slave trader and articled as clerk to a solicitor. Conscious of his lack of formal learning, Roscoe developed a life-long admiration for young men who exuded the confidence of an education in the classics and in foreign languages. His hero was James Crichton, 'the Admirable Crichton' (1560–82), a Scottish polymath who, at the university in Paris, was credited with disputing scientific matters in twelve languages. After fighting with the French armies in Italy, Crichton had become a wandering scholar, disputing in public at Italian universities, before being killed in a brawl at Mantua. Another role model was a local school-master, Francis Holden, under whose tutorship Roscoe mastered French and Italian, read widely, learned to discriminate, composed verse and taught himself to paint. Introduced to the tributary poem that, at the age of fourteen, another cynosure, Angelo Poliziano, had written in praise of the Medici, Roscoe immersed himself in the poetry of the Renaissance.[1] In 1773, aged 20, he and his band of enthusiasts launched a Society for the Encouragement of the Arts, Painting and Design. A chance meeting with Henri Füssli in 1782 led to an invitation for Füssli to show his work at the first of several exhibitions of European paintings to be shown outside London and to a long and fruitful friendship. The Swiss-born Füssli (1741–1825) had been lured to England after eight years in Italy, studying Michelangelo. He Englished himself as Fuseli and was celebrated for the dark fantasies that fascinated Blake and erotically aroused Mary Wollstonecraft. Roscoe was determined to introduce him to the people of his native city, to do this Roscoe wrote a long poem on *The Art of Engraving* (1785). The 1784 exhibitors included Sir Joshua Reynolds and Angelica Kaufman (1741–1807), another Swiss, a pro-lific painter of portraits, allegories and decorative canvases for country houses, who had been invited to England by Sir Joshua and been a founder member of the Royal Academy in 1768. But public interest was too small to sustain the Society, which languished until Liverpool was to enjoy its period of unparalleled commercial expan-sion following the opening of Brazil and the rest of Spanish America to foreign trade. Then the bread that Roscoe had cast upon the waters came back to enrich the city. The Liverpool Academy institu-tionalised the Society that Roscoe had helped to found, and became in 1817 the Liverpool Royal Institution. By this time Roscoe had become an attorney of the Court of the King's Bench, and a partner in a successful law firm. He prospered, married and begat a large family, most of whom were to achieve distinction in commerce, the law and science. All the time he bought books and pictures. His *Art of Engraving*, with which he had tried to familiarise the citizens of Liverpool with the work of Fuseli, had carried a reference to 'the Great Lorenzo'. A footnote identified him as Lorenzo de Medici, who, if a full inquiry were to be made into his life, would prove 'to be not only one of the most extraordinary, but, perhaps, upon the whole, the most extraordinary man that any age or nation produced'.[2]

If Roscoe saw in Lorenzo the Magnificent a successful merchant, deeply interested in the arts and the new learning, a role he might himself play in the renascent Liverpool, he did not trumpet it abroad, but set himself down instead to write Lorenzo's life, launching through his commercial contacts a search for books and manuscripts. *The Life of Lorenzo de Medici* appeared in 1796, and ran to three further editions in the next three years. The then rector of the university of Pisa, himself the author of a life of Lorenzo, arranged for the translation of Roscoe's book into Italian and its publication in 1799 by his own university: an act of singular generosity.

Roscoe retired from the bar early to enjoy the life of a scholar and administrator – he changed the lawyer's wig for the banker's balance – and to develop his growing interest in botany. By now, too, Roscoe had other causes for which to fight: the abolition of the slave trade, not popular in the city whose fortunes it had helped to make, and Catholic Emancipation, both of which he supported during a brief spell as MP for Liverpool.[3] His principal canvasser for the seat had been a Unitarian minister who, in 1802, under Roscoe's encouragement, produced a life of Poggio Bracciolino, private secretary to eight popes and chancellor of Florence in 1453.

Under the mesmerising influence of Gibbon's great work, finally published complete in 1788, Roscoe had originally wanted to write a general history of the Renaissance. But he soon realised that such a task was beyond him. Gibbon had spent 20 years on *The Decline and Fall* and Roscoe had too many commercial, cultural and charitable interests to want to spend all his hours in a library. So he decided to concentrate on *Il Magnifico* and his times, making Florence and its bountiful life of arts and sciences the hero, in the hopes that they might be replicated in one of the cities of Britain, perhaps Liverpool. The book, when it finally appeared, was a kind of treasure trove of raw facts lifted from his sources and accompanied by 84 appendices, including both supporting documents and poems. Roscoe was not a professional historian and his subject could do no wrong. He had a generally lenient view of sexual licence and was not disturbed by his hero's lusty *Canzoni a Ballo* and *Canti Carnascialeschi*, but he glossed over the cruelty and *realpolitik* that characterised the reigns of the Medici, and represented neither father Cosimo, nor son Lorenzo, as the assassins of Florentine democracy. For that he earned the contempt of Sismondi, who saw the Medici only in this light. Roscoe's readers, however, not only in Britain, but in Italy herself, were content to overlook the repetitive ramblings on subjects of which he knew little and the uncritical canonisation of a tyrant. There were too many other good things. Perhaps the most significant were Lorenzo's poems, many of which were incorporated in the text and appendices, and translated by Roscoe himself into verse. Some of these had lain unread in the Laurentian library in Florence until his agent dug them out. Their appearance in Roscoe's work gave it the seal of originality, imparting to his text the spurious glamour of a seminal work.[4]

The success of *Lorenzo de Medici* prompted Roscoe to follow it with a life of Lorenzo's son, Giuliano, who became Pope Leo X. The Magnificent had secured Giuliano a cardinal's hat when he was thirteen years old, but he did not live to see him pope. Instead of a general history of the Renaissance, Roscoe now aspired to write a history that would connect Gibbon, whose story ended at the fall of Constantinople, to William Robertson's *History of the Reign of Charles V.* He had the literary skill, but not the stomach of a scholar; he drew heavily – as he had for his *Lorenzo* – on the work of the generous rector of Pisa University, whose *Leonis Ponteficis Maximi Vita* had appeared in 1797, and amassed as many sources as he could. Writing the life of the son caused Roscoe more trouble than that of the father and the task took him five years, appearing at last in five volumes in 1805. Roscoe, moreover, was hardly a pioneer. Dr Johnson's friend, the poet William Collins, had projected such a life before he died in 1759, aged 39.[5] *Leo X* did not have the same success as *Lorenzo de Medici*, being greeted with savage hostility by *The Edinburgh Review*, which criticised it for prolixity, digression and inadequate historical rigour. The author's attempt to rescue Lucrezia Borgia from the accusation that she was her father's harlot was hardly popular in a land that cherished the legends of the Scarlet Woman. Nor was this the history of the revival of learning that Roscoe had unwisely advertised that it would be. It might do for dilettanti, but not for serious readers. Other, evangelical, critics found fault with his treatment of Luther. Nonetheless, the book did well enough in England, running to six editions between 1805 and 1883, and in translation in France, Italy and Germany. Despite, or perhaps because of, being admitted to the index of prohibited books by the Holy Office in Rome, it sold 2,800 copies in an Italian translation (from the French version of 1808), issued in eight volumes between 1816–17.

Sir Walter Scott was not tempted by Roscoe to set any of his novels in Italy, even though he was far from indifferent to the country. In a fragment of autobiography he confessed that Tasso and Ariosto, even in translation, had convinced him the Italian language contained a fund of romantic lore, and he had enrolled in a class of Italian, acquiring 'some proficiency', tackling Dante, Boiardo and Pulci in the original.[6] *Orlando Furioso* and *La Gerusalemme Liberata* were part of the inspiration for his crusading novels, *The Talisman*, *Ivanhoe* and *Count Robert of Paris*. Remembering the effort he had put in to translate the opening of *Orlando Furioso*, Scott makes Francis Osbaldistone, in *Rob Roy*, show his version to Diana Vernon, the Borders bluestocking, who knew her Ariosto in Italian![7] He also showed his acquaintance with *Orlando* in dubbing the chapter in which Waverley quarrels with the MacIvor 'The Confusion of King Agramant's Camp'.[8] (Agramant, a descendant of Alexander the Great, is the African emperor who leads his armies against Charlemagne in Ariosto.) Scott did not, however, have enough Italian to converse, many years later, with the King of the Two Sicilies. His French and the king's Italian were mutually incomprehensible.

If Scott did not publish an Italian tale, he certainly belonged to the 'stiletto school'. Writers on Italy were obsessed by knives. Forsyth reckoned that, for even the bloodiest ruffian, 'to shoot your enemy is held atrocious; to plunge a stiletto into his back, a proof of spirit.'[9] Statues, a French visitor told Mrs Piozzi in 1785, 'do not handle long knives to so good an effect as the others [humans] do, "qui aiment bien à s'égorger encore"'.[10] 'In Italy', wrote Mary Shelley, 'the secret stiletto was the weapon of revenge and the murder of one was avenged by the assassination of another until the list of expiatory murders ran high'.[11] 'Like a cowardly Italian', wrote Sir Walter, 'he had recourse to his fatal stiletto to murder the man whom he dared not meet in manly encounter'[12] In George Eliot's *Scenes of Clerical Life*, the Italian orphan, Catarina, on discovering that the heir to the house in which she has been brought up since childhood has trifled with her, seizes a dagger intending to destroy him.[13] Travellers entered Italy with a healthy fear of the stiletto. The French occupiers had banned the carrying of one, a prohibition that continued in the restored kingdom of Sardinia, otherwise resolved to remove every trace of French rule. Sydney Morgan in 1821 thought the crime of assassination there was as rare as in England.[14] Claire Clairmont, however, told Edward Williams of a servant recommended to a lady of her acquaintance as '*un bravo giovani* [sic] and tho' not twenty years of age, has already given *three stabs*' (Italics in the original).[15]

Scott's Scotland, however, was an *Italia* in itself, and could provide for 'the Master Spirit of the history of the Middle Ages ... spectres, magic, abbeys, castles, subterranean passages and praeternatural appearances' enough.[16] He confessed that he had once toyed with writing a romance about Giovanna of Naples, a figure who, like Mary Queen of Scots, was either 'a model of female virtue or a monster of atrocity'.[17] Giovanna I (1327–82) ruled as Queen of Naples from 1343, succeeding her Angevin grandfather, Robert the Wise. She was married four times, and was popularly supposed to have had a hand in the death of her first husband. She ceded Avignon to the papacy as public exoneration of that deed. Her detractors accused her of ruling Naples through favourites, some of whom were her lovers, and she was ultimately dethroned and murdered while at prayer by one of her nephews when she willed away the kingdom to another. She was the subject of Walter Savage Landor's Neapolitan verse trilogy, *Andrea of Hungary* (1839, husband number one), *Giovanna of Naples* (1839) and *Fra Rupert* (1840). But Scott was too good an historian to want to alter the past to achieve a novelistic effect. His portrait of Mary Queen of Scots in *The Abbot* is probably as near the mark as can be, and William Gell thought Scott gave up the idea of writing about Giovanna of Naples because he was inclined to take her part, as he had that of Mary. That would have been good history but a poor story.[18] Apart from *The Siege of Malta*, on which he tried to work during his visit to Italy in 1832, the nearest he came to selecting Italy as the locale for a story was *Il Bizarro*, an 'Italian story of corruption and assassination', never published in his lifetime. This was a Calabrian tale he had picked up on his travels, about a bandit who strangled his new-born child in case its crying revealed his whereabouts to his pursuers. His wife in revenge hacked off his head and claimed the reward for his capture dead or alive. Scott's handwriting, after his stroke, had become so bad that neither Lockhart nor Scott's publisher could read it, and what they could read they judged to be an absolute failure.[19] Nor was Scott well enough to profit from the treasure trove of horror he was offered in Rome by the Duke of Corchiano (sometimes known as Santa Croce), whose collection included 'all the murders, poisonings, intrigues and curious adventures of all the great Roman families over many centuries'.[20]

The first translation (into French) of a Scott novel was *Quentin Durward* (1816) and others followed quickly, so that by 1820 he was more widely read than any other novelist of the time, quite extinguishing the taste for the epistolary fictions of Richardson and Laclos, and eclipsing Voltaire and Madame de Staël. Most European readers without English would have read him in French and, as his Scottish novels were too alien, they read, mainly, his medieval romances. One exception to this was the Duke of Corchiano, who rebuked Scott for the death of Clara Mowbray in *St Ronan's Well*, one of his most delightful but less famous Scottish romances.[21] Scott's genius in bringing history alive through his characters who, in the 'Scottish' novels particularly, give an idiosyncratic commentary on their times, evaded most of his imitators, of whom there were few in Italy, but the novels did prove to be a quarry to which opera librettists turned to meet the inexhaustible requests for suitable subjects. Among the better known were Rossini's *La Donna del Lago*, Bellini's *Il Pirata* and Donizetti's *Elizabetta di Kenilworth* and *Lucia di Lammermoor*. There were nineteen others, drawing on *The Talisman*, *The Fair Maid of Perth*, *The Heart of Midlothian* and *The Bride of Lammermoor*. The *Bride* was translated into Italian in 1824 and inspired at least two other Italian operas in addition to Donizetti's.[22] Before Scott, plots for opera had been largely taken from the works of the Viennese 'Caesarian' poet, Pietro Metastasio. Tales from Greece, Rome and the ancient orient had hitherto formed the staple of tragic opera, but now librettists were ready to explore a wider range of plots, which repudiated the classical unities and the conventions of Italian opera that dictated how and when solos, duets, ensembles and choruses should be sung.[23] What they did with the plots is often pure travesty. A pastiche of *Ivanhoe* was mounted in Paris in 1826 provided by the Neapolitan Antonio Pacini with music from Rossini's other operas, its plot reduced to six characters among whom both Rebecca and the Jew had become Muslims, in order not to offend the powerful Franco-Jewish bankers.

Rossini, the Napoleon of music, had broken down the old frontiers, choosing not only stories from the Bible (*Mosè in Egitto*), the classical world (*Ermione*), the ancient orient (*Semiramide, Ciro in Babilonia, Aureliano in Palmyra*) but from the medieval world (*Tancredi, Sigismondo, Maometto II* and *Guillaume Tell*). Rossini dominated the romantic opera of the early nineteenth century as Scott dominated the romantic novel; and just as England had no indigenous operatic tradition – Handel, when he did not write Italian operas, presented his English work in the form of oratorio, Purcell in the form of vaudeville – so Italy had no romantic novels on which to draw for operatic plots. *I Promessi Sposi* (1827, translated first into English as *The Betrothed Lovers* in 1828) is often referred to as the Italian novel Scott never wrote. Or, at least, one of the novels that Bulwer Lytton could have written. The 1848 edition of *Rienzi* was dedicated to Alessandro Manzoni. In 1832 Scott wanted to meet Manzoni, whose novel he admired, but not enough to make the detour to Milan, so keen was he to return to Scotland.[24]

The early nineteenth century was rich in history novelists and painters who flocked to Italy for their subjects. It also had its history poets, of whom two were widely read: Barry Cornwall (actually Brian Waller Procter, 1787–1874) had been a school-fellow of Byron at Harrow and is probably more famous today as the father of Adelaide Ann Procter. A friend of Leigh Hunt and Dickens and a biographer of Charles Lamb and Keats, he became part of the literary establishment and was the author of poems with Italian historical subjects, notably 'Marcian Colonna, A Sicilian Story' (1820) and a verse tragedy *Mirandola* (1821), which was performed at Covent Garden in 1821 with Charles Kemble. Shelley and Thomas Love Peacock were not fans. Though 'A Sicilian Story' might be pretty enough, the other poems in the volume were imitation Hunt and Wordsworth. Peacock called it 'drivelling doggrel' [sic].[25] Eventually Procter's practice at the bar called for more dedication and he gave up verse. Alexander Kinglake was one of his pupils.

Felicia Hemans was more fortunate. Immensely prolific, there was hardly a subject she was not prepared to celebrate in rhyme: the last banquet of Antony and Cleopatra, Belshazzar's feast, Heliodorus in the Temple, Richard Coeur de Lion, the death of Conradin, Arabella Stuart, Inez de Castro. Born in Liverpool in 1793, Felicia Browne was the daughter of the union between an Irish merchant from Sligo and a Wagner, whose name, she claimed, was a corruption of the Venetian 'Veniero', a name borne by two doges and by the commander of the fleet of the republic at Lepanto. Felicia's maternal grandfather had been consul in Liverpool for the Tuscan government, and that was as near as she ever got to Italy. From childhood she was blessed with great beauty and a great capacity for self-instruction, living in the Welsh hills near Abergele in Denbighshire, in a house with a large library and a convenient apple tree in which she would sit to read Shakespeare. She had a remarkably retentive memory and could quote, as she was later to write, poetry by the yard. Her childhood was spent in a very nursery of Romantic sensibility, and she published her first book of poems at the age of fourteen. According to Tom Medwin, who had met her in Wales, her book made a powerful impression on Shelley who foresaw 'the coming greatness of that genius, which ... afterwards electrified the world'![26] Despite its otherwise sniffy reception she was not daunted, and duly fell in love, like Lydia Bennett in *Pride and Prejudice*, with a fine uniform inhabited by an unworthy soldier. She had to wait three years for him to complete his service in the Peninsula, before she married Captain Hemans of the King's Own Regiment in 1812. Six years and five children later the captain, whose eye was of a roving disposition, decamped to Rome, for his health. It was probably his presence there that prevented the author of *Lays of Many Lands* from going to Italy herself, but this prolific and cosmopolitan writer never left Britain's shores, being even less travelled than that other prolific and cosmopolitan writer, Ann Radcliffe, who at least got as far as the Netherlands. But the burdens of family and the education of her sons, two of whom went eventually to join their father in Rome, kept her, first, in Wales and then in Wavertree near the city of her birth.

Having taught herself to read French, Italian, Spanish and Portuguese, she gave herself free range among their historical figures and, setting herself to play the piano, even composed airs for her own lyrics.[27] Her reputation was at one time quite as high as her fellow Romantic poets, there being, in the opinion of William Michael Rossetti, 'probably no female poet in our language whose works are more affectionately remembered, and whose lyrics are held in higher esteem, by persons of cultivated taste'.[28] He was remarkably blind to the claims of other female poets, particularly of his own sister, Christina.

Felicia Hemans assumed her prophetic mantle early on, in 1816, with 'The Restoration of the Works of Art to Italy', a long poem demonstrating her extensive acquaintance with the pinnacles of classical and Renaissance art, largely culled from the popular *Classi-*

cal Tour through Italy by a clergyman, John Chetwode Eustace (1815).
It opens with what had become, by now, almost a habitual greeting
to the 'Land of departed fame!' and proceeds with a long allusive lit-
any of heroes of art and intellect, all dead and gone –

> ... glory's faded smile
> Sheds a lingering light o'er many a mould'ring pile;
> Proud wreck of vanish'd power, of splendour fled,
> Majestic temple of the mighty dead.

She almost reaches sublimity when she apostrophises the

> Eternal City! round whose Curule throne
> The lords of nations knelt in ages flown;
> Thou whose Augustan years have left to time
> Immortal records of their glorious prime;
> When deathless bards, thine olive shades among,
> Swell'd the high raptures of heroic song.

The poem continues in this Byronic strain, in the hope that the
return of the looted memories of their glorious past might rouse
young bosoms to noblest aims and 'a new Rome in phoenix grandeur burst'.[29]

Felicia Hemans also tried her hand at romantic drama and *The
Vespers of Palermo*, a play in five acts in blank verse, was performed
for one night only at Covent Garden. She wrote it in 1821, the year
that John Keats died, but she had to wait for two years until the
management was persuaded to put it on at the instance of the Reverend Reginald Heber. Heber, later the first Anglican Bishop of
Calcutta, was widely remembered for one poem, the hymn 'From
Greenland's Icy Mountains, From India's Coral Strand', like Mrs
Hemans herself, remembered chiefly for 'Casabianca'. John Murray
bought the copyright of *The Vespers of Palermo* for 200 guineas, and
the Hemans family in St Asaph waited all agog for a triumph. Alas,
it was a dismal failure. Though the lead was played by Charles
Kemble, the principal actress was hissed and when she decided on
an unscheduled and spontaneous 'death' in the last moments of the
play, for which there was no warrant in the script, she called down
derision. Kemble was not used to being associated with failure and
refused to appear again with the same player. Another actress not
being ready to learn the part, the play was not repeated, and Mrs
Hemans accepted the disappointment stoically as proper chastisement for the temerity of a female who had no business to write
tragedies.[30]

The play was originally to be called 'Procida', after its principal protagonist, but as the revolt was better known from its timing than from its leader, it was dubbed *The Vespers of Palermo*. The original rising had erupted as the church bells rang for Vespers on Easter Sunday, 29 March 1282, and was directed against the hated Angevin government. The French were slaughtered without mercy wherever they were found, men, women and children, even the Sicilian girls who had married Frenchmen, while the religious of both sexes who could not pronounce '*ciciri*', a Sicilian word the French tongue could not embrace, were torn from their convents and butchered in the streets. (The *ciciri* was a pea, peculiar in having only one seed per pod.)[31] None of this is the subject of Felicia Hemans's drama. The revolt was seen as the long overdue (and successful) reaction of a people to foreign oppression, but in 1282 – as in 1821 – Sicilians were not immediately thought of, by those who knew them, as Italians. They spoke a language strongly laced with Arabic words, and their island had been ruled by other European nations since the Vandal occupation of Carthage in the fifth century AD. Its incorporation into the Kingdom of Naples under the Bourbon King Charles in 1738, brought it into the embrace of a specifically Italian principality; and under King Ferdinand IV (of Naples) and III (of Sicily) and I (of the Two Sicilies) (1751–1825) – who spent most of the Napoleonic period under British protection in Palermo – it was ruled for the first time by a native Italian speaker, even if that Italian was Neapolitan.

Felicia Hemans knew nothing of Sicily, but she was ready to put any historical story into verse, and she had a model to hand. Jean François Casimir Delavigne (1793–1843) was a court poet, granted a sinecure in the Paris revenue office for a poem on the birth of the King of Rome. He was good at holding on to sinecures – after the Bourbon restoration he became an honorary librarian – and in 1819 was hailed for saving French theatre with *Les Vêpres Siciliennes*. Delavigne, whatever his merit, is now totally forgotten, a footnote in the history of literature, not unlike Mrs Hemans herself, and both their Vespers would be forgotten but for the tireless search for a plot by Eugène Scribe which gave us an opera by Verdi. It was Verdi's first opera for Paris (1855), and the massacre of a chorus of Frenchmen with which it ends – Wagner called it 'a night of carnage' – needed to be tempered with the suggestion that they did not wholly deserve their fate. Unlike Mrs Hemans and Delavigne, who both made Procida an agent of liberation from that thirteenth-century Napoleon Bonaparte, Charles of Anjou, Scribe made him 'a common conspirator with the inevitable dagger in his hand'.[32] No one should expect accurate history from tragedies in five acts or from libretti which require star-crossed lovers, usually on opposite sides, as happens in all three version here; but a stagefull of deaths before the curtain finally comes down should be expected. But these works can often suggest that, while this may not be exactly what happened, if circumstances were right, it could happen this way. The invasion of Sicily by a 1,000 red-shirts in 1860 was not a Sicilian Vespers, but, like the Vespers, it changed history. The Sicilians may not have risen to expel the Bourbon tyrant, Francis II, described by Tommaso di Lampedusa in *Il Gattopardo* as a mild-mannered, shy, devout, Italian-speaking 'seminarist dressed up as a general',[33] but they did not defend him, and Sicily was the first province to be offered to the King of Sardinia in Turin, the future first King of Italy. Poor Francis, however, did have his loyal admirers. William Moens, kidnapped by bandits, asked them what they would do if they met Vittorio Emmanuele. They would demand 'ten million ducats and then shoot him'. But if they were to catch the tyrant Francis II they would 'give him a good dinner and then release him'.[34] The Kingdom of the Two Sicilies never quite lived up to expectations. It was a Hispano-Neapolitan colony, not an Italian heartland like Lombardy, Tuscany or Emilia-Romagna. It was only deemed a part of Italy by those who read their Gibbon and Mrs Hemans.

In *The Vespers of Palermo* the Sicilian grievance is made quite clear. Sicily was

> ... no land of peace; unless that deep
> And voiceless terror, which doth freeze men's thoughts
> Back to their source, and mantle its pale mien
> With a dull hollow semblance of repose
> May so be called.[35]

Mrs Hemans rises at certain moments to real dramatic effect. The tyrant Eribert, the Angevin viceroy (Hemans, not being a historian, makes the occupants Provençal), has in true Macbeth fashion had all the children of the Sicilian grandee, Montalba, murdered. Montalba describes how, returning to his castle, he

> ... called – my struggling voice
> Gave utterance to my wife's, my children's names.
> They answered not. I roused my failing strength
> And wildly rushed within – And they were there
> Procida   And all was well?

Montalba   Ah well! for death is well:
And they were all at rest! ...
Raimondo [Procida's son]   Man of woe!
What words hath pity for despair like thine?
Montalba   Pity! fond youth – My soul disdains the grief
Which doth unbosom its deep secrecies
To ask a vain companionship of tears,
And so to be relieved.
Procida   For woes like these
There is no sympathy but vengeance.[36]

The massacre is not the climax of the play as in Verdi's opera, but happens in the middle of the tyrant's marriage to his bride victim, for which the Vesper bells are tolling. The theme of sexual as well as national liberation appealed to Scott, whose sympathies had often been with the insurrectionary oppressed, as in *Rob Roy* and *A Legend of Montrose*. Scott did not actually meet Hemans until 1829 and found her charming, but Joanna Baillie (1762–1851) had introduced him to the drama, her own play, *De Montfort*, a 'tragedy of hatred', having played for eleven nights at Drury Lane in 1800 with John Kemble and Mrs Siddons in the leading parts. In April 1822, Scott produced Hemans's play for the Edinburgh theatre. Mrs Siddons agreed to play the romantic female lead, Constance, the sister of the last Hohenstaufen emperor whom the Angevins had executed; it was prefaced by a special tribute to, and an epilogue by Scott, both recited by the *grande dame* herself. It had twice the success it had enjoyed in London, being performed twice. As a play, *The Vespers of Palermo* was no worse than many of its era and from time to time had moments that set the blood racing. Stripped to essentials it would have made a good opera plot, provided that the Vespers themselves, as Scribe saw to it, formed the climax rather than the end only of Act 3.

The heirs to the Gothic novelists were indeed the nineteenth-century opera librettists who were only too happy to sup full of horrors that could safely be ascribed to autocratic, clerical despots of whom there continued to be many in Europe until the third quarter of the century. Felicia Hemans was not a failed librettist, but a successful poet. Successful but now little read, she earned her place in the honoured ranks of 'awakeners' to the plight of Italy in the early nineteenth century, as well as being paraded today as an early feminist writer who helped to 'feminise' national history that had hitherto been a masculine preserve. Many of her works, including

The Vespers of Palermo, dealt with the 'suffering, victimisation or sacrifice, willing or unwilling of a female protagonist'.[37]

The other great giant of British Romanticism also paid his most substantial visit to Italy late in life, too late for it to influence his view of *Italia*. Wordsworth had made a foray into the Italian Alps in 1790, when he had rambled in the Alps with *Orlando Furioso* in his knapsack. In 1820 he penetrated as far as Milan, but he was not to go further afield until 1837, when he travelled with Henry Crabb Robinson. Wordsworth was now 67 years of age, and he regretted leaving the trip so late. Lake Como 'left its beauty with him', and he was sad that the innumerable images Italy would have given him had not been available for some noble purpose.[38] The rattling of the coach and of his travelling companion proved to be very exhausting. Though Crabb Robinson did his best to adapt to the needs and comfort of his older friend, Wordsworth resolved never to travel again without 'a female companion'. Crabb Robinson was too keen on 'loitering about towns, gossiping and attending reading rooms ... gabbling German or any other tongue' and then could not get up in the morning.[39]

Wordsworth on this visit was not looking for the *Italia* he had imagined as a boy, where herdsmen and their snow-white herd enjoyed

> ... a smooth life,
> To triumphs and to sacrificial rites
> Devoted, on the inviolable stream
> Of rich Clitumnus

and where the goat-herd 'under the pleasant brows of cool Lucetilis' heard Pan's piping'.[40] He had discarded this Poussinesque rubbish with the experience of real mountains in Cumbria, and of the rugged, ruthless people who lived in them. Over his long life, stimulated by Coleridge, he had assembled an extensive and recondite collection of Italian authors, most of them acquired in the years of his fame, and was as familiar with Tasso as Keats and Leigh Hunt were.[41] In 1802 he tried his hand at translating some of *Orlando Furioso*, echoes of which appeared three years later when, recording his musing by the banks of the Loire, he imagined that a traveller's 'speed and echoes loud of trampling hoofs'

> ... was Angelica thundering through the woods
> Upon her palfrey, or that gentle maid
> Erminia, fugitive as fair as she.[42]

Italian poets were part of his omnivorous diet and, though his tour in 1837 took him to the source of Italian culture, it had already woven what spell it had on his work. From his Cambridge days onwards he deplored the subjection of classical and Renaissance Italy to the physical and spiritual jackboots of Habsburg, Bourbon and papal oppressors, but he could not make up his mind between regret for the extinction of ancient, often imperfect liberties, and enthusiasm for the new emancipation introduced by Napoleon. His sonnet on 'The Extinction of the Venetian Republic', written at least five years after Napoleon had brutally snuffed it out at the Treaty of Campo Formio, reflects this uncertainty. 'Men are we and must grieve when even the Shade / Of that which once was great is passed away.'

Despite his contact, largely through Crabb Robinson, with Italian exiles, and despite his admiration of Mazzini, Wordsworth had no great hopes for Italy. He had found that 'few / Part from thee without pity dyed in shame'.[43] And in 'At Bologna, in Remembrance of the Late Insurrections' (1837) he railed against the 'great Italian nation, split / Into those jarring factions.' When passion rather than planning holds the scale;

> ... Nations sink; or, struggling to be free,
> Are doomed to flounder on, like wounded whales
> Tossed on the bosom of a stormy sea.[44]

The *Memorials of a Tour in Italy* is an '*Italia*' poem par excellence, not because it invokes *Italia* in recalling Lago Morto's

> ... dreary sight and name,
> Which o'er sad thoughts a sadder colouring threw,
> Italia! on the surface of thy spirit
> (Too aptly emblemed by that torpid lake)

but because, throughout its length, the author salutes only two living people.[45] One was a peasant woman at Albano who was confident it was going to be fine because prayers had been offered at Mass for good weather,[46] and the other an old man in Lombardy, bent with a load of mulberry leaves, whose lot he compares to that of an earthworm.[47] Otherwise it is a paean for the dead. Something similar is noticeable in Mary Shelley's work, never an admirer of the commonalty of Italy. In 'Recollections of Italy', a contribution to *The London Magazine* in 1823, her interlocutor summarises the pleasures of Italy as the beauties of nature and the works of man.[48] The Apennines compared ill with Wordsworth's beloved Lake District,[49] and a spirit of regret pervades the whole poem, perhaps as much induced by his philosophic meandering as by Crabb Robinson's ceaseless chat. The sequence ends with a proper obeisance to a desirable future; 'Awake / Mother of Heroes, from thy death-like sleep!'[50] After delighting 'in the rich stores of Nature's imagery and Divine Art ... how beautiful! how worthy to be sung / In strains of rapture, or subdued delight!' he was shocked, in the Alps, when delivering his last words in Italian in Italy, to be greeted in German. That

> ... greeting seemed to mock
> Parting; the casual word had power to reach
> My heart, and filled that heart with conflict strong.[51]

Apart from the almost, by now, ritual invocation to Italian freedom, Wordsworth did not succeed in awakening any devotion to that spiritual life of Italy so often dismissed as peasant superstition and idolatry. But in one place he felt a specifically numinous Italian presence. 'The Cuckoo at Laverna', that eyrie among the 'sterile heights of Appenine' where St Francis received the stigmata, echoed Wordsworth's love of heights and solitary places, oases of pure religion in convents that breathe the austere air in a discipline purified by simplicity. St Francis, 'rapt though he were above the power of sense' drew beasts and bird 'to his side by look or act of love' in an affection similar to that which our first parents 'held with all kinds in Eden's blissful bowers'.[52] Given the enduring devotion to St Francis today, it is surprising to learn that Wordsworth was the first Englishman of his century, perhaps the first European, to invoke the special qualities of the saint.[53] But St Francis was not going to lead a *risorgimento*.

Crabb Robinson in Florence introduced Wordsworth to another literary prolific, whose star the younger Wordsworth, at first little appreciated, had by now eclipsed. Walter Savage Landor had set off for Italy in the year that Napoleon burst out of Elba. Landor was looking for somewhere to live comfortably and cheaply with his wife, who had believed him an affluent resident in Bath, but who found that she had married a bankrupt. They first settled in Como, but if Landor had hoped to improve his fortunes with his pen, he was to be disappointed. The three years by the lake, apart from a few verses, were barren and, after a Stendhalian encounter with the censorship, during which Landor nearly got himself arrested, his residence permit was withdrawn. Disappointed by the expense of lodgings in Pisa, before it became a nest of singing birds, he moved to the benign climate of Leopoldine Florence and took an apartment in the Medici palace.[54] The next five years were the most fruitful of his life, during which he wrote most of the *Imaginary Conversations* and collected pictures. He was joined in Florence by the Leigh Hunts, by Keats's friend, Charles Armitage Brown, and by a growing cosmopolitan circle of poets and painters. His fiery and outspoken temper at one time dictated a prudent retreat to Lucca, until the grand duke's officials calmed down, after which Landor decided to move out of town to the Villa Castiglione, on the spot where Boccaccio 'led his women to bathe at the end of their first day of story-telling'.[55] Once installed, he told Henry Crabb Robinson that he would never leave Tuscany, though he was not fond of the Italian character. The Italians were too cowardly to assert themselves and demand representative government, which he believed they might have had for the asking, and they had contributed nothing to the cause of the constitutionalists who had just overturned the Bourbons in Paris.[56]

The following year he wrote 'High and Low Life in Italy', with many successors over the next two centuries, being a rather mannered account of everyday life in Italy, spoiled by the fact that it had 'fine writing' stamped all over it. It purported to be the letters of Mr J. J. Stivers, Secretary to Milord Raikes Esq., of Como, to and from various correspondents, English and Italian, in Italy. Neither Crabb Robinson nor his friend, Julius Hare, uncle of the ubiquitous pedestrian, Augustus, could find a publisher for the work, even John Murray declining it, and it only appeared six years later when Leigh Hunt was bullied into publishing it in the *Monthly Repository*. Landor was too epicurean a writer to sell well, and after a time he ceased to care. Though the cynosure of English *literati* in Florence, he found he could get on with neither his wife nor his children, who were growing up obstreperous. To spare them hearing 'such language as no decent person should even hear once', thus growing up to despise both parents, he decided in 1835 to leave the Italy he had hoped would be his home until death, and the children he still loved.[57]

Over the next 23 years in England, and despite his poor opinion of Italians, Landor continued to support the cause of an independent Italy. In 1848–9 he found the heroes, Daniele Manin and

Giuseppe Garibaldi, who were to transform that poor opinion. He entertained Count Orsini, whose attempt to assassinate Napoleon III for what he held was the emperor's broken oath to free Italy, triggered the French alliance with Sardinia to expel the Austrians from Italy. But he remembered Alfieri's advice to him as a young man that 'nothing good ever came out of France, or ever will. ... They have always been the curse of Italy; yet we have fools among us who trust them.' He knew where he put his faith. 'Rise Manin! rise, Garibaldi! rise, Mazzini. ... Strike and spare not; strike high.'[58] Landor died, back again in Florence, in 1864, writing to his last moment of life, dismayed that Garibaldi had been captured at Aspromonte by the Sardinians, for whom he had liberated Sicily and Naples.

Posterity has been unkind to Landor, whereas it has secured for the stay-at-home, Thomas Love Peacock, a secure affection. Like Landor, Peacock wanted to be a much-read poet, but was not tempted to join the flight to the Mediterranean, which had become almost fashionable. Despite his love of Italian poetry – he read Boiardo's *Orlando Innamorato* seven times and Ariosto's *Furioso* for the 'I-know-not-how-manieth time'[59] – Peacock had no desire to follow his friend Shelley abroad, wishing to travel 'as little towards Italy as to almost any other [country], France always excepted'.[60] For Italians he shared a then fairly general contempt: 'I deem it a moral impossibility that an Englishman who is not encrusted either with natural apathy or superinduced Giaourism can live many years among such animals as the modern Italians'.[61] This professed insularity was strange, considering his future job was with the East India Company, being responsible for drafting the letters that passed between the Company directors and their governor-general and governors in India. When Percy Bysshe Shelley wrote to enquire about a post in India at the court of an Indian prince, Peacock was sure that it would agree with neither his mind nor his body and declined to act, with the excuse that such posts went to covenanted Company servants, trained over many years.[62] His job left him time to write letters and continue writing novels and his income was sufficient for a literary production that was largely self-indulgent, reflecting the pleasures he received from his extensive classical education and his forays into Italian literature. Though he was deep into 'zamindars, ryots, mokuddims and putwarries' on behalf of his new employer, his linguistic inventiveness was not the result of exposure to the new almost phantasmagoric vocabulary of Indian administration, but to the work of the Florentine neologist and poetaster,

Benedetto Menzini, whose poems first appeared in 1782. Peacock was dazzled by Menzini's compositoconcatenated words, like *lattiporporifere* and *venericoribantentusiasmo*. Most of them meant no more than tethrippharmatelasipedioploctyphilous, reputedly the longest word in English fiction,[63] but in the Italian's *Anacreontiche* Peacock identified a spirit of poetry similar to his own. But Peacock's Italian enthusiasms are preserved in the Socratic symposia he inserted in his novels, which jaunted along with the rhythms of a Rossini opera. Indeed, the 20-year-old composer's *La Pietra di Paragone* (*The Touchstone*), which features a cast of talkative grotesques including, among titled gold-diggers and intriguers, a journalist and a poet seeking patronage from the rich hero, is a distinctly Peacockian affair.[64] Peacock revived the Gothic novel as a parody, set usually over dinner or a picnic in Italianate *sanguisemprappetenti* residences, or *gelidifontombriselvosa* rocks and glades.[65]

Peacock found a kindred soul in Byron's best man and fellow tourist, who had annotated the Canto IV of *Childe Harold* and been its dedicatee, John Cam Hobhouse. In 1835 Hobhouse became Peacock's political director, as President of the Board of Control for India, appointed to supervise the East India Company in its role of effective ruler of India. The two men shared literary, philological and philosophical interests, and their correspondence, after they had both retired from office, is punctuated by conundra posed by the interpretation of texts, and historical inquiries, such as whether the Matelda of Dante's *Il Purgatorio* was or was not the 'Great Countess of Tuscany'.[66]

Roscoe, Scott, Cornwall, Hemans, Wordsworth, Peacock and Landor had all immersed themselves in Italian history and literature as they believed was expected of any writer who intended to be poet or novelist. The land that had nourished and inspired their models, however, was betrayed by the spiritless attitude of its children, either too content to be slaves or too frivolous to break their chains. But none would have disagreed with the view that, even so, Italy should, as one nation, be free. The problem was how this was ever to be achieved.

7

'What Elysium Have Ye Known?'

Poets in Exile

> Souls and Poets, dead and gone,
> What Elysium have ye known?

> John Keats, 'Lines on the Mermaid Tavern', ll. 1–2.

I invented then a chain on which were engraved the names of 23 poets, both ancient and modern, the pendant being a cameo of Homer and a distich of mine in Greek saying:

> 'Alfieri founded a new Order
> and made himself a Knight of Homer.'

> Vittorio Alfieri, *Vita*, final page.

> *Tu non altro che il canto avrai del figlio,*
> *O materna mia terra; a noi prescrisse*
> *Il fato illacrimata sepoltura*

[You, land of my birth, will have only the song of a son. For us, Fate has in store only an unwept grave.]

> Ugo Foscolo, *A Zacinto*, ll. 12–14.

The play by Alfieri that Keats brought with him to Italy, from which he hoped to increase his command of Italian, was one of the playwright's first dramas. *Spumante* as the wine of Asti, his birthplace, Count Vittorio Alfieri was a Romantic before Romanticism, and a Byron before Byron, 'one whose temperament and character belonged as much to Italy as her Alps and her Vesuvius'.[1] Coming into a vast inheritance at the age of fourteen, he abandoned serious study to be a lawyer and dedicated himself to horse-riding, women and poetry. Being a *piemontese*, he was fluent in French – and the Franco-Italian dialect of his native province – and had to learn *il vero Toscano* when he came to translate his first dramas, written in French. *Filippo*, which Keats abandoned early on, was one of these. Unlike Byron, Alfieri did not distil his experience of travel into verse. He was bored by sightseeing but, like Byron, enjoyed the intimate company of women. In contrast to Byron's discovery of the Mediterranean, being a south European, he found his Arcadia in the gloomy forests and lakes of northern Sweden, relishing in their sublime loneliness a world free from the stifling trammels of mid-eighteenth-century society. Nourished on Plutarch and Metastasio, his future as a tragedian was sealed with the production of his verse drama *Cleopatra* in Turin in 1775.

While Italianising *Filippo* in Florence he met the unhappy wife of Bonnie Prince Charlie, to everyone in Rome the Queen of Hearts and, to a small coterie of Jacobites, Queen of England. Her marriage having proved childless and Charles declining further into drink and violence, the Countess of Albany slipped easily into the arms of such an experienced womaniser as Alfieri and, like Teresa Guiccioli later with Byron, tamed her poet into, first, a *cavaliere servente* and then, some averred, a husband. The liaison the two lovers formed in Rome was productive of fourteen tragedies and a model of extra-connubial bliss, and they were to stay together until Alfieri's death. His political views made him difficult to know and dangerous to publish while in Italy, so the couple exiled themselves to Alsace, moving to Paris just before 1789. There his aristocratic birth and a foray across the Channel to buy horses, made him suspect to the Jacobin authorities and, while he had initially welcomed the limitation of the monarchy – he indeed addressed a pamphlet to Louis XVI outlining how Louis might rule as a constitutional monarch like his 'cousin' the King of England[2] – he was disillusioned by the excesses of the convention and made his escape with his countess to Florence, where he died in 1803. If Sweden was Arcadia, England was Utopia. Since his first visit in 1769 he had become a regular Anglophile. He may have found the language unspeakable, the climate unbearable, the meals uneatable and the social life, because of the late hours it kept, unendurable, but he was impressed by London's streets, inns, horses and women, the 'universal sense of well-being', the cleanliness and comfort of its houses, the diffusion of wealth and industry into the provinces, and the whole impression that the country was better governed than any other he had visited.

But, though he admired England's general felicity, when designated an emigré in Paris, with all his possessions sequestered, he could not afford to take refuge there with the widow of the Young Pretender, and returned instead to his homeland.[3] Corinne praised his work to Oswald Nelvil, but admitted that, by and large, Italian drama had been pretty run-of-the-mill stuff until Alfieri's arrival on the scene. Metastasio, occupying an imperial appointment in Vienna, offered a stream of safely moral plays for the international world of classic drama and of baroque opera, but Alfieri had difficulty in getting his plays published, let alone acted. He was forced to leave Rome because the Cardinal of York, Prince Charles's brother, thought the attentions paid to his sister-in-law were damaging to morals.

Silvio Pellico, prisoner for ten years in the Spielberg and thus a proto-martyr to the Italian cause from his Gandhian account of *My Prisons* (*Le Mie Prigione*), having defined all liberals as romantics and all classics as extremists or spies, classified Alfieri as a classic, since with one exception his plots were all derived from Biblical, mythological and classical themes like those of Metastasio. But Alfieri's passion for the independence and freedom of his characters was a form of sedition, and made him a liberal and, thus, a Romantic.[4] He stripped his language of ornament, his scenes of incident and his stage of impedimenta, so that tragedy could march with a single-minded inevitability towards its dénouement. However, though both his vivid, if not lurid, autobiography and his plays were published and translated in England – where he enjoyed a brief *réclame* as an enemy of Bonaparte – his theatrical rigour, his dedication to the unities, his small casts endowed with long speeches, were unsympathetic to London audiences. In 1819, Byron in Bologna saw *Mirra*, in which the eponymous heroine, because her mother had boasted that Mirra was more beautiful than Venus, was fated to suffer incestuous love for her father. The fruit of that love was Adonis, who later became the goddess Venus's lover. Despite the improbable plot, Byron was thrown 'into convulsions' by which he meant 'the agony of reluctant tears and the choking shudder that I do not often undergo for fiction'.[5] He admitted that he and Alfieri had much in common; they both domesticated themselves with women of rank, they liked horses and were surrounded by pets of all kinds, and they shared a common sense of *cafard* and a passionate love of liberty.[6] Byron's debt to Alfieri was to be discharged in his own verse dramas, *Marino Faliero*, *Sardanapalus* and *The Two Foscari*, all published in 1821. But they were no more successful on the stage than the Italian's verse dramas: *Marino Faliero* (1821) failed at Drury Lane the same year and the other two could not find backers. Byron's Alfieri phase ended and he returned to drama of another kind in *Don Juan*.

Alfieri may have felt that he was striking a shrewd blow for revolutionary change, but he had little hope of its happening in his own country. The English may not have responded to his drama, but they were powerful, rich and politically influential. Italy was dead, his countrymen divided, weak, reviled and servile, so that he despaired that he was an Italian.[7] Yet, if he could not reanimate them, he could revitalise their language and, by making himself an international figure, passing like a meteor across all Europe, he cast his curse upon the *ancien régime*. Dante, Petrarch, Machiavelli, Boccaccio, Tasso and Ariosto had all been in their time the pride of Italy, conquering the heights of Parnassus. If peoples could follow their poets, as Shelley would have agreed, they could again be great. The day must come when Italians would spring to life, inspired by his songs, and the memory of what they were, and of what he was, would rekindle their ancient virtue. Armed then with the heavenly fury, which their ancestors inspired in him, his verses would prove fatal to the oppressor:

> *E armati allor di qual furor celeste*
> *Spirato in me dall'opre dei lor avi,*
> *Faran mie rime a Gallia esser funeste.*[8]

The oppressor was then Napoleonic France. Sydney Morgan, for whom the enemy was Austria, was a great admirer, and rated sublime Alfieri's uncompromising refusal to live under the government of Piedmont, where he had been born and raised, 'whose existence was incompatible with the independence he adored'[9]

Alfieri hoped to be added to those poets who had been the pride of Italy, but his champion was to come from the sleepier recesses of the Papal States. In 1818, the year that the Shelleys came first to Italy, the 20-year-old Giacomo Leopardi wrote

> *O patria mia, vedo le mura e gli archi*
> *E le colonne e i simulacri e l'erme*
> *Torri degli avi nostri,*
> *Ma la gloria non vedo,*
> *Non vedo il lauro e il ferro ond'eran carchi*
> *I nostri padri antichi.*

[Oh my homeland, I see the walls and arches
And the columns, the shadowy and abandoned
Towers of our ancestors,
But not the glory,
Not the laurels, not the weapons
Which loaded down our ancient forefathers.]

The foreign wars Leopardi had in mind in the poem were Napoleon's and, instead of the laurels and weapons of his ancient forefathers, he saw a half-naked lady of great beauty, manacled, her head between her knees, sobbing. Who had abandoned her, why were her sons not fighting for her but only as mercenaries in wars on foreign shores?[10] The spirit of the past, the spirit that led the Greeks to resist the Persian invasions at Thermopylae no longer animated his countrymen. It was a statement of fact. To put the great Italian poets, to which he had added Alfieri, back on their feet, the Italians themselves should be refashioned in heart and mind.[11] Leopardi did not urge his countrymen to redeem their past and make their future. His whole upbringing forced him to consult his own poetic freedom, his solipsism fed by fears that he would never achieve the fame he coveted, that his small voice would never be heard, because it would be silenced by its own melancholy. He developed an economy of style that made his work look puny beside the novel-length poems of his contemporaries. He wrote one long poem, when seventeen, a free translation of an epic attributed to Homer about the battle between the frogs and mice. His fame rests on the *Canti* or songs, in which the melancholy Romantic voice of an Italy in servitude speaks in almost unbearable pathos.

'All'Italia' was printed in Rome in the year that it was written, and Shelley soon had it by heart. But the Romantic recluse of Recanati met no English poets and was too shy and constrained to make the journey to Venice and beard Lord Byron. Nor was his verse known to the one British poet, to whose anecdotal, personal style his work was very similar. If Wordsworth had any knowledge of Leopardi, it would have come late to him, through his friend Henry Crabb Robinson, who got to know the Italian poet in Florence in 1831, when the *Canti* were first published.[12] Crabb Robinson doubted that Leopardi had ever heard of Wordsworth, but he identified in both poets a shared interest in despondency, Man and Nature, memory and the springs of poetic inspiration. But in the year that Wordsworth and Crabb Robinson came to Italy, Leopardi died in Naples.

Leopardi was virtually an exile in his own country and the poet whose career uncannily mirrors Leopardi's was another, as well as being for three months a true exile in Italy. John Keats and Leopardi never met; they never knew of each other's existence; they wrote not only in two quite different languages, but in different styles. So what Elysium did these two poets know? If such a question had been put to Leopardi his answer could have been that there was 'nothing in life desirable but the joys of the heart and the contemplation of beauty'.[13] Keats's answer must surely be found in 'Ode on a Grecian Urn', written in the same year as 'All'Italia', in which 'Beauty is truth, truth beauty, that is all / Ye know on earth, and all ye need to know.' On 31 December 1819 Keats wrote to his brother George that 'I never feel certain of any truth but from a clear perception of its beauty'.[14]

Both poets tried to find a new language that would allow science to 'establish the precise point beyond which the effects of virtuous belief must not extend'.[15] A voice that would allow poetry to use

> All lovely tales that we have heard or read,
> An endless fountain of immortal drink;
> Pouring unto us from the heaven's brink.[16]

That heavenly ichor also inspired Leopardi's *Canti*, simple, subtle invocations of the world seen from the windows of the palace that served him both as home and prison, just as it did the sonnets Keats dedicated to the friend who sent him roses, and to his brothers 'who had been long in city pent'.[17] But whereas Keats used language in a way that it had not been used in England since the Jacobean age, as a reckless cornucopia of metaphor, images and colour, Leopardi used his with a spareness and economy that was in stark contrast to the rhetoric of his contemporaries. Keats used the whole lexicon of medieval and modern English usage. Leopardi's use of synonyms and imagery has only been rivalled for its pungent and effective economy by Federico Garcia Lorca.

Despite the distance and the cultures that separated them, Keats and Leopardi had an almost uncanny set of shared experiences. Giacomo Leopardi was born in the family palace in Recanati, in the eastern Marches, on 29 June 1798. His father was Count Monaldo Leopardi, a scion of the local aristocracy, a loyal subject of the pope and a cautious conservative at a time when revolutionary change had already swept through northern Italy in the wake of Napoleon's armies. Both poets were deprived of the demonstrative and nurtur-

8. John Keats (1795–1821), after a portrait by Joseph Severn.

9. Giacomo Leopardi (1798–1837), by Dominico Morelli, 'a miraculous likeness' painted from his death mask in 1839. Keats and Leopardi neither knew nor knew of one another, yet their poetic histories were strangely similar.

ing love of parents, what Alphonse Daudet called, in Leopardi's case, *'la caresse chaude, la Mamma'*, for most of their childhood.[18] They were both first children and both had a devoted younger sister. Keats had three younger siblings, Leopardi nine, only four of whom survived infancy. Leopardi's father had an old-fashioned view of children: that they should be dependent on their parents until they died. He gave his sons no pocket money and virtually forbade Giacomo to leave the family house unaccompanied. His mother was a religious bigot, who professed herself glad that five of her children were taken to the Lord early in their lives, thus sparing her the grief and expense of rearing them. The Keats children were finally orphaned when John was fifteen, and they passed into the guardian-ship of a severe Lancastrian self-made man chosen by their grandmother, who abused his position by keeping them apart and perpetually short of money. Leopardi, habited like the abbé his father hoped he might become, was taught by his father's old tutor whose knowledge he soon outgrew, taught himself Greek and French, and spent his days in the university of his father's library, an eclectic collection of books bought in bulk lots and at random, resembling a second-hand bookshop, full of surprises. Count Mon-aldo secured special permission for his son to read the forbidden books, kept in locked cases – to which Giacomo's own works were later to be added. Keats at least went to school, where he had a repu-tation for fighting, and where the proprietor was, for his time, an enlightened educator, allowing his students to study where they liked, so that Keats supplemented his formal education by setting himself a vigorous scheme of reading. Neither had enough money to buy the books they wanted and were dependent on the collec-tions of others. Leopardi ruined his eyesight, poring over the musty volumes for twelve hours a day, without the possibility of open-air exercise which Keats regularly took, walking what are, for today, immense distances, to visit his brothers and friends.

Leopardi as a child was reconciled to his destiny as a priest and launched himself on studies in philosophy and philology, writing at the age of sixteen a commentary on Porphyry's *Life of Plotinus*. Keats qualified as a surgical dresser at Guy's Hospital. Both abandoned their avocations for a life of poetry. Keats had just enough money to live without working for the few years that were left to him. Leo-pardi cajoled and schemed to be allowed to take up a position outside Recanati so that he could escape from the family home, 'this hermitage, or rather seraglio, where the delights of civil society and the advantage of solitary life are alike wanting'.[19]

Both were saved from a deadly introspection by the love of their siblings; Carlo Leopardi who shared Giacomo's young ambitions and their sister, Paolina, who with her own hands was proudly to place her brother's poems in the locked case of banned books. Both, too, found a friend and spiritual mentor who encouraged their first creative efforts and their spirit of rebellion: Keats the radical poet and pamphleteer James Leigh Hunt, who was imprisoned for his political views from 1813 to 1815, and Leopardi the scholar and patriot priest, Pietro Giordani. These men became to their young acolytes the fathers the poets did not have, older men who understood and supported genius greater than their own, to whom they looked for encouragement and advice.

Both Keats and Leopardi early understood the intimations of their own mortality. In February 1820, Keats had recognised his death warrant. Leopardi's curvature of the spine which deformed him, his long, sick headaches which condemned him to rest for hours in the dark, the psoriasis which corrupted his flesh and made him stink were all presages of the death from chronic congestive heart-failure, caused by the progressive deformity of his thorax, that overtook him in 1837 at the age of 39.[20] Both were to find devoted companions during their sickness and decline, Keats in the history-painter, Joseph Severn, and Leopardi in the young Neapolitan poet, Antonio Ranieri, who, with his sister, sustained and nursed Leopardi through the last four years of his life. And final irony, they both developed an eventually hopeless passion for women called Fanny. Fanny Targioni-Tozzetti, whom Leopardi met in Florence in 1830, though she admired the poet's mind, could not reciprocate his passion, as she was already married, in love with Ranieri, and could never overcome her repugnance to his smell. Keats's love for Fanny Brawne is well known.

Leopardi spent almost as little time in Rome as Keats, spending five months there in 1822 and finding it all a terrible disappointment, his uncle's palazzo in the Via Condotti little better than his 'prison' at Recanati, the society frivolous and the monuments too big. Failure to find the spiritual and intellectual uplift he expected from Rome inspired in Leopardi the persistent thought that life was a permanent state of suffering, that happiness was an illusion, and that there was no point in expecting things to get better. Keats's death in Rome linked him with that city in a way it did not deserve, any more than it deserved the hopes and expectations of Leopardi, who finally chose to live in Naples; had Keats done the same, it might have prolonged his life long enough for him to write something while he was in Italy. The only person to express any interest in Leopardi's work was the Prussian ambassador, Barthold Neibuhr, himself the author of the first modern history of Rome. No one of similar public distinction recognised Keats, and what seemed to be the failure of his life's work prompted him to ask for his headstone to carry the simple inscription: 'Here lies one whose name was writ in water'. Leopardi's hopelessness *per essere intera e continua, e fondata in un giudizio fermo e in una certezza* ('being absolute, continual, founded on a firm judgement and on certainty') did not allow him to indulge *a sogni e immaginazioni liete circa il futuro, né animo d'intraprendere cosa alcuna per vedere di ridurle ad effetto* ('in dreams and happy imaginings for the future, nor to embark on any enterprise in order to bring them to fruition').[21] Like Keats, he despaired even of his poetry, 'If I were a poet', he wrote to an admiring French philologist, Charles Lebreton, on 6 April 1836. 'I have never achieved any real work. I have only made attempts, always believing them to be preludes – but my career has gone no further.'[22]

Both Keats and Leopardi had premonitions of death, and Keats protested against going before his 'pen has gleaned my teeming brain', against not living to trace 'huge cloudy symbols of a high romance'.[23] Leopardi greeted it as the most desirable element in life's two experiences, love and death: *Due cose belle ha il mondo / Amore e morte* ('Two beautiful things can the world offer, love and death').[24] In the end the power of destruction always triumphs over the spirit of creation; indeed they become synonymous:

> Sola nel mondo eterno, a cui si volve
> Ogni certa cosa,
> In te, morte si posa
> Nostra ignuda natura;
> Lieto no, ma sicura
> Dall'antico dolor.[25]

[Alone on earth eternal, to whom all created things must come, our naked self finds peace in you, o Death, not happy but safe from the ancient anguish.]

Keats did allow himself one last illusion, that he might swoon to death on his fair love's ripening breast.

Leopardi also died fighting for breath, joking to the end that asthmatics always lived long lives:

> Ma la vita mortale, poi che la bella
> Giovinazza sparì, non si colora
> D'altre luce giammai, né d'altra aurora.[26]

[Life, once lovely youth is gone, is lit by no other light, no second dawn.]

All roads lead to the tomb and to nowhere else. The shared experience of life of both poets, which seemed to deal both of them a consistently unhappy hand of cards, can be summed up in Leopardi's words from his daybook: 'There are two truths which most men will never believe. One, that they know nothing and the other that they are nothing. And there is a third, … that there is nothing to hope for after death.'[27] Both poets had rejected the comforting myths of religion.

If Keats had been too ill in Rome to struggle up to Sant'Onofrio to see Tasso's tomb, Leopardi did and wept at the sight, 'the only pleasure that I have felt in Rome!'[28] Like himself, Tasso was 'a man who has yielded to adversity. Even if all his calamities were imaginary, his unhappiness most certainly was real'.[29] Leopardi may have believed that the Viennese court poet, Count Pietro Metastasio, librettist to both Mozart and Salieri, was the only Italian poet worthy of the name since Tasso, but Tasso 'put religion and the opinions and popular spirit of the time, and all other things that lend themselves to poetry to the use of … preserving civilisation, freedom, the political structure and the well-being of Europe as a whole'.[30] Poets were the unacknowledged legislators of the world. Keats loved to peer up 'at the morning sun, / With half-shut eyes and comfortable cheek', seeking in the tales of Italy 'a region of his own, / A bower for his spirit'.[31] Everything that combined colour, pleasure, joy and the simple pleasures of uncomplicated people was grist to his poetic mill, whether it was Greek or Roman, medieval and Renaissance Italian, or French chansons.

How his spirit would have leaped at Leopardi's tribute to Silvia, where

> Petrarch, outstepping from the shady green,
> Starts at the sight of Laura, nor can we wean
> His eyes from her sweet face.[32]

The Keatsian exuberance is replaced by the Leopardian economy, but the same accent of melancholy delight is there.

> Sonavan le quiete
> Stanze, e le vie dintorno,
> Al tuo perpetuo canto,
> Allor che all'opre femminile intenta
> Sedevi, assai contenta
> Di quel vago avvenir che in mente avevi.
> Era il maggio odoroso e tu solevi
> Così menare il giorno.[33]

[The still rooms, the silent streets rang with your continual singing, as you sat at your woman's work, happy with the blissful future of which you were dreaming. It was fragrant May, and thus you passed your time.]

In his poetry Leopardi disencumbered himself of his philosophy and his philology. He deplored the existence of 'an ever growing wall between the writers and the people'.[34] Poetry should be *popolarissimo*, a view shared by Manzoni, by Byron, by Shelley and by Keats, even though Shelley believed that Keats 'never was, nor ever will be a popular poet'. The voices of both Keats and Leopardi were barely heard in their lifetimes. 'If I were a poet ...', lamented Leopardi. 'If I should die', wrote Keats to Fanny Brawne after a fearful haemorrhage in February 1820, 'I have left no immortal work behind me.' But their pursuit of beauty, of a new language of poetic sensibility, their battle with the sense of nihilistic failure, of exile from the great company of poets – all gave both Keats and Leopardi heroic status in the international Romantic movement.

The poems of both Leopardi and Keats, so different in style, in form, and in almost every other way, were drenched in the influence of myth. As a young man, Leopardi collected and analysed folk tales and country superstitions. To him they represented the authentic speech of the people whose language he wished to revive and make potent through poetry. John Keats immersed himself in classical legend and lore, when the world was young and lovely. His longest poem, *Endymion*, opens with perhaps his most quoted line – 'A thing of beauty is a joy for ever' – and is a pastoral epic, in which he attempted to rescue the world of nature from its prevailing eighteenth-century rococo artificiality, and to recreate it as something to which humankind could re-dedicate itself. Leopardi would have understood. Two voices and a common destiny. Neither advanced the cause of Italian freedom, but each invoked that Romantic spirit which was beginning to bind Europe into a shared articulacy of nationalism. Neither achieved any public fame during their lives but in their poetry they spoke most intimately to the romantic spirit of the day. By the time the future of Italy was exercising the chanceries of Europe, Keats had been glorified by his death in Rome, in a land of poets and poetry, the new Elysium.

Whatever in Italy was best worthy of the attention of a foreigner was, according to Sydney Morgan's husband, being printed in London, 'the obscurantism of the sovereign tyrants of Italy not tolerating any work not dedicated to the propagation of falsehood and the retrogradation of intellect'.[35] Sir Christopher had found no shortage of poems; instead, 'an intolerable flux of verse', escaping from the contrived brevity of the sonnet and boosted by the reputation of *improvvisatori*. In 1816 the London literary scene welcomed an Italian refugee from Bonapartism. Born in Zante in 1778 to an Italian physician from Spalatro, both Venetian outposts, in the Adriatic, Ugo Foscolo had studied at Padua under the Italian translator of Ossian, and was seduced by the romantic idyll of Celtic mists and prophetic liberators. He welcomed the overthrow of the Venetian Republic in 1797 unreservedly, with an ode to Napoleon the liberator, at nineteen becoming an ardent member of the various committees that sprang up to return democratic freedoms to the republic. But his retreat from Bonapartism started when, in the squalid pact of Campo Formio, Napoleon exchanged the old oligarchy he had overthrown for the modern tyranny in Vienna.

Taking as his model a young Paduan student who had committed suicide in political and moral despair, Foscolo poured out his sense of shock in *The Letters of Jacopo Ortis* in 1798. In the absence of actual power to change events, the moral authority of suicide to change minds as a sacrificial protest, *à la Cato*, both disinterested and noble, appealed to those whose ideals were under attack from more ruthless ideologues. Just as the Girondins had gone to the scaffold in France in the hope that their sacrifice, when the bloody harvest of power had been fully reaped, would ultimately usher in a more liberal age, so Foscolo saw suicide as the ultimate triumph of the human spirit over tyranny. It was not, however, to be Foscolo's way. Instead he gave Bonaparte the benefit of the doubt and enrolled in the armies of France. He saw battle at Trebbia and was wounded and taken prisoner at the siege of Genoa, returning to Milan, then under French rule, to become one of Shelley's unacknowledged legislators, a poet. Among his enterprises was a version of the *Iliad* and a translation of Lawrence Sterne. As a volunteer, Foscolo had been sent as far as Boulogne, Yorick's starting-point in *A Sentimental Journey*, where the French were amassing an army for the invasion of England. Foscolo's attraction to this strange, quirky and, in literary terms, revolutionary book, appealed to his own pursuit of originality and became, in his hands, a Romantic text.

Foscolo's liberal dreams became subversive when asked to contribute to the *consulta* on the state of Italy, which 450 chosen Italian delegates were invited to present to the new Consul for Life at Lyons in the winter of 1802–3. Despite this pretence at consultation, Napoleon had already decided what was to happen to the Cisalpine Republic he had brought into being, and it did not include the nationalist ideas of Foscolo. Unable to reach the emperor's ear, Foscolo expressed his disappointment in the *Carme sui sepolcri* (1807), a romantic and melancholy threnody on the past compared to the misery and despair of the present. Appointed two years later to the chair of Italian eloquence at Pavia, he urged his students to study literature, not just as an academic discipline but as a vehicle for achieving self-fulfilment and freedom of the soul. His example was to be followed several thousand miles away by a young Indo-Portuguese lecturer in Calcutta, Henry di Rozio, who believed that the great works of European letters had the key to intellectual liberty from native religious and foreign political thralldom. Napoleon (unlike the British) recognised the subversive power of the imagination by suppressing all chairs of eloquence in Italian universities. Despite the emperor's final defeat and fall, the Austrians had no reason to believe that Ugo Foscolo was anything other than a troublemaker so that, when the Austrians re-entered Milan in 1813, Foscolo was branded a collaborator and withdrew to Switzerland. Three years later he removed to England.

There he became a lion, a contributor to the *Edinburgh* and *Quarterly Reviews*, in the first of which he favourably reviewed Cary's Dante and wrote an influential but critical account of Petrarch on both of whom, with Boccaccio, he gave public lectures, casting himself as teacher to a generation. The fortunes of literary exiles are not, however, always happy. Foscolo was improvident and spent time in a debtors' prison. He quarrelled with those who had befriended him, and managed to upset even the easy-going Walter Scott, who was not impressed by the exile's spurious panache, likening him to

a baboon.[36] Foscolo died in 1827, and in 1871 his bones were transferred to the first capital of the Italian nation, to be interred in the
national pantheon of Santa Croce in Florence.

Like Mazzini, Foscolo searched for the spirit of a free nation in its
poets. He found in Byron, who had exiled himself from the illiberal
administration of Lord Liverpool, an obvious inspiration, but it was
the 'heroic' stanzas of *The Corsair, Lara, The Bride of Abydos* and the
lyrical invocations of Italy in *Childe Harold* that inspired him, not the
mocking heroics of *Don Juan*. Byron's flirtation with *carbonarismo*
elevated him to the rank of saint and, though Foscolo himself was
anything but Byronic, it was Byron's sprit that informed his romantic nihilism.

Foscolo was responsible for launching one exile from Italy into a
brilliant career. Antonio Panizzi, fleeing Naples after the collapse of
the 1821 revolution, arrived two years later in Britain, completely
destitute. Foscolo was able to introduce him to William Roscoe in
Liverpool, who secured him pupils of Italian until he was able to
obtain a post for him, first as professor of Italian at University College, later as assistant librarian in the printed books department of
the British Museum. As professor, between 1830 and 1834, he
decided to rescue Boiardo's *Orlando Innamorato* from obscurity by a
new edition. Written in 1486, while its author was governor of
Modena for the Duke of Ferrara, it was the first of the Carlomagnian
romances that reached their apogee with Ariosto. Milton had not
been able to resist its roll-call of Agrican, Albracca, and Gallaphron,
like a list of galaxies from *Dr Who*.[37] As chief librarian, Panizzi persuaded the trustees to buy new books, catalogued its holdings,
designed the great domed Reading Room and ended up a knight of
the realm.

Another failed revolutionary, Gabriele Rossetti, wanted by the
Neapolitan authorities for his part in the 1821 revolution, passed
himself off as a British naval officer, and escaped on a complaisant
British man of war to Malta. He eventually got himself to England in
1824, and kept himself alive by giving Italian lessons. In 1831 he
acquired a substantive post as professor of Italian at King's College,
created in rivalry to University College, where Antonio Panizzi held
the rostrum. Italian was now publicly recognised as one of the
accompaniments to civilised life, a basic tool for the study of art,
architecture, history and letters, and its study was accepted by the
intellectuals of the day, as probably never again since. Even so, Italian was never a popular language at university, and neither Panizzi

nor Rossetti had many students. But Wordsworth and Scott learned enough to read the poets. Keats took it in through his poetic pores; Shelley and his wife learned to speak it well and write it reasonably accurately. Byron became fluent. Leigh Hunt and Hazlitt could not have developed their critical faculties without it; Macaulay thought that few people had been more thoroughly penetrated with the spirit of a great work than he by the *Divine Comedy*. Southey moved easily between Italian and Portuguese, and of Landor's 39 *Imaginary Conversations* selected by Oxford for inclusion in its World's Classics five were between Italians. Coleridge, apart from being the instrument to broadcast Cary's translation of Dante, also read deeply into the works of Giordano Bruno and Giambattista Vico, and advised Wordsworth on what Italian books he should buy. Hookham Frere in retirement parodied Pulci. Italian remained caviar to the general public and not a language of tourism, while visits to the past glories of Italy did not promote its use. For tourists, the lingua franca was Latin, of which Italian, in the words of Leigh Hunt's usher, was but a bastard.[38]

8

'Metropolis of a Ruined Paradise'
Venice, Naples and the Lure of Volcanic Power

Those who alone thy towers behold
Quivering through aerial gold,
As I now behold them here,
Would imagine not they were
Sepulchres, where human forms,
Like pollution-nourished worms,
To the corpse of greatness cling,
Murdered and now mouldering:

> Percy Bysshe Shelley,
> 'Lines written among the Euganean Hills', ll. 142–9.

Thou heart of men which ever pantest
Naked, beneath the lidless eye of heaven!
Elysian City, which to calm enchantest
The mutinous air and sea! They around thee, even
As sleep round love, are driven!
Metropolis of a ruined Paradise
Long lost, late won, and yet but half regained.

> Percy Bysshe Shelley, 'Ode to Naples',
> Epode 2, strophe 1.

The broad and beamless moon sinking behind the tall elms of Posillipo – the broken starlight on the surface of the wave – Sorrento's purple promontory – the solitary grandeur of Capri's mountain island, rising out of the middle of the bay, a colossal sphinx guarding two baths of azure light – Vesuvius breathing its smoke and flame and sparks into the cloudless ether …

> Mary Shelley/Claire Clairmont, 'The Pole'.[1]

The condition of the common people here is abject and shocking. I am afraid the conventional idea of the picturesque is associated with such misery and degradation that a new picturesque will have to be established as the world goes forward.

Charles Dickens on Naples.[2]

Southern peoples had a poor idea of northern countries: 'all snow, wooden houses, great ignorance and plenty of money',[3] and it was to escape the first that their inhabitants came to Italy. The traffic the other way was small. Even the educated had little notion of the geography of the British Isles. The Liverpool of Donizetti's opera, *Emilia di Liverpool*, was a small town near London, and the action took place in an Alpine valley a few leagues from London! First performed in Naples in 1824, the cast included an English sea-captain returning from 20 years in captivity among the Moors, a Neapolitan nobleman who sang only in Neapolitan, and a sundry mixture of villains, crossed lovers and incoherent parents. It was set in England for exotic effect. Vincenzo Bellini, born in 1801 in Catania, had had some distant contact with the erstwhile rulers of his island during the Napoleonic wars and felt comfortable enough to set his first opera in Ireland. *Adelson e Salvini*, also first performed at Naples, in 1826, had at least a credible Irish setting, the 'park' of a large Anglo-Irish house. Though the *primo tenore* was an Italian painter, apart from the villain and the comic manservant, a variant on the Figaro character, the rest of the protagonists were recognisably non-Italian. Lord Adelson, the owner of the house was, of course, immensely rich.

To the Italians, this is what all the English were, judging from their single-minded acquisition of art treasures. There was a general supposition that they were all noblemen. In 1756, the architect Robert Adam, enjoying the hospitality of a well-to-do farmer near Monte Cassino, was mistaken for an English cardinal. His man denied the charge but did admit his master was an English prince, whereupon pretty well the entire entourage of the local duke came to pay court with bands and music and invitations to dinner. Adam, unable to sustain the imposture, decided to escape early the next day, but not before the entire village, about 300 people, had turned out to see what an English prince looked like and what he would tip.[4]

Mrs Piozzi found that the Italians believed most English were consumptive from the numbers that came for the climate, and indeed many were. They attributed it to English coal fires, remarking that they could only be so short of wood that they must dig into the soil for fuel.[5] Health was certainly one reason for a visit to Italy, but for most it was the crowning episode of a classical education. The Grand Tour had charted Italy like a schoolbook, so that 'a Man who is in Rome can scarce see an Object that does not call to Mind a Piece of a Latin poet or Historian'.[6] Observations and recollections poured from the pens of visitors to recapture for the tourist the grandeur that was Rome, in turn regurgitated by local *ciceroni*. In Joseph Forsyth's, one can recognise every tour guide: 'our[s] ... was a local Latinist. Though as ignorant of the language as any other parrot, he quoted, with good accent and good discretion, all the ancient poets that bore upon his rounds.' From the artists for whom he had formerly carried their impedimenta, 'he had picked up the best remarks on its scenery, he stopped us at the finest points of view, he lectured, he grinned with admiration, he amused us and was happy.'[7] Charlotte Eaton was less enthusiastic: her guides were too ready to pass off their own theories as given, and to give different names to certain ruins, in the hope of seeming better informed than the others.[8] And to accompany the vastly increased numbers of tourists who set off south after the end of the Napoleonic wars, an average of seven travel books on Italy, Forsyth's *valets de place* in print, appeared in Britain every year after 1819.[9] There has been very little let-up since.

But the fate of Italy also served as a reminder that Great Britain could, if she were not watchful and prudent, become like *Italia Romana* and *Magna Graecia*. If Rome represented the epitome of power and absolutism, Florence the cradle of modern art, and Naples a ruined paradise, the fate of Venice carried an awful warning. The republic of the lagoons was a once great democracy, an icon of freedom. No act of Napoleonic despotism had seemed so arbitrary and capricious as its cynical cession to Austria in the Treaty of Campo Formio in 1797. Its sinister reputation, summed up by Byron apostrophising Venice in the mouth of Jacopo Foscari as

> ... your *sbirri*, and
> Your spies, your galley and your other slaves,
> ... your midnight carryings off and drowning,
> Your dungeons next the palace roofs, or under

> The water's level; your mysterious meetings,
> And unknown dooms, and sudden executions,
> Your 'Bridge of Sighs', your strangling chamber and
> Your torturing instruments

had all done a disservice to the splendid city in the eyes of northern Europe.[10] The name *Venetia* was used by liberal Conservatives, who constituted what they called a 'Fourth Party', to describe the government of Tory diehards in mid-nineteenth-century Britain.[11] 'Monk' Lewis had produced his supposed 'translation' of *The Bravo of Venice* in 1804, his first work of Gothic nastiness, and few visitors could remain unaware that, under its veneer of pleasure, surveillance was close and sudden disappearance common. The network of canals was a convenient depository for the *Sparafuciles*, so adept at the use of the stiletto. Yet, when the transfer was made to the Austrians, whose ancestors had over centuries threatened the integrity of the city in its lagoon fastness, it seemed like a great betrayal. Wordsworth's resonant words, learned by heart by generations of schoolboys, were the ultimate lament for the loss of liberty.

For Byron, Venice was not just a subject of political depravity, 'everything about [her] is or was extraordinary – her aspect is like a dream, and her history is like a romance'.[12] He plunged himself into the Italian histories of the former republic, and out of them emerged two five-act dramas, written in rapid succession in 1819 and 1821. The first, after Alfieri and originally intended for dedication to Goethe, was written to satisfy Byron that he could write a poetic drama, and not for the stage.[13] The action of *Marino Faliero* takes place in 1355, and Byron had nursed the story ever since he had seen the site of the corpse on the Giant's Stairway in the Doge's Palace, the painted veil over the space where Faliero's portrait should have appeared among those of past doges, and his humble tomb *outside* the church of SS Giovanni e Paolo. Byron may have felt a special empathy for the patrician doge, snubbed and traduced by his social equals and an icon to his social inferiors, but he wanted to write a historical play, not a political tract. The aged Faliero, who had done the state some service, is outraged that a traducer of his young wife's honour is only lightly punished by the Venetian politburo, the Council of Ten. Considering it degenerate and disrespectful to him, the conqueror of the Hungarians (Byron refers in the preface to Faliero's victory over the Huns, the title he gives the Austrian rulers of Venice in his letters to John Murray[14]), and saviour of the republic, joins a conspiracy of *popolani* to overthrow the oligarchy of 'swollen silkworms'[15] and establish a purer republic. The plot is betrayed, the conspirators, including the doge, are rounded up and condemned to death. Faliero curses the republic to be 'bought and sold, and basely yield / Unto a bastard Attila', when

> ... she shall stoop to be
> A province of an empire, petty town
> In lieu of capital, with slaves for senates,
> Beggars for nobles, panders for a people![16]

Four hundred and forty-two years later, the curse is fulfilled. Venice's fall is like the crumbling of a proud cliff into the sea, long expected but shocking when it happens. Byron's second Venetian drama,[17] *The Two Foscari*, in which the ruling doge has to consent to the attainder and torture of his own son because the state so demands it, was intended to be a play about suppressed passions, free from the rant and rave of popular drama, not absent even from Alfieri.[18] The plot looks with uncanny foresight to the despotic states of the twentieth century, when absolute obedience is owed to the central committee of the party, and rank and reputation are made and unmade on anonymous information and on the corporate wish of its members.

> Had I as many sons as I have years,
> I would have given them all,
> To the state's service, to fulfil her wishes,
> On the flood, in the field or, if it must be,
> As it is, alas! has been, to ostracism,
> Exile, or chains, or whatever worse
> She might decree.[19]

What had been a Roman virtue in the green days of the Roman Republic had become an outrage in the seared and yellowed age of Venetian gold.

Austria's may have been the least oppressive government Venice had enjoyed for centuries, but in its new role as a rest and recuperation city for Austrian and Hungarian white-coats, the reckless glitter of its palaces of pleasure faded, and the rich gamblers and pathological partygoers were replaced by solemn tourists, students of Titian and Tintoretto and collectors of Canaletto. 'Thirteen hundred years / Of wealth and glory [had] turned to tears', and 'the harsh sound of the barbarian drum, / With dull and daily resonance, repeats / The

echo of the tyrant's voice'. The people 'only murmur in their sleep
... / and thus they creep, / Crouching and crab-like, through their
sapping streets'.[20]

The merits of *The Two Foscari* were obscured by a blazing public
row with Robert Southey over Byron's insult to the poet laureate in
the preface, and it only succeeded on the stage in its adaptation as
an opera by Verdi. (*Marino Faliero* was also made into an opera by
Donizetti, after a dramatic makeover by Casimir Delavigne). It was
1843 and Verdi was looking for a subject for his debut at La Fenice.
But *Foscari*, over-simply described as the attempt of the doge's son
to defend himself against trumped up capital charges, while the
doge as head of state is powerless to intervene, was almost intract-
able. Like *Faliero*, Byron had not intended it for the stage,[21] and had
poured his poetry into long speeches in which the doddering doge
and his tormented son argued the primacy of obedience over affection; the play may have struck Verdi as 'a fine subject, delicate and
full of pathos', but he was the first to admit it did not have the theatrical grandeur needed for an opera.[22] The management of La Fenice
advised him to think again, as Byron had not particularly flattered
the republic's reputation for justice. Verdi made his debut, instead,
with *Ernani*, but kept *Foscari* on the stocks and it was finally performed at the Argentina theatre in Rome. It never fell completely
out of the repertoire, though Verdi came to think little of it, dubbing
it monotonous. His librettist, Piave, had been instructed to stick
close to Byron, but Byron's Venice was not the one with which La
Fenice's patrons were comfortable. His was a city of dreadful instru-
ments of state terror, theirs the familiar one of masked balls,
barcaroles, midnight intrigues and reckless gambling, more a Mediterranean Blackpool than Byronic Wormwood Scrubs. For Venice
was an unreal city in which ordinary people scarcely lived. Even
Contarini Fleming thought 'the life of a Venetian is like a dream,
and you must pass your days like a ghost gliding about a city fading
in a vision.' A vision such as Shelley saw with Count Maddalo: 'Its
temples and its palaces did seem / Like fabrics of enchantment
piled to heaven.'[23]

It was a vision painted by Turner with 'a melancholy magic and a
coldness in their very splash of colour and luminosity'. It took
Ruskin to rescue the city from its deliquescence of cloud and water
and render it again in stone, while he rhapsodised over 'the pillars
of variegated stones, jasper and porphyry, and deep green serpen-
tine spotted with flakes of snow, and marbles that half refuse and

half yield to the sunshine, Cleopatra-like, "their bluest veins to kiss"'.[24] The merchant's son, Ruskin, had no interest in the city's special charms and fleshpots that had attracted Byron. But the moral was as clear to the author of *Stones of Venice* as to that of *Don Juan*: let its gawping visitors take warning. Smug complacency and tolerance of the malversations of a financial oligarchy could also reduce London to a similar plight, to Shelley's 'corpse of greatness'.

The Romantic trajectory had begun to be set by the end of the eighteenth century. Visits to Milan, Venice, Florence, Pisa and Rome remained mandatory, but the grandeur of nature was now as great an attraction as the works of man, and artists responded to the taste for the picturesque of the post-bellum traveller. Myth and legend were more evocative than the exploits of a people so decidedly pragmatic and materially successful as the Romans. Ruins assumed a magic of their own, sparking fewer elegies to past greatness and homilies about hubris, and more appreciation of their own stark beauty and appeal to the soul. To one drenched in the culture of Greece and Rome like Shelley, no evocation of the landscape was entirely naked of classical allusion. But to those who had not experienced that total immersion, something of more instant appeal was required. This was supplied in 1818 by James Hakewill who published his *Picturesque Tour of Italy*, in which he invited the tourists to taste the splendours of the Alpine passes, the northern lakes, the Vale of Clitumnus in Umbria, the bridge over the gorge of the Nar (Nera) at Narni, the great cataracts of Terni, the misty falls of the Anio at Tivoli, the woods and volcanic tarns of the Alban hills, the haunted sites of Campania Felix, the Phlegrean Fields, until they reached Naples, and its live volcano. The Hakewills were a family of artists and architects. James's father was a landscape and portrait painter, his brother an architect, and James claimed at different times to be both. He had come to public notice with a *History of Windsor and its Neighbourhood*, published in 1813 with 20 plates. As soon as the war was over he and his wife, also a talented artist, went to Italy and the resultant *Picturesque Tour* aimed 'to attract the notice of the traveller in Italy, whether for the beauty of the landscape, the historical interest which they inspire, or their architectural elegance'.[25] He followed very closely an itinerary plotted by Eustace's four-volume *Classical Tour through Italy* (1813), to which his drawings might also be illustrations. John Murray brought out the first part of *The Picturesque Tour* in 1818 but, when Hakewill commissioned eight other artists to produce watercolours from his pencil drawings, Murray refused to meet the additional expense of printing them in the second. He made one exception, agreeing to print those by Joseph Mallord William Turner, and throughout 1820 *The Picturesque Tour* continued to appear in parts. It was a financial failure and Murray was forced to try to recoup his losses by selling the Turner watercolours for fifteen guineas each. Hakewill was able to find another publisher for his *Eight Views of Rome*, advertised as being by the author of *The Picturesque Tour of Italy*, and the two works, if not money-spinners, spun a reputation for both Hakewill and his collaborator Turner.

No one captured demonic nature better than this Paganini of paint, this virtuoso of virtuosi.[26] He improved on Hakewill's dull sketch of the Terni cascade – after all, these were the falls before which one visitor had apostrophised 'Well done, water' – by elevating them to a proper height, while over the gorge where

> the hell of waters! where they howl and hiss
> And boil in endless torture; while the sweat
> Of their great agony, wrung out from this
> Their Phlegethon, curls round the rocks of jet
> That gird the gulf around, in pitiless horror set.

'he suspended a rainbow arching over the base of the cascade'.[27]

The English public who did not know Italy at first hand took their image from paintings Turner made long before he got there himself in 1819. For over 25 years beforehand, Italy had been the subject of his imaginative longing. He had pored over the works of Poussin and Claude, he had copied painters who had got there before him, and he had sketched classical subjects in the style of Claude for his first patron. He read the guide books and made extensive sketches from the descriptions in the best of them, Eustace's *Classical Tour*. He approached Italy with a profound knowledge of what he wanted to see and a curiosity whetted by Canto IV of *Childe Harold*, which had appeared the year before. Over a period of four months he filled nineteen books with sketches of Rome, Tivoli, Pompeii and the surroundings of Naples, on which to work at leisure.[28] Fourteen of them were crammed with swift pencil sketches, the merest impressions, but he also made 50 watercolour sketches which captured the silvery, luminous atmosphere of this wonderful new country. The influence of *Childe Harold* has been sought and found in Turner's Roman paintings of 1819, especially of the Forum with a rainbow, the latter feature being read as a symbol of the regeneration Byron's poem had prophesied when Italy's freedom was secured.[29]

Hakewill had used both the *camera obscura* (whereby a wide panorama could be projected onto a screen in a darkened box) and the *camera lucida* (an instrument by which the image was reflected by a prism onto a flat surface on which its outline can be traced or sketched), but the camera effect was quite overwhelmed by Turner's Romantic impressionism. Apart from public exhibitions, Turner's first Italian visit was to be commemorated in a book of 'Picturesque Views of Italy', which never appeared. He went to Rome again in 1828 and possibly twice more to Venice, once in 1833 and again in 1840. The poet laureate of Venice in paint had already established his credentials from the 1819–20 sketches, when his views of the Bridge of Sighs, ducal palaces and the Custom House 'displayed a brilliancy, breath and power killing every other work in the exhibition' at the Royal Academy.[30] From that visit, Turner produced the vignettes that made the 1830 edition of Samuel Rogers's long poem, *Italy*, outsell more prosaic guide books and travellers' memorials. He also produced illustrations for two lives and collected works of Lord Byron, thus reinforcing Byron's paramountcy as the poet laureate of Italy,[31] but of an Italy still bathed in the romantic illusion of an age long past and a future uncertain. 'The glory has parted, the eternal city with its splendours – its stupendous temples and its great men – all have become a mockery and a scorn.'[32]

Few travellers proceeded further than Naples, a city quite unlike any other. John Evelyn 'was assured there was little to be seen in the rest of the civil world ..., but plain and prodigious barbarism'.[33] After leaving the papal domains at Terracina, travellers felt they were at last reaching the Italy they had imagined among their English fogs.[34] Mary Shelley's spirits rose when she arrived from Rome in 1818, 'the sky, the shore, all its forms and the sensations it inspires appear formed and modulated by the Spirit of Good alone unalloyed by any evil. Its temperature and fertility would, if men were free from evil, render it a faery habitation of delight.' But, she added, a Neapolitan had called it *'un paradiso abitato dai diavoli'*.[35] It remained a paradise, John Ruskin sniffed, to 'the common English traveller, if he can gather a black bunch of grapes with his own fingers, and have his bottle of Falernian brought him by a girl with black eyes'.[36]

10. The tarantella, symbol of the romantic allure of the Neapolitan *lazzaroni*, who impressed tourists by their active cheerfulness in the face of poverty.

What with the mild air, the shining mountains, the colourful, shiftless peasants who danced to work in the fields with a violinist at their head,[37] the barefoot, knickerbockered *lazzaroni* with their hair in snoods, the orange and lemon groves, the myrtles and aloes among the olives, and all the noise and bustle of a major port, Naples had its own special romantic allure. It was picturesque, though Charles Dickens saw in the *lazzaroni* not the artless children of nature but 'mere squalid, abject, miserable animals for vermin to batten on; slouching slinking, ugly, shabby, scavenging scarecrows'.[38] It was also the centre of a huge tourist park, wherein was to be found the Cumaean Sibyl's cave, the mouth of Hades and Charon's cave, the Elysian fields, Virgil's tomb, Cicero's villa, the seaside sulphur spa of Baiae, and the columns of the temple of Serapis at Pozzuoli that rose from and sank into the sea with every rise and fall of the earth's crust. It also contained St Paul's landfall, Martial's lampreys that answered to their names, the tomb of Nero's mother, temples, Caesarian palaces, rotundas and amphitheatres galore, all of which made the place seem more genuinely Roman than Rome itself.[39] As the seat of a monarchy, and of an opera house over whom first Rossini, then his wife, had presided like benevolent despots, Naples had its own social life, and it was cheap and easy to winter in style. Only Dickens was not impressed. 'Oh the raffish counts and more than doubtful countesses, the noodles and the blacklegs, the good society!'[40] Moreover, it was not a dead city of the past, like much of Rome, but the teeming capital of an independent kingdom, the third largest city in Europe, after Paris and London. In 1831 Berlioz, bored as a *stagiaire* at the French Academy in Rome, was liberated by Naples: 'What life! what animation! what dazzling bustle! How different it is from Rome and its sleepy inhabitants and untilled desolate, denuded soil. The austerely melancholy Roman countryside is to the plain of Naples as the past is to the present, death to life, silence to vivid, harmonious noise' (Shelley thought the Roman *campagna* was 'a flattering picture of Bagshot heath'[41]). Goethe compared Rome to 'an old, badly situated monastery', Shelley to 'a sepulchre, beautiful but the abode of death'.[42] By contrast, Naples in its glittering countryside, nurtured on the rich volcanic soil, the product of its copious easily worked tufa, was a cynosure for artists, less for its classical remains than for the sensational beauty of its site and the colourful lifestyle of its citizens, 'made up of the Corso, the church and the opera'.[43] As the Blessingtons had found, accommodation was not cheap but it was splendid, the great baroque palaces letting rooms on a self-catering basis.

The English by 1820 occupied Naples during the winter. Its reputation as a suitable recovery asylum for sufferers from venereal disease made it a popular resort, along with Montpellier and Lisbon, for young men who may have been clapped before setting out or after, in Boswell's favourite brothel in Rome perhaps. 'Residence at the seaside and warm bathing' were recommended by venereologists 'as being especially advantageous to the lingering arthritic ailments of syphilitic patients'.[44] Sydney Morgan would have found it the most agreeable residence in Italy were it not for the despotism of its government.[45] Foreign visitors enjoyed the liberal attentions of a church hierarch, the Archbishop of Tarentum, who entertained intellectuals in his palazzo in Naples. He had been sentenced to death for collaborating with the 1793 revolutionaries but, being too popular with the prelates, princes and people, was pardoned and rehabilitated. That popularity saved him also from persecution after years of collaborating with Joachim Murat, and the restored Bourbon merely retired him from his archbishopric. A patron of learning and the arts, he continued to keep a good table and became a favourite of the foreign community, with whom his *conversazioni,* followed by cards, became one of their principal entertainments.[46] A visit to him was almost mandatory for any visitor to the city with pretensions to rank or celebrity, including Walter Scott, the Blessingtons and Samuel Rogers, who was much taken with the cats that formed the principal members of the archbishop's household.[47]

From 1764 to 1800, however, British social life had centred round His Britannic Majesty's ambassador to the court of Ferdinand I, diplomatist, collector, patron, intellectual and cuckold-in-chief, William Hamilton. Sir William had abandoned Parliament for Naples because his first wife had weak lungs, and first arrived in Naples in November 1764, the year of Ann Radcliffe's birth and Gibbon's conception of *The Decline and Fall of the Roman Empire.* The new ambassador delighted in his post, which enabled him to indulge his Voltairean spirit of mischievous inquiry, unveiling among other things the survivals of Priapic worship in the customs of southern religion, thus establishing a tradition of sceptically anthropological enthusiasm for the people of Italy that survived until Norman Douglas, D. H. Lawrence and Harold Acton. Hamilton's embassy was in the centre of the city, his official residence at the Villa Angelica near Portici, and his 'nest' a little casino in Posillipo. The last was where he most liked to be. It had an uninterrupted view of the crater of Vesuvius, while the sea lapped at its steps.[48] There he received his visitors, who included Goethe and the musical journalist, Charles Burney. Hamilton quickly became an expert volcanologist, observing and recording the activity of Vesuvius, and was commissioned by the Royal Society in 1783 to study earthquake effects in Calabria. His collections, in addition to Greek vases, statuary and books, included the products of Vesuvius, mainly crystal formations in petrified lava, as well as ex-voto offerings, particularly male genitalia in wax, either petitioning or in gratitude for a cure for syphilis, and fossils, pressed plants and insects, all the natural detritus of a garden of Eden. They inspired Goethe to make nature his special study for the rest of his life, confident that he could make discoveries to add to human knowledge.[49] In 1786, four years after the death of his wife, Hamilton imported, on the advice of the then President of the Royal Society, a gardener to create an English garden at the royal palace at Caserta, while his nephew, Gavin Hamilton imported his model, the 'fair teamaker', who was to make his uncle the most famous tourist attraction in Naples and to be the unhappy partner in a cuckolding that rocked England and, in 1800, brought his diplomatic career to an end.[50]

The Kingdom of the Two Sicilies never seemed to the English to be properly Italian. It did not belong to the *Italia* that was being revealed by Gibbon, Sismondi, Roscoe and Byron. It was anthropologically curious, its inhabitants – unlike the inhabitants of the rest of the peninsula – being improvident, cheerful, egalitarian and poor. They spoke a dialect that sounded more Arabic than Italian. Venetians, Florentines, Romans were Italians. The inhabitants of Naples were Neapolitans. Things were done in Naples that would not have surprised a visitor to savage lands, such as wet nurses being put to suckle lapdogs for ladies of quality which so shocked Mrs Piozzi (though she was probably unaware that puppies were used in England to relieve a nursing mother of her milk if her child died or was denied the breast. Mary Wollstonecraft, dying of puerperal fever after Mary Shelley's birth, was subjected to this treatment when Mary was taken off the breast for fear of infection.[51]) 'One need not', the remarried widow Thrale added,

wander round the world with Banks and Solander,[52] or stare so at the accounts given us in Cook's Voyagers of *tattowed Indians*. The man who rows you about this lovely bay, has perhaps the angel

Raphael or the Blessed Virgin Mary, delineated on the brawny sunburnt leg, the saint of the town upon the other: his arms represent the Glory, or the seven spirits of God'.[53]

The outlandish devotion to saints and relics, especially to St Januarius, the burning of images of the saints on to torsos and arms, could have been the practices of *Terra Australis*.

The origins of Naples were Greek not Latin, and its culture, architecture, religion and language more Hispanic than Italian. Naples's importance to Britain was that she took vast quantities of English wool and broadcloth, and offered a temporary if lengthy asylum to a large number of British grandees and tourists. English broadcloth provided much of the clothing of the peasants against the penetrating cold of the mountains of Calabria and Sicily and its export was so important to English weavers that the conquest of India can be traced to the illusion that India would be as good a market for English cloth as Mediterranean Europe. King Ferdinand also sported the empty title of King of Jerusalem, claimed by indirect descent from the Crusader Latin kings, and feudal lord of Malta, whence the Knights of St John of Jerusalem had been obliged to offer the annual tribute of a falcon. This claim he never abandoned, even though the island had been granted to Britain at the request of the Maltese themselves at the Congress of Vienna. Pietro Giannone, whose anticlerical *Civil History of the Kingdom of Naples* (1723) was published in translation in Edinburgh by a group of Jacobites to emphasise their distance from the ultra-monarchist tendencies of Rome and the Old Pretender, had been a primary source for Gibbon, and proved that Naples owed more to Byzantium, Normandy, Anjou, Aragon and Castille than to Italian states further north.[54]

The first Bourbon king, Charles IV, son of Philip V of Spain and Elizabeth Farnese (r. 1734–59) had inaugurated an Italian renaissance at his court, assisted by his Saxon queen. The Farnese collection was brought back from Rome to grace the royal palaces. To prove that Naples was in the forefront of artistic skills, Don Raimondo di Sangro, Prince of Sansevero, commissioned the Genoese, Francesco Queirolo, to sculpt a dead Christ in his shroud, so close that every detail of his broken body could be discerned, and a bizarre memorial to Delusion, represented by a man bursting out of an imprisoning net with the help of his intellect, represented by an angel. The Estese Antonio Corradini carved Pudicitia (Modesty) as a naked woman clad in a skin-tight diaphanous marble veil from

11. Francesco Queirolo's *Delusion*, bursting out of an imprisoning net with the help of his intellect, represented by an angel.

12. Antonio Corradini's *Pudicitia* (Modesty), a naked woman clad in a skin-tight diaphanous marble veil from head to foot. Both this and Queirolo's *Delusion* (opposite) displayed a virtuosity that encroached on the macabre, a sense that appealed to the Romantic imagination.

head to foot. Both sculptors had come down from Rome, but in the thick Baroque air of Naples, and particularly of the Palazzo San-severo, with its intricate model of the human blood system, they displayed a virtuosity that encroached on the macabre.[55] Nothing was quite what it ought to be in Naples. The king, Charles's third son, Ferdinand I, in addition to speaking only Neapolitan, was as 'merry and fat, dirty, rude and savage' as his subjects and 'rides and rows, and catches Fish and sells it, and eats Macaroni with his Fingers – resolves to be happy himself and make no Man miserable'. He competed with the watermen in the Bay, exacted the wager when he won, and returned double what he had won to the waterman's family.[56] Palatial facades hid warrens of slum dwellings, the air might be thin with brilliant sunshine or black with volcanic ash, miracles replaced medicine and life mirrored opera. Beggars were often part-time employees, between jobs. Even the style of clothes and furniture was borrowed from the dead cities of Pompeii and Herculaneum, slowly being uncovered to the world. The Neapolitans were convinced that their land was as near a paradise as this wicked world could provide, and found the visitors from the north sad people. Marguerite Blessington thought the Neapolitans were like children let out of school, but Goethe knew them better. Their industry, such as it was – and the poor were industrious, if only to survive – was 'not to make them rich but to live a life free of care'.[57]

Mrs Piozzi was sure that the drunken Faun and the dying Gladiator she had seen in Rome would fade from her remembrance and leave the glow of Solfatarra and the gloom of Posilippo, and the terrifying Vesuvius, indelibly impressed upon it.[58] Travellers who got as far as Naples went primarily to confront the sleeping terrors of its volcano. 'That's our mountain', a Franciscan friar told her, 'which throws up money for us by calling foreigners to see the extraordinary effects of so surprising a phenomenon'.[59] On first entry into Italy visitors saw man living in a comfortable Wordsworthian harness with nature; at journey's end, they met man quailing under her unpredictability. Vesuvius was never wholly quiet and usually provided a display for visitors throughout the eighteenth and early nineteenth centuries. It erupted several times in 1822, sometimes sensationally. Turner, when in Naples, surprisingly made only sketches of the conventional panorama. Perhaps he felt he could not improve on his lurid *coup d'imagination* before he ever went to Italy when, based on Hakewill's sketches of the 1817 eruption, he represented the sea, blood red, reflecting the fireworks in the sky, with Castel dell'Uovo in dark relief and tiny figures on the Riviera di Chiaia securing their boats from the boiling waves. Coleridge paid a visit from Malta to Italy specifically to study volcanoes that presented a fine example of the grandeur and misery of nature when out of man's control.

Painters loved Vesuvius. In 1765 William Marlow had witnessed the volcano in action and in his later renderings placed tourists far too close for comfort, especially as one viewer thought that if he approached within three yards of the painting it would scorch him.[60] Joseph Wright of Derby on his return from Italy in 1775 showed the mountain bathed in sunlight, with a flame of fire like a gas jet. Even when quiescent, the crater promised a sight of the descent into hell. For John 'Warwick' Smith, summit and crater were like an open boil on a dry and devastated landscape. Henry Tresham, peering over the curled lip of rock into rising steam, made a rapid sketch of his mountain party beginning a hurried descent. Getting to the top posed its own challenge. Tourists were usually roped to a guide, for the surface was constantly changing and loose cinders and ash could be perilous.[61] Progress was tedious and fatiguing, as one slipped back as often as one went forward. An alternative to being roped to a guide was to go up on mule-back, like Goethe on his first ascent on 2 March 1787. He was among the bolder visitors who went to the summit when the crater was active, braving the torrid heat and the stones and ash belching forth. Berlioz and his party were as courageous, climbing up at night, while the crater was filled with red-hot motionless lava, six inches from their feet.[62] More timid visitors like King Ferdinand would watch flows of lava pouring down the slopes, while they were safe in the company of Sir William Hamilton who understood the vagaries of the mountain.[63]

At La Scala, Milan, in 1827 Vesuvius erupted with a wonderful concatenation of brass and timpani. The astonished spectators were confronted with a backcloth of a Roman city on fire before a great mountain belching flame and rocks, having blown off its top. This was in *L'Ultimo Giorno di Pompeii*, an opera by Giovanni Pacini, with a sensational backdrop by Alessandro Sanquirico. In 1828 Vesuvius erupted, this time off-stage, at the end of Auber's *La Muette de Portici* as heaven wreaked its wrath on those who had rebelled against their lawful rulers. In this Romantic, and iconic, story of Naples, the volcano broods over a drama of hopeless and betrayed love, participating to tragic effect in the uprising of the fishermen of Portici against the Spaniards, one of whom – no less a person than the viceroy's son – has taken advantage of a dumb girl from their community, *la muette*, Fenella. Her brother, Masaniello (Tommaso Agnello), is the leader of the rebellion and, to show his magnanimous spirit, he vows to respect all those who wish to leave Naples. Fenella, recognising her seducer and his wife among the refugees, persuades her brother to protect them. This act of collaboration is seen by his followers as weakness and, when the viceroy's son leads the forces of reaction against the rebellious city, Masaniello is accused of being a friend to tyranny and poisoned. He lives long enough to march out to meet the avenging army backed by an erupting volcano, and perishes among his routed *lazzaroni*. La Muette, betrayed, dishonoured and unprotected by either brother or lover, jumps into the crater. James Kenney's *Masaniello*, adapted

13. In 1827, at the Teatro San Carlo, Naples, later at La Scala, Milan, Vesuvius erupted with a wonderful concatenation of brass and timpani in *L'Ultimo Giorno di Pompeii*, an opera by Giovanni Pacini, with a sensational backdrop by Alessandro Sanquirico.

from Auber's opera and performed in London in 1829, had Fenella throw herself into the lava that had burst out of the mountainside.[64]

The most famous victims of Vesuvius were the cities of the plain at its feet, like 'the bones that strew the ground at the mouth of a Lion's den, who is only sleeping within – & growling in his slumber'.[65] Herculaneum was still largely underground, a network of subterranean roads, an infernal theatre, all reflecting in the wavering light of pitch torches the horrid anterooms of hell. Pompeii, on the other hand, had been gradually unpeeled since 1748 to reveal a civilisation petrified at a precise moment in recorded history. From 1817 to 1819, the former chamberlain to Prince George's rackety wife, Princess Caroline, Sir William Gell, who had 'topographised and typographised King Priam's dominions in three days', began in a more leisurely way to sketch in dull but accurate detail the Pompeian finds, making this, in the event, his life's work, and serving as an indispensable guide for foreign visitors, and the inspiration for Bulwer Lytton's most famous novel, *The Last Days of Pompeii*.[66] Gell, knighted on carpet consideration, was no scholar and liked almost too much the society of the noble or famous, and became their indispensable *cicerone*. The Naples galleries were full of the finds, a consummating attraction to visitors, all of whom had read their Pliny and their Gell, like Marguerite Blessington, and some of whom had bought Pompeiian pots from the Wedgwood factory in Staffordshire.

The ruins of Poseidonia (Paestum), with its three temples and basilica still skeletally intact in the midst of a malarial swamp, attracted only the hardy. The haunt of buffalo, it was hard to visualise the site as all that remained of one of the great cities of Greek Lucania, famous for its gardens and roses that bloomed twice a year. Man had undone it first. What the Saracens had begun in one of their Viking-like raids from Sicily, the Norman Robert Guiscard had completed. The Silarus River silted up, and by the sixteenth century Paestum had virtually disappeared from the map. 'Buried in the night of woods', the temples had become as inaccessible as the ancient cities of North Africa and mainland Greece, until opened up in the reign of Charles IV, when a road was driven along the coast from Salerno. These were the finest remaining Greek buildings in Italy, rivalling Agrigento in Sicily, and their existence, open to the sea, sky and mountains, roused the same emotions that Tintern Abbey raised in the sensibilities of Romantic travellers, of a glory all departed.[67] In her short story, 'The Heir of Mondolfo', Mary

Shelley's peasant Viola, fleeing from her father-in-law – who intends to ship her out of Italy away from her noble husband – blunders into the temple complex at night. What seemed so desolate and threatening in the darkness appears, in the light of day, to be 'temples of some god who still seemed to deify them with his presence; he clothed them with beauty, and what was called their ruin might, in its picturesque wildness and sublime loveliness, be more adapted to his nature than when, roofed and gilt, they stood in pristine strength'.[68] (Mary never actually visited Paestum, put off by the dangers and discomforts of the journey.) Despite their Romantic appeal the temples were not much visited, for most people thought, like John Evelyn, that Naples was the last outpost of civilisation. After that it was high prices, poor, often non-existent inns and outlaws. Many travellers read Samuel Rogers and decided that his description was better than a visit:

> No cornice, triglyth or worn abacus,
> But thick with ivy hung or branching fern;
> Their iron-brown o'erspread with brightest verdure!
> ....
> The air was sweet with violets, running wild
> Mid broken friezes and fallen capitals –
> > Nothing stirs
> Save the shrill voiced cicala flitting round ...

That was enough for most travellers.

Mount Etna was an even more formidable monster than Vesuvius, but less visited. It had created Catania at its feet (its name in ancient times being Catetna, or city of Etna), successive eruptions having formed a gigantic mole of lava jutting into the sea and forming a protected harbour. After a disastrous earthquake in 1693, which buried most of the inhabitants under rubble, St Agatha took the city under her protection.[69] Etna's chief danger was that she could erupt from any part of her surface, small craters appearing in her sides, or huge clefts from which lava boiled over. Local observers, as in Naples, had concluded that those inhabitants who lived near these vents were rendered by the sulphurous air peculiarly wicked, a discouragement to exploration. The approach to the summit was made perilous by snow and ice, which occasionally melted to form large pools that were then covered in ash which camouflaged them from the unwary traveller.

The crater area was a huge amphitheatre about three and a half miles in circumference, from which dense sulphurous smoke emerged from soft and moving rock. Within that turgid pustule, Patrick Brydone was told in 1770, an English queen was condemned to boil for eternity for having made her husband turn Protestant. Only with difficulty did he establish that she was Anne Boleyn.[70] Brydone had succumbed to the romantic lure of the fiery mountain. His party ascended 'over "Antres vast and deserts wild", where scarce any human foot had ever trod. Sometimes through gloomy forests, which ... from the universal darkness, the rustling of the trees; the heavy, dull, bellowing of the mountain; the vast expanse of ocean stretched at an immense distance below us; inspired a kind of awful horror.'[71] With his companions he collected rock samples, took temperature readings and experimented with the behaviour of sound waves in the rarefied atmosphere by firing a gun and being surprised that it made no more noise than that of a stick on a door. He satisfied the credulity of the 'wicked' peasants, who found the behaviour of his party suspiciously incomprehensible, believing that, back in England, the tourists would transmute the volcanic rock samples into gold.

In the popular imagination of the day, the inhabitants of these growling and capricious mountains always numbered a hermit with mysterious powers and a dark history. Berlioz, in October 1831, discovered that the hermit of Vesuvius actually had to apply for the position and was licensed to run a tavern, where the composer enjoyed a 'vigorous Lacryma Christi'. Germaine de Staël had imagined the hermit living at the border of life and death, where natural vegetation ended at the rim of volcanic rock where the fires glimmered, but Mrs Piozzi was surprised to find that the successful recruit was her French hairdresser from London. Sydney Morgan found his successors were two Franciscan monks, who dispensed 'prayers and provisions, Litanies and Lacryma Christi'.[72] For the rest, the 'wicked peasants' were *banditti*. The slopes of Vesuvius were too well policed to harbour more than petty thieves, but further south, even as late as 1865, visitors to Paestum could be seized by brigands for ransom.[73] Among the deterrents to travel beyond the hinterland of Naples was the endemic problem of outlawry, so that the bandit was one of the principal Romantic images of Italy.

9

'The Kings of Apulia'
Banditry and Brigandage

Tutti, tutti li franzisi
avimmo noi d'ammazzare.

[We must kill all the French]

The song of the Sanfedisti.

Brigands abstain from meat on Wednesdays and Fridays ... and raise their hat at the name of Jesus or Mary or at the Vesper bell.

William Moens, English Travellers and Italian Brigands,
Volume ii, p. 224.

The genuine banditti ... of the seventeenth century, were no vulgar cutthroats, who, like the Maestrillos and Fra Diavolos of modern times, confined their exploits to road robbery and indiscriminate plunder and assassination.

Sydney Morgan, Life of Salvator Rosa, p. 44.

Ann Radcliffe had created an appetite for bandits among her readers, without having met any herself. Salvator Rosa had made them almost household denizens. The legends of Jonathan Wild, Jack Sheppard and Dick Turpin, all safely hanged, provided frissons of fear in Englishmen and women on a dark night. Footpads and highwaymen, however, were to bandits as muggers are to the Mafia, and banditry had been for centuries one of the accepted hazards of life in southern Europe, pandering to the Protestant prejudice against Catholic laxity when it came to law-breaking. Byron had fuelled a fancy for its macabre history. The rude-carved crosses that marked the highway round Cintra in Portugal were not Devotion's offering but

> ... memorials full of murderous wrath;
> For whereso'er the shrieking victim hath
> Pour'd forth his blood beneath the assassin's knife,
> Some hand erects a cross of mouldering lath;
> And grove and glen with thousand such a rife
> Throughout this purple land, where law secures not life.[1]

Sydney Morgan likened the bandits of the seventeenth century to

> brave, bold *condottieri* ... living at large and wild, with their hands against every man and every man's hand against them, yet they occasionally rivalled in dignity and importance the standing armies of existing legitimates, fighting like them for hire in any cause that paid them, and attacking the rights and liberties of all who stood in the way of the ambition, cupidity or despotism of their employers, with all the pride, pomp and circumstances of legitimate warfare.[2]

Though she conceded that the contemporary bandit was more treacherous cut-throat than brave bold *condottieri*, Lady Morgan reinforced strongly the Robin Hood myth of banditry. To redress the record in 1833, Dr Charles Macfarlane published *The Lives and Exploits of Banditti and Robbers in All Parts of the World*. Charles Macfarlane (d. 1850) lived and travelled extensively in Italy from 1816 to 1827, and in 1832 dedicated three volumes on the country as part of a series, *The Romance of History*. In addition to his bandits, he wrote *Popular Customs, Sports and Recollections of the South of Italy* in 1846, and on the strength of his knowledge of the Kingdom of Naples attempted to defend its government from attacks by Gladstone.[3] Half his book on *banditti* was devoted to those of Italy, some of whom he had met. From the outset he expressed a certain sympathy for his subject, 'for I scarcely heard of a career of crime in Italy but what had its origin in the passion of love'.[4] The murder of a rival in love was considered a peccadillo and punishment by the civic authorities (as opposed to revenge on the part of relations) constituted persecution. Both the victims of love and fugitives from justice tended to congregate in communities of similar social outcasts, providing further opportunities for more rivalry and murder. The distinction between bandits and brigands was often blurred, but it mattered when determining the fate of prisoners or *pentiti*. Bandits were those who had come under proscription for crimes committed against persons or property, whereas brigands had become outlaws in protest against social and political conditions. Brigandage was an endemic condition in largely peasant societies. Some might also be bandits but most of them were rebels against social oppression or breakdown, fugitives from taxation, unjust laws, involuntary enlistment, or persecution by landlords. Their principal hope was to see a restoration of the golden age when harvests were good, landlords kind and princes just. When the social order and harvests failed them, peasants resorted to brigandage to stay alive by plunder rather than agriculture. The band that took William Moens captive in 1865 was composed partly of former soldiers, all of whom, like Don José in Merrimée's *Carmen*, had been in trouble over infringements of discipline, and partly of peasants and shepherds who had killed someone.[5]

Gangs of outlaws had congregated for centuries in the mountainous terrain that separated the Kingdom of Naples from the Papal States, especially round Terracina, and in the impenetrable *maquis* of the Abruzzi. 'If the frontiers are mountainous', Dr Macfarlane volunteered, 'it seems almost impossible that they [the inhabitants] can be honest, until the contiguous states are both highly advanced in civilisation', an opinion that would have been heartily endorsed by any British officer stationed on the north-west frontier of India in the nineteenth century.[6] Despite their romantic baggage, the lot of brigands was neither profitable nor comfortable. Their chiefs took the lion's share of what booty there was, and none of them was a Robin Hood, or cast in the romantic mould of Schiller's *Robbers*, agents in the transfer of wealth between rich and poor. The chief of the band that kidnapped Moens had gambled away the half the ransom money allocated to himself within hours of receiving it.[7] They were perpetually on the run, deprived of both physical and spiritual consolations; capture meant almost certain execution, for many of them had escaped from the galleys to which they had been once consigned for former crimes. At least on the scaffold they would be shriven and not depart into the next world with their sins still upon them. They were religious in the strength of their devotion to images rather than to the Decalogue, and often carried a medallion or portrait of the Virgin Mary pinned to their clothes, so that in combat with soldiers or *sbirri* a quick prayer, accompanied by a kiss to the Mother of God, might assist their souls to make a safe, if sudden, passage from this world to the next. The bandit/brigand was more often to be pitied than feared. A miserable wound, in the absence of medical care, would fester and sometimes maim him for life. Occasionally the bandit could be credited with fine feelings, like the ferocious sixteenth-century chief, Marco Sciarra, who held up Torquato Tasso and his entourage. Learning who his victim was, Sciarra knelt, kissed the poet's hand and sped him unharmed on his way.[8] But most of them were desperate characters, even though they might abstain (other viands permitting) from meat on Wednesdays and Fridays, and doff their hats at the name of Jesus or the Madonna or when they heard the church bells rung for Vespers.[9]

Many of them were survivors of guerrilla warfare and found it hard to rejoin peaceful society. The French occupation of the Papal States and the Kingdom of Naples in 1798–9 and 1805–14 extended rather than abbreviated the history of *banditti*. What had been small bands of hated outlaws became large partisan armies; the *lazzaroni*, who saw the French destroy their sacred images and who were forced to exchange their snoods for the Phrygian cap of liberty, enrolled in their hundreds; the peasants, whose provender was rifled without compensation by French armies, took to the hills with their agricultural tools and joined their brothers in reaping heads rather than wheat. The excesses of the French, required to live off the land, raised legions of irregulars in Calabria and the Abruzzi. The countryside was closed to all except armed groups, and the brigands, now warriors for King and Church, were plentifully supplied from Sicily with guns by English and Sicilian flotillas. A popular song hailed the 'One and Indivisible Neapolitan Republic'. Cardinal Fabrizio Ruffo, having landed on 8 February 1799 with six companions at Pezzo in the toe of Italy with the royal brevet as vicar general, became a most unlikely liberation priest, raising the standard for *Fernando e la Santa Fede* in south Calabria. No questions were asked of the antecedents of these holy warriors, any more than in the Abruzzi, where the bands were led by another priest, l'Abate Proni. Together they closed on the Parthenopean Republic which stretched, as one song had it, 'from Posillipo all the way to the Capuan gate'.[10] Statues of Our Lady were seen to open her eyes in horror at French sacrilege, and the pope instituted a special mass *De apertione oris et oculorum Beatae M Virginis*.[11] The cry of '*Viva la Santa Fede*' brought the *lazzaroni* onto the streets. It was like another Sicilian Vespers. The French retreated to the Castel Sant'Elmo, while the city was looted in the name of Christ, anyone not wearing the standard Neapolitan pigtail proudly worn by their exiled king was presumed to be a Jacobin and butchered. The Parthenopean

Republic collapsed in 1799 with the capitulation of the French garrison. An unexpected result of Ruffo's campaign was that the Papal States were briefly brigand-free as the brigands had all joined either the cardinal or the abbé.

The French returned in 1806, this time as imperialists not republicans, seeking a kingdom for Napoleon Bonaparte's brother, Joseph. Ferdinand IV and his queen, Marie Antoinette's sister, Maria Carolina, went back to Palermo under the protection of the Royal Navy. This time, in the year of Austerlitz, things were different. The French armies, led by Generals Masséna and Reynier, were systematic and efficient. They had come to stay, and though General John Stuart was able to defeat Reynier at Maida on 4 July 1806, he had no cavalry with which to turn victory into rout and, being too weak to withstand both French armies, he withdrew to Sicily. Cardinal Ruffo knew he could not repeat his exploits of seven years before and, though Maida gave a great fillip to bandit armies (and a name to the burgeoning London suburb), they were soon confined to the most inaccessible heights of Calabria and Campania and to the chestnut forests of the Abruzzi. There they were joined by fugitives from the enlistment policies of the French, who wanted men to fight in Austria, Poland, Spain and Russia but who indirectly enrolled them in *une guerre de brigands*. The French reacted with savagery; prisoners were submitted to slow hanging and peppered with shot as they hung dying, unshriven, before being tumbled into pits dug by the next to die, or thrown into streams and brooks, polluting the water of the peasants. Women and children of communities that were suspected of harbouring brigands ('terrorists') were imprisoned without trial or the simple necessities of humanity.

Mary Shelley tells a tale that perfectly illustrates this ferocity. It was 'inspired' by a plate of Turner's showing Italian *contadini* meeting a pedlar in the hills near Rome, and the author claimed to have been told it by the Countess Atanasia D—. A peasant in the Alban hills has two daughters. One has become a nun, the younger has unwisely fallen in love with a bandit. One day, while taking provisions to him, she is arrested by French soldiers and instantly sentenced to death. Her sister, visiting home on sick leave from her convent, goes off to intercede for her, and finding the French implacable, she secures a visit to the condemned girl, and changes places with her, fully expecting them not to shoot a nun. She is wrong. Though the bandit and his followers make an attempt to rescue her, all are killed, and the younger sister enters the convent in

her elder sister's place, to pray perpetually for their souls.[12] Mary
Shelley's bandits behave with a hopeless chivalry in their attempt to
rescue the innocent girl. Usually, the partisans killed the French,
when they could, without mercy and disfigured any who had col-
laborated with them, in particular scalping any compatriot who had
incautiously cut his hair short *al francese*. Church sympathies were
not with the godless French and many a priest acted as decoy to
French hunting parties, so the execution of a nun by the exasperated
French was an act of prudence.

Among the most famous of these bandit partisans was Michele
Arcangelo Pezza (1760–1806), known as Fra Diavolo. Apprenticed to
a saddle maker in Itri, a small castellated town in the Auruncian
mountains, dominating a stretch of the old Appian Way near
Formia in the Campania, he killed his master in a brawl and, when
his victim's brother threatened revenge, he killed him too. He fled to
a distant part of the *Regno*, where he became a cattle drover. In 1798,
answering a call to arms, he commuted his two murders for thirteen
years as a fusilier. He served less than a year. Part of the force that
pushed the French out of Rome in November 1789, he deserted as
soon as the French returned and drove the Neapolitan army south
in confusion. Disgusted by the craven incompetence of his regiment's foreign officers, he returned to Itri, enlisted the help of his
brothers, and recruited deserters and vagabonds into a *masnada* or
guerrilla band which soon numbered over 1,000 men. Michele Pezza
had never been, as popularly supposed, a friar. His priestly school-
master had, in exasperation at his truancy and pranks, protested
that he should have been called Fra Diavolo rather than Arcangelo;
now he became Fra Diavolo in fact. He established contact with the
British gunrunners and impressed their officers as a man who
meant business. They reported on him favourably to his Austrian
queen, who dubbed him 'honest and brave'.[13] Though his men
tipped carriages from Rome over precipices without inviting their
occupants to descend, Pezza did not go in for horrors, like his fellow
guerrilleros, Mammone, who affected a thirst for human blood,
which he drank from a skull, or Matteo Cesarini, who dressed as a
woman and executed his prisoners with an axe. Pezza had taken the
oath of a soldier to his king, and a soldier he would be.

'General' Pezza – he was actually breveted colonel of infantry in
October 1799 but elevated himself at Velletri in September, to commander and general in charge of the left wing of Ruffo's army
marching on Rome – had rallied to Ruffo's standard, but a double

murderer and protégé of the queen was scarcely the champion of the Faith for whom the cardinal was looking. When his makeshift army had the French bottled up in Gaeta, Ruffo refused to let Fra Diavolo lead the attack on the city, fearing that his men were only interested in its sack. He negotiated its surrender instead to John Acton, Ferdinand's prime minister, and Horatio Nelson. Ruffo also used regular Neapolitan troops to prevent Pezza from being the first to enter Rome, upon its second 'liberation'. Indeed, because Fra Diavolo was unable to stop his men from treating Albano like a city to be plundered, he entered Sant'Angelo under armed escort as a prisoner. But Michele Pezza had a ready tongue and, back in Palermo, he talked himself back into royal favour. His colonelcy was confirmed and, upon the second French invasion of the *Regno* in 1805, he was put into Gaeta to assist in its defence by Admiral Sir Sidney Smith, the hero of Acre.

Being beseiged was too tame for Pezza, and his failure to return from night forays with baskets of French heads, as he had boasted he would do, irritated the Hessian prince in command, who suspected him of being a go-between with the French and had him shipped back to Palermo. Smith put him back into Calabria with 200 liberated galley-slaves to wage guerrilla warfare and rouse the province as Ruffo had done seven years earlier. Although he worsted a French general at the mouth of the Amate River, for which he was created Duke of Cassano and which caused Napoleon to admonish his brother Joseph never to mention Fra Diavolo until he had been captured and executed, times had changed. Ruthlessness on the part of the French, fatigue, carelessness and overconfidence on that of the *banditti* told against the *masnadieri*. Colonel Hugo, the father of the then three-year-old Victor, was charged to bring him to heel. One by one his men were killed or deserted, and eventually he was a solitary fugitive. At the end of his tether he entered the house of a village apothecary who turned out to be a member of the national guard. Fra Diavolo was too weary to deny the challenge. The French, despite appeals from both Sir Sidney Smith, and Colonel Hugo, were determined to execute him as a common criminal. They agreed that he could wear the uniform of a royalist soldier and, on 11 November 1806, wearing as a further mockery a placard inscribed with his ducal title, he was hanged in the main square in Naples. The executioner botched the job, and Pezza had to be shot.

Itri was to retain its bad reputation. In the 1840s, the Ruskins stayed there, though it had been 'hinted darkly to us … [as] … of no good repute … that the entire population consisted of banditti'. Having met none, we 'never troubled ourselves about banditti any more'.[14] Fra Diavolo is now only remembered as the subject of Daniel Auber's opera, with a libretto by the prolific Eugène Scribe. It is the bandit opera par excellence. Auber was 24 when Pezza died, and Scribe fifteen, but both were French and had supped on the legend, not of an ardent partisan, but of an unprincipled thief and murderer. The action takes place at an inn near Terracina, where Lorenzo, commanding a detachment of French *carabinieri*, is lodged while

14. Programme cover for Auber's opera, *Fra Diavolo*.
The cowering victim reveals that the plot concerns Michele Pezza, not as a gallant patriotic partisan against the French but as a common thief.

engaged in hunting Fra Diavolo, on whose head there is a hand-some price. Two English tourists, Lord and Lady Cockburn, come to the inn, complaining that they have been robbed by the bandit on the highway. Lorenzo, who loves the innkeeper's daughter, Zerlina, goes off with his men to find him, but the arrival of the Cockburns is closely followed by that of the Marquis de San Marco, who is, of course, Fra Diavolo himself. The action that follows consists of a plot by 'San Marco' to relieve Cockburn of the rest of his wealth, secreted about his person, by hiding in the bedroom of Lorenzo's sweetheart, next-door to the Cockburns'. The plot miscarries because Lorenzo, having failed to find Fra Diavolo, but claiming to have killed a score of his followers, returns unexpectedly and wakes the household. 'San Marco', bent on revenge, whispers to Lorenzo that his sweet-heart has been unfaithful to him and the two men decide to fight a duel. The duel never takes place, since Zerlina is able to prove her innocence and the duplicity of 'San Marco'. His plot is uncovered and his identity revealed, whereupon, when Fra Diavolo turns up for his duel, he is either shot or arrested, depending on which ending the producer adopts. *Fra Diavolo*, first performed in Paris in 1830 and at Drury Lane in 1831 followed Auber's runaway success with *La Muette de Portici* (1828/9),[15] and in Act 3 truth flew out of the window on the wings of a cantilena on the joys of a bandit's life. Reality was harsher. The 28-strong band which captured William Moens was harried from one hide-out to another for twelve weeks by the soldiers hunting them, hungry, ill, wet and cold. When his ransom was finally paid, it was shared among only seventeen survivors.[16]

When the Napoleonic wars were over, the brigands expected grati-tude from the restored king and pontiff, but economic conditions were bad and it was impossible to reintegrate so many people into productive life. So bands of outlaws continued to harass the roads from Rome to Naples, especially in the Volscian hills (Monti Ausoni) between Sonnino and Frosinone, at times operating as close to Rome as Tivoli, not 30 miles from the centre of Rome. In 1819, Byron's biographer, the Irish poet, Thomas Moore, joined an expedi-tion to Tivoli on a party of pleasure, 'armed' as a precaution 'with pistols, daggers, sword-canes etc.', and Mrs Hinde was shot at, about three miles from Rome, by a lone brigand, whose gang had seen her party leaving the city and lain in wait, only one member managing to stay awake.[17] That same year, Captain Graham and his wife Maria, making their *villeggiatura* at Poli in the Prenestine hills, found themselves in the middle of bandit activity, which was severe enough to cause them to cut it short and return to Rome. Maria Graham was an experienced naval daughter, wife and traveller, and she liked to amass as much information about her surroundings to make a book. Her husband was a Royal Naval captain on half pay. In Poli she intended to record 'the state of easy poverty, above want but below ambition' and uninterested in any form of government but one which let 'him sit under his own vine and fig tree'.[18] Maria Graham kept a journal of her experiences, as she had done in India and was to do in both Brazil and Chile, whither she accompanied her husband in HMS *Doris*. The bandits they met were ready to stand as painter's models and their mildness, even boredom, persuaded her that they were more like Robin Hood of legend than thugs like Fra Diavolo.[19] In fact, they were a dangerous nuisance. The Grahams were intrepid people, and during her residence after her husband's death in Brazil Maria single-handedly drove off a *quilombola* (escaped slave), who was breaking into her house in the mountains round Rio de Janeiro. But in Poli rumours of a band of outlaws in the vicinity who had enquired about the English and their movements, and the discovery of a murdered man on one of their walks in the countryside unsettled the Grahams. They had little confidence in the civic guard of Poli, whose comic-opera manoeuvres proved almost more dangerous to each other than to any bandits they might meet, and the limitation imposed on their movements, for their own safety, proved irksome. They decided to return to Rome via Tivoli, escorted by a Mozambican man with a long gun and twelve armed peasants. Whether because of the black man, a figure so uncommon as to be a figure of terror in himself, or the peasants with their muskets and double-barrelled fowling pieces, they were not molested, though the bandits were actually encamped in Hadrian's villa. An attempt was made at that time to kidnap Lucien Bonaparte, Prince of Cannino, from his summer house in the site of the ancient city of Tusculum. The marauders seized his secretary and butler in error, and had the prince not paid the ransom money, the kidnappers would have been obliged to cut their throats; their 'honour was engaged'.[20] The prince also hired a hunting party to track the brigands down, without success, though they had been bivouacking in the ruins of Tusculum by day and roamed the streets of Rome by night.[21]

Bands like this would make their headquarters on a virtually inaccessible peak and range freely round the countryside, using shepherds and goat-herds to obtain food and intelligence. Their number was about 140, divided into gangs of 20, and their principal occupation was hostage-taking in order to raise a ransom; if a hostage turned out to be valueless, he would be constrained to act as go-between for those for whose liberty their families or villages might pay. Hostages included even teen-aged students at a minor seminary.[22] The *banditti* affected a kind of uniform, all pretty tattered, linen shirts, breeches of broadcloth and velveteen jackets with large pockets between the outer fabric and the lining, into which were stuffed food and spare clothing and loot of whatever kind. The most exotic part of their apparel was a waistcoat festooned with silver *filigrana* buttons and stolen jewellery, especially watch chains, seals and rings taken from the 'rich English', and gay silk handkerchief or scarves, usually too dirty to be elegant. A sort of 'wide-awake' or else conical Alpine hat and ostrich feather was an almost indispensable part of the dress, as it was important for bandits to be quickly recognised for what they were, so that transactions were not prolonged. A bandolier of cartridges for their long hunting rifles, and a hunting knife – the preferred weapon of injury, being silent – completed the dress. William Moens, when he described the bandits who captured him near Paestum in 1865, could not have known that their dress was unchanged in essentials from the days when Salvator Rosa painted *banditti*.[23] The cry *faccia a terra* required instant obedience. More often than not the guards accompanying a tourist carriage put up no resistance and had not even loaded their carbines in case of accidents. Sydney Morgan's two guards between Terracina and Gaeta, one sitting with the driver, the other covering the rear perched on the luggage, had stuffed their guns with paper![24] Unless soldiers or police (*sbirri*) had been sent out to hunt bandits down, the only guardians of law and order were the civic guards of the townships, composed of peasants who were enrolled by the day when bandits were reported nearby, and who were often almost as disaffected as the regular outlaws. Bandit *masnade* frequently acquired *manuténgoli* or protectors, who found them useful to scare off government inspectors and tax assessors and to settle personal scores. But they would often fall to bickering and private warfare, so that anyone straying from the highway was more likely to be murdered in crossfire between rival gangs than killed in a hold-up. Where brigands still ruled, the countryside was neglected and barren, strewn with the carcasses of dead horses and cattle, like some blasted landscape out of *Melmoth the Wanderer*.

Before the Grahams went to Poli, Pius VII, the supreme representative of the *Santa Fede* which had sanctified the banditti, had tried to
end the nuisance by sending papal zouaves to clear the countryside
round Frosinone, but as the bandits merely retired to more inaccessible places, His Holiness decided to try personal treaty with their
leaders. He offered them a token year's imprisonment in the notori-
ously lax Roman gaols in return for rehabilitation in society, aided
by a public subsidy. As a result, wagonloads of brigands trundled
into Rome. The most fearsome of them all, one Masocco, came with
his wife, whom the Duchess of Devonshire, taking time off from her
excavations, rewarded with a valuable necklace. Masocco, now
poacher turned game-keeper, was invited to bring in a recalcitrant
rival, Cesari. But Cesari callously shot him down at their first meeting. This was no way to treat a reformed bandit. As Cesari's family
were in the hands of the papal *sbirri*, Masocco's friends seized and
murdered six of his women in cold blood. Cesari then slaughtered
every one of his prisoners who was or had been in papal service,
and the bloodshed only ended when he was shot by a papal *carab-
iniere*, thus bringing the pontiff's initiative to an end. Bandits who
did turn themselves in could be sure of a reasonably comfortable life
behind bars. Charlotte Eaton joined a party to view them in Castel
Sant'Angelo, 'apparently enjoying the novelty of their situation',
and admired their 'fine limbs, fine features, fine flashing dark eyes
and hair and bright brown complexion, expressing undaunted confidence and fearless resolution'. As she had already been part of a
coach party which was robbed at gun point, she felt obliged to add
that she could give 'no idea of the sinister expression – the confirmed villainy that many of them wore'.[25] Stendhal as consul in
Civitavecchia would make the arrangements for newly landed tourists to view a notorious bandit, one Gasparone, who, with his 20
followers, could be viewed in their cell, for a modest fee, between
the hours of ten and twelve each day. As he commented sourly, of
100 French visitors landing for the first time in Italy on their way to
Rome, half would want to see Gasparone, while only four or five
wanted to see him, Stendhal.[26]

Banditry was never extinguished in the papal domains. Indeed
towards their end, when the future of the pontiff's rule was in grave
doubt, it was out of control. In 1844, Charles Dickens, on approaching Bologna, entered the Papal States, 'which is not, in any part,
supremely well-governed, Saint Peter's keys being rather rusty
now', so that his driver and 'Brave Courier' were afraid to travel in

the dark.[27] Joseph Severn, taking the baths at Tolfa in July 1867, hoped that none of the many gangs which held the countryside to ransom would wish to kidnap a simple painter.[28]

Tourists in search of excitement would venture into bandit country where they might be politely relieved of their few valuables, but by and large bandits did not want trouble with foreigners.[29] Hector Berlioz, while a student in Rome, was intrigued by the life of an outlaw and would go off to shoot in the hills south of Rome, carrying nothing of value except his fowling piece in the hopes of meeting one. He spent some time in Subiaco where he made friends with a man who claimed to be a brigand, but Berlioz was convinced that he could not have killed so much as a monk, and treated the story that he had been condemned to the galleys with some scepticism. If he was a bandit, he was the nearest Berlioz ever came to one, though it was not for want of looking.[30] On the whole they wreaked their havoc among the landlords who had not paid them tribute. When the menace of revolutionary *carbonari* began to preoccupy the papal authorities, the bandits proved adept at carrying out counter-espionage in country they knew like the backs of their hands. For most of them were staunch supporters of the pope and of the Holy Faith, and their struggle against the French had already passed into folklore. They showed their loyalty by turning in so-called revolutionaries, most of whom came from a social class that had done little for the rural poor.[31] The middle-class *carbonari* found the bandits their most deadly enemies, as there was no hiding from them, and the authorities were not above hiring them as trackers. The legend that bandits were often used by the authorities to carry out their dirty work, the assassination and kidnapping of liberals, was widely held in the north. In George Henty's *Out with Garibaldi*, the Neapolitan secret service used bandits for this purpose.[32]

Bandits were not always people of the mountains. The heel as well as the toe of Italy was infested by brigands and for several years, after Joachim Murat's reign in Naples was snuffed out by a firing squad at Pizzo, the province of Puglia, with its lonely *masserie* (fortified farmhouses), its network of stone walls, orchards and vineyards and lonely hilltop villages was ideal for outlaws. One of them, Gaetano Vardarelli, a former trooper in Neapolitan service, styled himself King of Apulia. He would only accept a pardon if the king gave him substantively the power he already exercised over the area. His was 'a good trade ... One lives like a king, the great people fear us, the poor look up to us, the women adore us. We get

plenty of money and spend it freely. It's no bad thing to be account-
able to nobody and above all law.'[33] The region round Lecce in
Puglia was in thrall to a notorious renegade cleric who held much of
the province to ransom. Don Ciro Anacchiarico, a native of Grot-
taglie, was an ordained priest, but quite early on in his priestly life
he fell in love with a village girl. Don Ciro shot the girl's suitor and
his whole family but one, to remove the possibility of vendetta. For
this offence he was sentenced to fifteen years in the galleys but
escaped after four and took to banditry. So fearsome was his reputation as a dead shot that the lad who survived the family slaughter
never left his house until he heard that the assassin was dead. Don
Ciro did not join the Sanfedistas, and acquired so horrible a reputation that every murder and robbery in Puglia was attributed to him
or his gang. Though he tried to take advantage of a general amnesty
on the restoration of King Ferdinand in 1815, his outrages were too
notorious for pardon. Don Ciro's attitude to his priestly vocation
would have afforded a study for Graham Greene. Though rejecting
the ministrations of the regular clergy, even at the moment of execution, he said Mass frequently for his followers and allowed people to
believe his cloth rendered him immune to earthly punishment. An
antinomian like Rasputin, he was credited with supernatural powers. Even the troopers who assisted at his execution could not kill
him outright by musket fire but had to finish him off with his own
musket loaded with a silver bullet.[34]

For three years Don Ciro played at being a *carbonaro*, drawing up
an elaborate constitution for a bandit society, and adorning his
notices with skulls and crossbones and the motto 'Sorrow, Death,
Terror and Mourning'. The Resolute Society of Jove the Thunderer
(*Società Deciso del Tuonante Giove*) known as the *Decisi*, were murderous freemasons, who only qualified for membership, it was claimed,
after committing two murders. Their induction into the fellowship
followed horrendous rites of passage, the final stage of which was to
face his comrades drawn up as a firing squad ready to execute 'a
scoundrelly republican, an enemy to the king'.[35] Once professed, the
Deciso went back to his home, being called out, like the Ku Klux
Klan, for brigandish assignments. He was not a *fuoruscito* or outlaw
who could be easily identified and denounced, but masqueraded
outwardly as a law-abiding citizen. The threat of revenge by brother
Decisi deterred denunciation by an informer until there was a demonstration of overwhelming force on the part of the agents of law
and order.

Law and Order was eventually provided by an Irish major whom Sismondi's description of Ezzelino da Romano, by chance, fitted like a glove. The Cork-born Richard Church (1784–1873) 'was an extraordinary man', wrote a compatriot, Sir John Lennie, who met him at Lecce in 1820, 'below the middle size, ... extremely well-built, spare, sinewy and active, with a well proportioned head, sharp piercing eyes, rather aquiline nose and a closely compressed mouth, denoting great firmness and resolution'.[36] A veteran of the Peninsula War, he had helped to form the Maltese fencibles after the release of the island from French occupation, and in 1806 was captain of the Corsican Rangers, who fought at Maida. His skill in commanding meridional troops tempted him to pass into Neapolitan service as a major-general, charged with the reduction of brigandage, with powers to 'condemn and execute such malefactors without any form of trial'.[37] In 1820 he was transferred to command the royal troops in Palermo, found them disaffected and ill-disciplined and eventually had to flee the island when the revolution broke out. He was arrested on arrival at Naples by the constitutionalists and spent several months in the Castel dell'Ovo until released by the efforts of the British ambassador. He passed, at the age of 43, to the service of the new Greek state in 1827, became generalissimo of its armies, partnering Thomas Cochrane who was admiral-in-chief. Church stayed in independent Greece until he died. He was famous as a raconteur of bandit stories.[38]

Though an Irishman, he had acquired all the arrogant sang-froid of the victors in the 20-year war with France, which baffled and intimidated men who thought little of taking life openly or by treachery. To those who practised the rough peasant democracy of the secret societies, Church behaved as a classic Renaissance tyrant. He knew when to be merciful and when to be inflexible. Almost wholly without fear, he was a good judge of men, and in his war against the *masnadieri* he practised all the wiles of a medieval *condottiere*. His first encounter with a band of brigands while accompanied only by his Swiss aide-de-camp and valet was worthy of a novel by Anthony Hope. While conceding nothing to Don Gaetano Vardarelli, who was their leader, he invited him to submit to the king and, when that ploy failed, he insisted on inspecting the hundred or so brigands as if they were regular troops. He found Don Gaetano a likeable rogue, it being in his favour that he had killed few people himself; but perhaps Church did not know that Don Gaetano had

killed his own sister, wounded in an affray with the Neapolitan sol-
diery, to prevent her falling into their hands. When Church
threatened to bring Don Gaetano to heel, the outlaw decided to
make his peace but, before he could do so, he was waylaid by villag-
ers his band had pillaged and was shot dead.[39]

There were said to be 70,000 'sectaries' in the Lecce region alone at
the end of the Napoleonic wars, in gangs which had adopted *carbonaro* titles and attributes. In addition to the *Decisi*, there were *Filadelfi*,
Patrioti Europei, *I Calderari*, all of whom professed libertarian slogans
and an ambivalent attitude to the king. The *Decisi* even aspired to a
Salentine Republic (the Salentine peninsula being the heel round
Otranto and Lecce).[40] Many of these were discharged troopers who
had gone home with their arms and preferred to poach rather than
dig for the pot. Their numbers, perhaps, were inflated by the fear
they induced in the countryside. Church destroyed their *masnade*
methodically, as if on a tiger shoot. Outrunners would beat through
the Puglian scrub, criss-crossed by stone walls that afforded prime
sites for snipers, until the quarry had retreated to their headquarters
in a *masseria* which had always been able to beat off earlier royal
forces. This time it was different. Church was not a Neapolitan and
could not be bribed or twisted. He made it his business to be affable
and sociable, visiting the landlords and *latifundisti* who had more or
less protected the gangs in order to keep their game and their harvests from pillage, and he convinced them that, this time, the king
meant business. Landlords who employed bandits as agents to
enforce their will on tenants found Church inexorable and impervi-
ous to the corruption of southern hospitality and, as confidence
grew, so the terrorised peasantry turned on the gangs in their midst.
By 1820, Puglia was largely cleared of them, (though they were back
by the 1860s[41]) and where they still existed, in the more mountainous parts of Calabria, they were now hunted by peasants as well as
the armed countrymen of the Urban Guard. Indeed, in 1838, the
landscape painter, Arthur John Strutt, with a number of companions, on a walking and sketching tour in the countryside near
Catanzaro, were mistaken for brigands and viciously attacked by a
group of armed peasants. Their assailants robbed them of their possessions, thus behaving no differently from bandits themselves and
things could have gone badly wrong for the tourists had not a
detachment of the local urban guard happened to pass by.[42]

Banditry never completely vanished from the mountains of
Calabria and in 1865 a party of four travellers were apprehended by

bandits on the road from Paestum to Salerno, having been escorted to the temples by a military contingent who had then gone to negotiate the ransom of two Italians seized on the road a few days earlier. While the Reverend Murray Aynsley and the two wives were sent back to Naples to raise the ransom, negotiated down from £1700 (100,000 ducats) to £850 (a sum they had great difficulty in raising), the hostage who was retained, William Moens, spent thirteen weeks almost continually on the run with the outlaws. To make pursuit harder they repeatedly moved camp, little more than a large bonfire on which they cooked in a cauldron whatever they had been able to pillage, and were always wet, cold and hungry. With so many troops on the look out for them, it was surprising that the gang remained undetected in what was a comparatively small area of the mountains near Salerno, which city and the place of his capture being often plainly visible to Moens from where he was being kept. Rumours having reached the band that Moens was a relative of Lord Palmerston and rich, he was always afraid either that the agreed ransom would prove to be insufficient, or that the troops who had been sent to rescue him would kill him by accident. The British consul attempted, in return for Moens's safe release, to arrange a safe passage out of Naples for the leader and his gang on a British man of war, but they all feared that they would be slaughtered either before they were on board or thrown into the sea when they were. The kidnapping was reported in *The Times* and when no news of Moens's release had been received, his wretched wife was assailed by reports that Moens had joined the bandits to raise his own ransom by brigandage, and she was plagued by letters suggesting that 'life with brigands cannot be so unpleasant after all ...!'[43]

Twenty-first-century banditry has demonstrated the same truths that Moens averred: that kidnapping and being kidnapped is no fun for either party, and that often a feeling of affection grows between them. When the gang was convinced that Moens was not a rich English milord, they accepted a rather reduced ransom, and he was finally released. Before he left, the gang leader had a whip-round for him, most of the gang contributing 'a napoleon or two, or parting with one of their rings'. One even went so far as to give him his much prized and lethally used stiletto in return for a penknife.

Moens was convinced that the only people who profited from banditry were the shepherds and peasants on whom outlaws depended for their supplies. Bread and meat were sold at such a high mark-up on market prices that it could cost a gang of 25 to 30 men the equivalent of £4,000 sterling a year just to subsist. Peasants too were often the source of information on possible kidnap victims, and they would act as intermediaries in ransom deals. Bandits who were captured were often shot, those who surrendered themselves usually did a spell in prison, where they were often more comfortable than on the run, having cash available to buy little luxuries and special treatment. Banditry persisted in those parts of Italy which were inefficiently policed, where peasants with grievances against landlords could laugh at the blood-curdling threats against anyone who aided bandits or conveyed ransom money. They were most oppressed when there was a system of neighbourhood watch, which had rescued Strutt and his party from a beating, and which was abandoned in the south after the fall of the Bourbons in favour of policing by the military, often from other parts of united Italy, who were ignorant of the local patois and other conditions. The unification of the kingdom, too, was often accompanied by higher taxes and a fall in the value of land which, combined with a novel interpretation of the meaning of freedom, revived the causes of brigandage.[44] It has never completely disappeared.

William Moens wrote his account to dispel the romantic aura that hung round banditry, which for 50 years or so had fascinated foreign artists. They swallowed the false legend of Salvator Rosa, which now, 100 years after he had peopled his landscapes with outlaws, clothed the bandit in the mantle of romantic rebel. And, as Macfarlane was to claim, bandits had more often than not been reduced to crime either in protest against injustice or as the result of hot temper. Sydney Morgan glamourised the bandit of Salvator Rosa's time: 'these *fuori citti* [sic], these *condottieri* of romantic history, whose graceful forms and noble bearing bespoke their high caste, natural and social, were capable of chivalrous deeds and generous sympathies.'[45] Her long description of a Rosa engraving, of a bandit chief's wife pleading for the life of a prisoner, reeks of *Carmen*. Despite being flung out of the pale of society for her strong passions, her countenance was full of stern melancholy. Hers was a figure of command.[46]

In 1816, the future president of the Royal Academy of Arts, Charles Eastlake (1792–1865) came to Rome, where he was to stay for fourteen years. He had been a pupil of Benjamin Robert Haydon and had made his name with a portrait of Napoleon solemnly contemplating his bleak future on HMS *Bellerophon*. As a history painter he was patronised by the sixth Duke of Devonshire, but by 1819 he had decided that he was a landscape artist. Eastlake wanted to paint the peasants in their habitat and bandits in their lair. So he went off with Captain and Maria Graham, whom he had befriended in Rome and nursed through attacks of fever, to live in bandit country. Eastlake did not like an unpeopled painting, so he peopled his with *banditti*, and these, some of which illustrated Maria Graham's account of their uncomfortable three months, were the sensation of the exhibition at the British Institution in 1823. He could have sold each one many times over. So great was their commendation by the great Sir Thomas Lawrence that he was elected a Royal Academician *in absentia*, the first ever to be so. Eastlake was merely following a fashion, set by earlier artists. John Hamilton Mortimer (1741–79), many of whose works were shown posthumously towards the end of the century, had made pastiches after Salvator Rosa, as well as original sketches of outlaws engaged in outlawry. Joseph Wright of Derby had embellished a romantic grotto near Naples with desperados. Jacques David's pupil, Louis Léopold Robert (1794–1835), who sold his big canvases of the seasons in Italy to both Bourbon and Orleanist monarchs, portrayed his model outlaw and his woman as free spirits, who had thrown off the trammels of civilisation and chosen a life of freedom in the wilderness. For the artists who flocked to Rome after the French had withdrawn, seeking a return to romantic nature and the quaint, colourful people who lived their intense life within it, the outlaw began to exert a special fascination. Here was the Byronic hero for whom the scowl of Conrad/Lara or the Giaour was a perfect fit *à la Rosa*, set apart from his fellow man by law and order that were both unjust. The reputation of the freedom fighter and partisan against the French lingered on, despite the gruesome stories that were attributed to them, and proved strong enough for artists to go and live in the campagna in the hope of sketching bandits 'at home'. Eastlake had hoped that the experience would be profitable, which for a time it was, but he and the Grahams only too soon discovered that outlaws mostly deserved to be outlaws. They were content, in the absence of readier prey, to pander to the romantic illusions of artists who were, on the whole, too indigent to be worth robbing, and if they gave convincing performances as men of mystery, they only too quickly showed that they were also men of violence.[47] But it was a violence about to be rendered redundant as revolution and liberation began to shake the land.

10

'The Mingled Beauties of Exalting Greece'

Feminising Italy

Came packages by water-carriage, containing an infinite variety of Venuses. There were the Medicean Venus, and the Bathing Venus, the Uranian Venus, and the Pandemian Venus; the Crouching Venus, and the Sleeping Venus; the Venus rising from the sea, the Venus with the apple of Paris and the Venus with the armour of Mars.

> Thomas Love Peacock, *Crotchet Castle*, Chapter vii.

So stands the statue that enchants the world,
So bending tries to veil the matchless boast,
The mingled beauties of exalting Greece!

> James Thomson on the 'Venus de Medici',
> 'Summer', *The Seasons* (1727).

Maybe in a frolic daft
To Hague or Calais takes a waft,
To make a tour, an' take a whirl
To learn 'bon ton' or 'see the world' ...
... Or down Italian vista startles
Whore-hunting among groves o' myrtles.

> Robert Burns, 'The Two Dogs' (1786).

The women are particularly empty, and though possessed of ... superficial grace are devoid of any cultivation or refinement.

> Percy Bysshe Shelley to William Godwin, 25 July 1818.

Far from terrorising the women who visited Italy after the end of the war, bandits intrigued and fascinated them. The Grand Tour had been largely a male thing; most tourists being either unattached men or content to leave their women at home. It was not surprising that the women they met in Italy were only too often whores or, if not, so debauched that they are 'hardly to be considered as moral agents, but as inferior beings',[1] like the dancers at the Opera, whose costumes often simulated nudity, and whose lives were so depraved that they were often dead before they had survived two years with the company. 'Victims of Vice and Misery, ... their places are filled by other miserable creatures who as quickly share the same fate.'[2] Percy Bysshe Shelley, on first arrival in Italy, formed an appalling view of its women: 'the most contemptible of all who exist under the moon; the most ignorant, the most disgusting, the most bigotted, the most filthy'. Even ladies of quality smelt so strongly of garlic no Englishman could approach them. He was so disgusted by Lord Byron who had his 'gondolieri pick up in the streets' and allowed 'fathers and mothers to bargain with him for their daughters', that he tarred the whole sex with the same brush. By the time he had reached Rome he had a formed a slightly kinder opinion of them. They had become gentle savages, even interesting, despite being totally devoid of any kind of information or culture of the imagination or affections or understanding.[3] An innocent encounter with a pretty maiden was, therefore, cause for comment. Mary Shelley, in her summary of the pleasures of Italy, described one extremely pretty girl who served her at a picnic as if she were a rare specimen.[4] Chroniclers of the time generally appreciated Italian women when they reflected the beauty and grace of ancient statues.

The eighteenth-century taste had been for male models, warriors, wrestlers, *discoboli*, senators, emperors, but classicism began to be feminised with the cult of the 'Venus de Medici'. In 1727 James Thomson declaimed:

> So stands the statue that enchants the world,
> So bending tries to veil the matchless boast,
> The mingled beauties of exalting Greece![5]

This feeling was carried to a peculiar intensity in 1821 by the epicene enthusiasm of Samuel Rogers in Florence, 'worshipping, / In her small temple of rich workmanship, / VENUS herself, who, when she left the skies, / Came hither'.[6] He could be observed every morning admiring the statue as if he hoped, like Pygmalion, to animate her,

15. Painting of a brigand by Charles Alphonse-Paul Bellay (1826–1900). The brigand was a much-painted subject, as he increasingly became the only Italian peasant to preserve a distinctive dress.

'or rather perhaps that the statue might animate *him*'. As a practical joke a young Englishman put a poem between the statue's fingers, beseeching Rogers not to come ogling her every day. His friends might think he was still alive but she knew 'he had come from the other side of the Styx'![7] In 1800 the statue had been despatched from Florence to Naples to save it from the French but since 1803 had been exposed in the Louvre, after diplomatic and military pressure secured its transfer to Paris. There at six o'clock in the morning of 16 August Napoleon himself had come to render homage.

The statue was probably the most copied in history; five being made for Louis XIV, and she appeared repeatedly in English gardens throughout the eighteenth century. Not everybody, however, thought she represented the angelic and chaste ideal of perfect beauty: Smollett found no beauty in her features and her attitude awkward, and only conceded that her buttocks would 'excite the admiration of the most indifferent spectator'.[8] Winckelmann thought her navel too deep, others that her fingers were too long. Kotzebue considered the young women of Berlin were more attractive, Hazlitt found her insipid, Flaxman declared that she was a poor copy of a finer original, while Wordsworth went to sleep with his back to her while admiring a Raphael. Sydney Morgan reported that the new science of craniology showed that the goddess was an idiot, but at four feet eleven she was the 'Madonna della Conforta to all who "found the blessedness of being little"'. On the other hand Napoleon's artistic commissar, Vivian Denon, reckoned that her foot was 'a monument in itself',[9] and most admirers were prepared to accept the judgement of the young Ruskin in 1840, that the 'Venus de Medici' represented one of the purest and loftiest images of woman that it was possible to conceive.[10]

In 1815 the Venus returned, with an escort of cavalry and beating drums, to her home in Florence where, in the meantime, visitors to the Uffizi had had to be content with the *Venere Italica* by Canova. She had been finished only in 1812 and, with her faintly roseate flesh tints, hot from the bath (which inspired John Gibson's *Tinted Venus*, and challenged Lord Leighton to imitate it in paint), she held court in the Tribuna at the Pitti Palace where the more famous Venus had been, until her return. Then *Venere Italica* was consigned first to the grand duke's cabinet, where she was surrounded by mirrors, then to a *tempietto*, and finally to a corridor in the Uffizi. Catherine Hinde, predictably, felt she must give the palm to the Medicean Venus but acknowledged Canova's 'a most beautiful woman'.[11] Like her rival she had most beautiful nates, but was otherwise largely concealed by a drape modestly clutched to her bosom. Antonio Canova had established new canons of pulchritude when he selectively allowed living women to enter his sculptural pantheon in all their contemporary splendour, both clad and unclad; Pauline Borghese as *Victorious Venus*, Mme de Recamier as one of the three graces, Josephine Beauharnais as a *danseuse* – the sculptor was besieged by requests by the *elegantissime* to be models, some of which he accepted, most of which he refused.[12] His combination of naturalness and virtue desexed the subjects and made his statues ideal representations of beauty, collector's pieces for the public to ogle.

The most famous living beauty in Italy was also on public display in Naples towards the end of the century. Emma Hart, later Hamilton, specialised in living attitudes taken from statues, vases and legend, and no visit to the city was complete without an appearance at one of her displays. She was more of a 'must' than the Archbishop of Tarentum.[13] As she grew stouter, voluminous robes concealed the flesh and enhanced the emotions of serenity, voluptuousness, hatred or love that epitomised her chosen 'character' for the evening. She was assisted in her pantomimes by Charlotte-Louise-Eleanore-Adelaide de Boigne, the future wife of a grizzled old *condottiere* from India, the Savoyard Benoît de Boigne (1751–1830), who had been generalissimo to Mahadji Scindia's Maratha army.[14] On one occasion Emma took her, unceremoniously and without warning, by the hair and brandished a dagger. All present applauded, shouting '*Bravo la Medea*', 'Then clutching me to her bosom as if to ward off the anger of heaven, she drew from the same voices *Viva la Niobe*'.[15] Goethe certainly enjoyed the show, which he attended on two nights. Emma Hamilton, like Marilyn Monroe, started as a model and ended by marrying an intellectual, achieving her celebrity by the intelligent use of her pantomimic skills, encouraged by her ambassadorial lover. When Hamilton bought Emma from his indigent nephew, he was acting Pygmalion to his own collection of antiquities, bringing the beautiful images to life for carnal enjoyment. He had soon realised that her performances provided a frisson of pleasure to his visitors, otherwise quickly bored by a museum. Emma herself became an art object.[16] The male world of otherwise dusty antiques had become a woman's preserve at a time when women were beginning to undertake a grand tour of their own.

What was it that women expected from *Italia*? Readers of Ann Radcliffe may have leaned out of their prisons and thought of Italy (so that when they had finished the novel, they could lie back and think of England).[17] England still represented a social, intellectual and physical prison and to most women, slow to throw away the stays and hoops and other impediments to free and easy movement, Italy had the allure of liberation. Englishwomen might experience a Radcliffean adventure, one that did not entail real danger, more a frisson of the unexpected such as had excited Catherine Morland about Northanger Abbey. Denied a classical education, they were little interested in poking about ruins and examining the reputed homes of classical dignitaries (mostly male), unless, that is, they were Lady Mary Wortley Montagu – who was denied the pleasure of the antiquities of recently discovered Herculaneum because the king would not part with the key – or the second wife of the fifth Duke of Devonshire.[18] Many of them knew more Italian than their escorts and, encouraged by the greater freedoms that the French Revolution had encouraged women to demand, they applied themselves to arts they had hitherto practised in private. The most famous woman of the Romantic period in Italy, before Mary Shelley shot to fame with *Frankenstein*, was, however, make-believe. If Emma Hart was a beautiful but silent *improvvisatrice*, Germaine de Staël made her mouthpiece a famous and articulate one. Corinne, in her first appearances in the novel which bears her name, is on the Capitol, giving an improvised speech before the people of Rome. Her subject is the past and present state of Rome, a call to arms which sets the head of the Scottish nobleman in her audience spinning. Improvisers had been a feature of Italian poetic life for centuries. They amazed tourists, who, not always able to understand what was being improvised, were impressed by the conviction and passion of what poured out of the performer's mouth. Sydney Morgan assisted at a performance by Carlo di Negro in Genoa, whose speciality was to improvise sermons in *terza rima*, not without danger as he once fell foul of the ecclesiastical authorities.[19] But perhaps the most famous of the *improvvisatori* in Italy in the first quarter of the nineteenth century was Tommaso Sgricci (1789–1836), partly because of the notice Shelley and Byron took of him. Shelley first heard him in December 1820, improvising in Pisa upon the future independence of Italy; and Mary Shelley heard him soon afterwards in Lucca. Shelley described, in his far from immaculate Italian, a long 'improvisation' on the death of Hector, 'improvised' in the Pisa theatre. '*Mai non fu un esibizione*', he wrote, '*cosi maraviglioso della forza della umana mente; l'immaginazione del poeta pareva ch'agiva senza l'agiuto dell'intelletto, ed appena sembrava conscio delle parole ditate a lui da qualche superna possa.*' ('Never was there such a marvellous exhibition of the power of the human mind; it seemed that the imagination of the poet acted without the aid of his reason, and he scarcely seemed conscious of the words dictated to him by some superior power.')[20] The Shelleys were bowled over by the experience, which they treated as an exhibition of poetic bravura, even brilliance. Charlotte Eaton heard him improvise on the subject of *Medea*, which he had recently performed in Florence. As many of his auditors could have heard this, he gave an almost entirely different presentation. 'For four or five successive hours he continues to pour forth a flood of unpremeditated verse without the smallest hesitation or apparent effort and with far more ease than any of us could, after hard labour, recite a composition by rote.'[21] Byron was more reserved. According to Thomas Medwin, Byron warned Shelley that 'there is a great deal of knack in these gentry ... their poetry is more mechanical than you suppose'.[22] And being a 'celebrated Sodomite' Sgricci appealed especially to women who thought 'it as a pity in a man of talent', hoping that 'he may yet be converted to Adultery'.[23] The loose, almost conversational style of *Don Juan* may well have been influenced by his performance.

Corinne, too, was possessed by what Mary Shelley described as 'the deity who spoke within' her. As it poured from her, as it had from Sgricci, 'poetry was brilliant flowing & divine ... music eloquence & poetry were combined in this wonderful effort of the imagination – or rather ... the inspiration of some wondrous deity'. In 1802, Forsyth described the performance of another *improvvisatrice*, La Fantastici, who impressed him by 'her rapidity and command of numbers'. The poetry was pretty standard. Tired of demi-gods, Forsyth suggested the sofa as a subject for improvisation. Fantastici soon turned it into a Cytheran couch. In this he thought she sang as Homer might have sung![24] De Staël's Corinne, however, was an unlikely *improvvisatrice*, for she was only half Italian. Her father was a Scottish laird, and much of her upbringing had been in Northumberland. She was a mixture, therefore, of the two races de Staël admired, exhibiting the cosmopolitanism of a citizen of the world. There was, in fact, an *improvvisatrice* by the name of Corilla, born a peasant girl in Pistoia and blessed with a remarkable capacity for memorising and rhyming. She first engaged the heart of

16. *Girl Seated in a Romantic Gorge*, Richard Bonnington, charcoal, wash, sepia on paper (c. 1825). The Grand Tour had been largely a male thing, but after 1815 women were not content to be left at home.

the Marchese Ginori in Florence, and then of a certain monsignore in Rome, through whose influence she was crowned on the Capitol, like Corinne. She died in 1798. Charlotte Eaton thought the daughter of a comedy actor, Rosa Taddei, even better than Corilla, who was but a dunce compared to Rosa. Rosa could improvise on subjects like the expulsion of Adam and Eve from Eden, the parting of Titus from Berenice, Venus and Adonis, and the battle of Maxentius and Constantius (her weakest performance!).[25] Corinne, however, was the clothes horse upon which the garments of romantic disappoint-ment and tragedy were to be cast.[26] To circumspect English ladies, her freedom was suspect. French freedoms in Italy appeared gener-ally shocking: from the two French women at the Medical School in Bologna, who accompanied their escorts to see the anatomical mod-els in wax – 'for the credit of the nation we will hope that all her women are not devoid of decency' – to the woman who managed to climb to the topmost lantern of St Peter's dome with '*une grace incon-cevable*'. Eustace in his *Classical Tour* hoped 'no English lady will emulate such inconceivable grace'![27]

An English Corinne had already blazed her trail to Italy, the land of her second husband's birth, between 1785–6. For Hester Lynch Piozzi, formerly Dr Johnson's Mrs Thrale, it was not a Grand Tour, though she followed the path of Grand Tourists, for Piozzi was showing his wife the sights and introducing her to polite Italian society. Mrs Piozzi took a generally understanding and tolerant view of the customs and manners of her new husband's compatri-ots. After all, this was the man, a musician and a Roman Catholic, whom she loved, despite the consternation, even mockery of her friends, and she was disposed to find Italy and the Italians *simpatici*. She found the cooking excellent, she liked the healthy egalitarianism that existed between master and servant, making comprehensible the impertinences of a Figaro or a Leporello. 'Candour, and a good-humoured willingness to receive and reciprocate pleasure, seems indeed one of the standing virtues of Italy.' As an intellectual, and a friend of Dr Johnson, she had literary pretensions, and her *Observa-tions and Reflections of a Journey made into France, Italy and Germany* was not, like so many effusions from other English women who had travelled to Italy, just a travelogue, wrapped round social contacts with their own countrymen and women abroad.[28] Hester Piozzi penetrated Italian society, such as it was, being freely accepted into aristocratic *conversazioni*, and exercised a shrewd eye for quirky or quixotic behaviour, both among her fellow Englishmen, of whom she met many, and among Italians, of whom, being the wife of one, she met more than most.[29]

Unusually, for an Englishwoman, she could sympathise with the position of the young wife who was obliged to spend her leisure time in the presence of a *cavaliere servente*. The young woman

> had ventured to choose her own Partner, as all the others are disposed of in their Cradles; so I thought she might possibly remain true to her original Taste. 'What can I do replied She but follow the Crowd? my Husband will not go out into Company with me, nor sit an Hour Tête a Tête with his wife – *lest people should laugh at him.*'

She had no money of her own and her husband liked to see her dressed at someone else's expense.[30] She loved her husband and gained little from the institution of the *cavaliere servente*, 'except wearisome attentions from a man one cares little about', but it was the custom and custom was all.[31] Though spiritual advisers may not have liked it, they had to accept a convention that enriched the lives of couples ill-matched in their interests. After the birth of a son and heir, a respectably married woman was free to find her *cavaliere*; as 'a woman who has no *cavaliere servente* at all and makes her husband her companion, is despised and ridiculed by all her female acquaintance', her parents, who had arranged the original match, might find him for her.[32] The French director of the Paris observatory, Joseph Lalande (1732–1807), found the custom unexceptional. Deprived of choice over whom one might marry, '*chaqu'un se content de la dame qu'il sert*'.[33] Edward Williams, Shelley's companion on their last fatal voyage, heard of an amorous Venetian widow of 72, who fell for a young Swede. Not wishing to upset her *cavaliere servente* of more than 30 years, who was himself getting on in years, she married the *cavaliere*, and allowed the attentive Swede to take his place.[34] Sydney Morgan, who encountered the institution of *cavaliere servente* in Genoa, where he was known as a *patito*, or sufferer (for love), put the institution down to Jesuit education which had rendered young men 'ignorant and feeble and threw them on gallantry and gambling for their sole occupation and resource'.[35] Mary Shelley summed up the fate of affluent couples in Italy in her short story 'The Trial of Love', which ends with a couple living 'the usual life of Italian husband and wife. He was gay, inconstant, careless; she consoled herself with a cavalier servente.'[36]

The tourist in the post-bellum years may well have read *Corinne*, but more accessible were the notes of a lively Irishwoman, writing a popular account of Italy for money, and already much quoted. Lady Morgan, née Sydney Owenson, produced her three-volume account of *Italy* in 1821. Like Hester Piozzi's *Observations*, it was part guide book, part diary, part showing off, describing all the grand houses she had visited and dinners she had eaten. Sydney Owenson (1783/5–1859) had some of the attraction and liveliness of Emma Hart. Born in Dublin and brought up in the bohemian company of her father's friends, she made the most of the education she received in a variety of Dublin schools, and danced, sang and played the harp, becoming the belle of many a party. Her father having got his affairs into a muddle and needing financial support, she began to write, having seen how well Fanny Burney had managed to make a living from her pen. Her novels all had Irish settings, like Maria Edgeworth's, but were much more overtly nationalist, one of them, *The Novice of St Dominick* (1805), providing William Pitt's deathbed reading. Owenson was taken into the household of the Marquis of Abercorn as a social companion to his wife, acquired some of the graces of high society and was then, under strong prompting by the marchioness, who found her charms disturbing, married to the marquis's doctor, for whom the marquis obligingly obtained a knighthood. Lady Morgan needed no longer to write defensively; her next Irish novels were intensely 'patriotic', and when the war ended she was off to visit France and Italy. She traded on her title, as Hester Piozzi had on her Italian husband, to gain entrée into polite society and meet intellectuals and, like Hester, she boasted of her entry into the salons of Italian intellectuals and implied that it was her profound knowledge of Italian culture which attracted them to her.[37] She decided that the 'stormy, bustling tyranny' of France's occupation chiefs in Italy was infinitely preferable to the 'lethargic, lumbering despotism which under Austrian and Papal governments converted a paradise into a desert'.[38] The Austrians (she meant the Habsburgs but never referred to the dynasty, only the nation) were the enemy, and had been ever since the middle ages. Austrian rulers had clamped the Inquisition onto the chivalry and pride of old Castile, the faggot and sword of the Austrian oppressor had afflicted the Low Countries and degraded and barbarised Naples, just as England had Ireland.[39] Byron, who despised women writers on the country on which he was establishing a monopoly of wisdom, was forced to praise *Italy* as 'fearless and excellent'.[40] Too much so. It was banned as seditious in the Kingdom of Sardinia; this was hardly surprising when Lady Morgan had described the king, also self-styled monarch of Jerusalem and Cyprus as 'the King of Anchovies'. Her account of his return, after the social upheavals of French occupation and government by Napoleon's brother-in-law, the Prince Borghese, was not unfair. Vittorio Emmanuele I had spent the war in the island of Sardinia and determined to restore his kingdom to what it was before the war, entering 'his good city of Turin, habited in the same costume, with the same peruke, and the same prejudices, in which he had left it'. He was accompanied by 'a little army of tin soldiers which he had daily exercised in the Queen's dressing room'.[41] Morgan's book was also banned in the Papal States and in all Austrian territories, but it sold well in England, where the feisty national spirit of the author was admired. She followed it with a life of Salvator Rosa, written in the style of Roscoe with much learning and little enlightenment. Like most Irish writers, if they wanted to get on at all, she was a Protestant, and dutifully described the medieval Church as 'founded in sacrifice, enforced by persecution, with terror in its spring, and human degradation for its object, dark, despotic, exclusive and sanguinary'! But she was sympathetic to the ordinary Catholic faithful and the simple priests. She disliked prelacy, both Protestant and Catholic and clerical rule, stating that the Archbishop of Canterbury was richer than the pope and that the Protestant Prince Bishop of Durham was worth at least ten Italian bishops![42] She was far from unsympathetic to the condition of Roman Catholics in her native island; as far as she could observe only the Irish revered the papacy, as the Italians certainly did not.[43] As for nuns, she believed the denizens of the Turkish seraglio were just as much victims of the tyranny of man, both equally violating Nature's laws.[44] In 1850 she was to engage in a pamphlet war with Cardinal Wiseman over the pretensions of the see of Rome.

Despite her opinion that Leo X was the arch-traitor of that family of parricides, the Medici of Florence, Sydney Morgan was a good disciple of Roscoe and she bustled about in the art and history of the Renaissance. When she took her head out of the guide books, she could be both shrewd and understanding of the Italian people.[45] She was quick to understand that the gold and silver ornaments of the peasants were not evidence of idle wealth or squandered improvidence, for they were carrying their assets about their person as there was no other way to bank them or lay them out in profitable speculation. Gold and silver were always good in an emergency and held their value.[46] Her essay on the characteristics of the *Trasteverini* in Rome is a small classic,[47] and she was to prove more percipient than many better-qualified politicians. Of Austrian-ruled Italy and those states ruled by Austrian satellites, she prophesied, rightly, that

> these additions to the Imperial crown will ... be of no avail in supporting Austria against the usurpation either of France or Russia; but rather will paralyze its military movements, by the known disaffection of the Italians to their masters. As a balance of power, therefore, the act of political cruelty which thus enslaved the Italians ... will eventually prove vain.[48]

She had no doubt that the epoch of Italy's deliverance would come.[49] Throughout her long work she made constant comparison between the efficient despotism of the French, when Bonapartists ruled Italy, and the dead hand of the Austrians, whose rule was 'pure and unmixed despotism, ... a studied and designed aggregation of every abuse that can tend to desolate and oppress, to break the spirit of the species, to damp industry and to quench hope'.[50] The two chapters devoted to Austrian rule in Lombardy in her first volume are full of comparisons to British rule in Ireland.

Sydney Morgan's feminine empathies were never far from the surface. She had had no classical training, had been reared in the oppressive colonialism of Dublin and had no male admiration for the Romans of old. Ancient Rome offended her for its glorification of arrogance, as she apostrophised the abuse of power while contemplating the Tarpeian Rock from which felons and traitors were hurled; she mocked the boast that modern Rome had ever been the instrument for communicating those great blessings of civilisation, science and religion, after seeing the 'tin noses and wooden legs, old wigs and woollen petticoats', with which statues were decked in the Pantheon; she could not enthuse about any of the monuments to male power and cruelty. 'Here is no resting place for hope of man's amendment, of the diminution of his sum of suffering, his mass of error – all here is monumental to his folly or his crime, his credulity or his imposture.'[51]

Indeed, Lady Morgan enjoyed being contumacious, challenging the accepted opinions and looking for the perverse and unexpected. Her colourful, if basically uninformative, life of Salvator Rosa reflected this interest in disorder for its own sake, a protest against the protective world in which men wished to cocoon their women.[52]

Italy abounded with feminine images, apart from Radcliffean dam-
sels in distress (for the most part heroines of opera), the most
common being images of Our Lady. In addition there were smooth
anatomical hills, lambent lakes, gaudily dressed *contadine*, nuns, *cav-
alieri serventi*, coffee houses patronised by women, suggestive cakes
and biscuits, aphrodisiac *canzoni*, swooning arias. *Italia* was a she,
not a staid Britannia but a conspiratorial Rosina; not a fierce strum-
pet like Marianne, but a passionate maidservant like Susanna, not a
Gretchen but a Madonna and child. Men had raped *Italia*, women
now wooed her. They came to sympathise and understand. Charlotte Eaton, visiting Rome in the immediate aftermath of the war,
surprisingly reproved the French for their archaeological rearrange-
ments round the Colosseum, preferring to be impressed by the
symbols of decay 'of a city that has successively been the temporal
and spiritual tyrant of the world'. Gazing at the Forum, she saw the
'fall of tyrants' and 'the contrast of past greatness with present
degradation', and mused that 'man is great only when he is free,
that true glory does not consist in the mere possession of
unbounded power or extended empire, but in the diffusion of
knowledge, justice and civilisation', sentiments that were beginning
to fire the rulers of India, whose Romantic impulses had not yet
been crabbed by utilitarianism.[53] The women's interest in Italy was
different from that of their menfolk. The feminisation of ideas about
Italy made it seem less likely than ever that the men would rise to
throw off tyranny by violent action and provoked a very male moral
reaction. As attitudes under the influence of the evangelical revival
and the challenge of Tractarian Catholicism hardened, it seemed
that the women who had written about Italy had too easily identified with the loose morals and infantile religion that they described.
By 1827 one father was quoted as never having met or heard of any
man who 'did not loathingly recoil from the idea of matching himself with any girl who had gone the round of Italy'.[54] Even poetry
came under suspicion. The discovery that Petrarch's Laura may
have been a respectably married lady with many children or, worse,
'a matron so prolific that she was delivered of eleven illegitimate
children', and that her 'amorous swain'[55] was a corpulent cleric,
short of breath, cast a shadow over the *Canzoni di Vita di Madonna
Laura*, so admired by Shelley, and over his leman, Laura de Sade,
who had become an icon for the Romantics. While Dante was associated with his robust defence of dying liberty, Petrarch had been
content to accept servitude to an unattainable woman, thus prepar-

ing 'the inglorious heritage of servitude for the next fifteen generations'.[56] Byron was more brutal. 'I detest the Petrarch so much, that I would not be the man even to have obtained his Laura, which the metaphysical, whining dotard never could.'[57]

By the 1840s, the men and women who had visited Italy were both agreed on one thing. Whatever greatness the Italians had once enjoyed, they were not worthy of it any more, and unlikely on recent evidence to achieve greatness again. Of course they should be free and, possibly, united, but how, and were they capable of sustaining either freedom or unity? That very feminine nature which Italy's women visitors had applauded meant that Italians needed the rule of firm men, but not the brutal tyrannies from which they mostly suffered. One woman deplored this image. Elizabeth Barrett Browning when she thought about this, gazing out of the Casa Guidi windows, believed that the portrayal of a suffering woman ruined by her own beauty, the myth of *Italia*

> ... childless among mothers,
> Widow of empires, ay, and scarce refrained
> Cursing her beauty to her face, as brothers
> Might a shamed sister's – Had she been less fair
> She were less wretched,

merely trivialised the cause of Italian freedom.[58] It suggested that only an external liberator could free her. Until then, like pale Hibernia, an *Italia* of the north, which nestled under the benevolent armour of stern Britannia, she should find a protector, preferably not Marianne, and not the licentious Hun, but whom?

11

'Thou Crimson Herald of the Dawn'

Italians Arise

For this was the theatre of the world in its spring glory. It was the school of man where he passed from infancy to maturity. That season has gone by – His strength is decayed – He has fallen into old age – Now time itself, nor fate can make another Rome. The phoenix shall never rise from its ashes – Rome is no more!

Charlotte Eaton, *Rome in the Nineteenth Century* (1820), i, p. 147.

> *Sei pur bella cogli astri sul crine*
> *Che scintillan quai vivi zaffiri*
> *É pur dolce quel fiato che spiri,*
> *Porporina foriera del di.*

> [Thou art fair with the stars in thy locks
> Sparkling like living sapphires,
> And sweet is thy breath,
> Thou crimson herald of the dawn.]

Gabriele Rossetti, saluting the 1821 constitution in Naples.[1]

> I heard last night a little child go singing
> 'Neath Casa Guidi windows , by the Church
> *O bella libertà, O bella!* – stringing
> The same words still on notes he went in search
> So high for, ...
> And that the heart of Italy must beat
> While such a voice had leave to rise serene
> 'Twixt church and palace of a Florence street.

Elizabeth Barrett Browning, 'Casa Guidi Windows',
part II , strophes 1–10.

Between the publication of Sydney Morgan's *Italy* (1821) and of
Charles Dickens's *Pictures from Italy* (1844) nothing very much
seemed to have changed. Lady Morgan's long narrative, punctuated
with large slices of the history, legends, art and letters of *Italia*, had
recorded a dismal picture of the life of her inhabitants. The only
parts of the peninsula that showed any dynamism were those that
had, until recently, been governed by the French. Otherwise the
dead hand of Austrian rule stifled Milan and the rest of Lombardy,
while reaction ruled in those ancient fiefs restored to princes (with
the exception of Tuscany) both benighted and frightened. The religious orders had been restored, and what social and industrial
change had been inaugurated by the French was in full decline. Sydney Morgan's description of Piacenza (which inspired a long
reflection on the state of her native Ireland where the peasant, 'the
happiest class of the Italian population', suffered even greater degradation) will do for the rest of Italy. 'To judge by its silent empty
streets and dismantled edifices, it seemed to have been lately swept
by pestilence, or depopulated by famine.'[2] Adjectives like sad, old,
mean, miserable, hopeless, dirty, lazy, dreary, mouldering, pepper
the text (these all appear within ten pages of consecutive prose).
From time to time (as in Modena) 'rays of intellectual lustre have
played over the gloom of that saddened land, like the lightnings of a
summer night; the more brilliant, the denser the clouds through
which they penetrate'.[3] Otherwise the population of the capital of an
Italian provincial despotism consisted of monks, friars, soldiers,
chained galley-slaves and begging nuns.[4]

Twenty-three years after Morgan, Charles Dickens spent a year in
Italy, feeling that he needed a break after the comparative failure of
Martin Chuzzlewit and the runaway success of his first three *Christ-
mas Books*. Unashamedly he made no attempt, as had Sydney
Morgan at inordinate length, to reproduce information freely available to his readers in the host of guide books. Artists and their works
were barely mentioned. He bowed once to the contemporary icons
of art and referred to GUIDO, DOMENICHINO and LUDOVICO
CARACCI (in capital letters) as being among the sights of Bologna,[5]
and in defiance of educated taste called the works of Bernini and his
school 'the most detestable class of productions in the wide world'.
He abominated the drapery blown inside out, the veins as big as a
forefinger, the hair a nest of lively snakes.[6] Even Shelley had
thought that Michelangelo lacked any sense of 'moral dignity and
loveliness', finding no majesty in *The Last Judgement* fresco in the

Sistine Chapel and rating him wholly inferior to Raphael. Visitors to Italy at this time were barely interested in the artists who preceded the sainted Raffaello Santi, and passed, for example, through Padua without visiting Giotto's frescos in the Arena Chapel; until the Rossettis 'discovered' them, the pre-Raphaelites were ignored.

Dickens's trained and eager eye turned almost wholly on the present, and the Italian present, for the most part, depressed him, just as present-day India depresses travellers for whom poverty and squalor conceal the brilliance of an alien culture. Sydney Morgan had found the palaces of the Genoese aristocracy virtually standing ruins, with floors hired out to mattress cleaners and laundresses, cobblers and stocking-grafters. Dickens did not like to conjecture what went on inside the multiplicity of storeys and their labyrinth of rooms.[7] Like Sydney Morgan before him, he found Piacenza 'a brown decayed old town, ... A deserted, solitary, grass-grown place, with ruined ramparts, half filled up trenches'.[8] Ferrara was 'more solitary, more deserted ... The grass grows up in the silent streets, [so] that anyone might make hay there, literally, while the sun shines'. Tivoli was squalid, and Albano's wine had not improved since the days of Horace. Like Morgan's, Dickens's adjectives – sleepy, ruined, decayed, dark, dirty, deserted, melancholy – were put to work regularly. All that penetrated this drabness were the colourful people, at market, at work, at festa, in church: 'drowsy masses, curling incense, tinkling bells, priests in bright vestments: pictures, tapers, laced altar cloths, crosses, images and artificial flowers'. Otherwise the church ceremonies are 'tedious and wearisome'.[9] *Italia* it is; Italy, as a dynamic modern society it is not.

There was one wavering but hopeful exception to this picture of gloom. Under her benevolent grand dukes, Florence seemed like an oasis of reasonable government, an Italianised Austria rather than an Austrianised *Italia*. Leigh Hunt loved the good-natured, intelligent inhabitants and admired the reigning family, 'Austrians but with a difference, long Italianised, and with no great family affection'.[10] The city relied on the fabulous collection of buildings and art that established it as the showroom of Renaissance art. A relatively efficient and stable agricultural economy allowed cheap living, and its aristocrats were prosperous enough not to have to let out their palazzi as in Venice and Naples, or to bother much about the foreign residents who could find spacious apartments at reasonable cost, like the Brownings, whose apartment in Casa Guidi was/is large enough to house whole companies of Eton schoolboys on school excursions, or like Landor's family, who rented a villa in the neighbourhood of Boccaccio's plague refuge in *The Decameron*, at Maiano. Florence was an oasis of expatriates, an enclosed, liverish sort of place, where visitors lived on communal gossip. Byron spent very little time there, his first visit lasting only a day, hotfoot as he was for Rome; but he fitted in a sight of the Venuses, both the Medicean, more to be admired than loved, and Canova's, and both of whom left him 'drunk with beauty'. He found the '"entusimusy" [i.e. enthusiasm]' of his fellow tourists, however, a form of cant, and the nearest that he could later be persuaded to live to the city was Pisa.[11] The tribute to the Etrurian Athens in *Childe Harold* is almost perfunctory, and he leaves to the 'vile breath' of *entusimusiasts* to describe the undescribable.[12]

'Entusimusy' may have been one of the vices of the English who lived in Florence, where it seemed easy to study Italy's great past in comfort and cheaply, without being deafened by the resonance of Ancient Rome. The grand duke was ready to keep that climate peaceful and benign as long as people recognised their advantages and refrained from revolutionary intrigue. He was ready to receive the Gambas when their activities eventually had them expelled from papal territory, but he could not tolerate the sort of affray in which Byron, Shelley and Trelawny were embroiled, which involved the nearly mortal attack on a Tuscan guardsman with a pitchfork.

To nearly every English visitor, a people whose peasantry alone inspired any warmth of feeling was unlikely to live up to its past. Whatever had inspired its greatness then had vanished beyond recovery. By the time Dickens had finished with the Italians, his readers had been persuaded to give up on them too, or rather on the governments that had reduced them to such misery. The residents of the peninsula scarcely deserved to be called Italians and, indeed, as late as 1855 he referred to the human flotsam in Marseilles harbour as 'Hindoos, Russians, Chinese, Spaniards, Portuguese, Englishmen, Frenchmen, *Genoese, Neapolitans, Venetians*, Greeks, Turks, descendants of all the builders of Babel'.[13] Like Indians, Italians had no nationality. It was time to turn to the other 'geographical expression' of contemporary Europe, that was also showing signs of looking for unity and great power status, and gave greater promise of succeeding: Germany.

Despite the existence in Britain of a general conviction that Italians deserved better than the oppressive nightmare that, for all liberal-minded people, characterised the administration in

Austrian-held Italy, the Papal States and the Kingdom of the Two Sicilies, there was little hope that much could be done about it. Mazzini's solution of a loose union of independent republics was acceptable to none of the monarchical states of Europe, including Great Britain. His followers, moreover, did not speak for an Italy accustomed to throne and altar, and the notion that Italian states could be brought under one ruler barely crossed the mind of international politicians. How could an, admittedly very limited, parliamentary democracy like the Kingdom of Sardinia join a papal theocracy, and how could either act in common with an ancient, completely separate kingdom like that of Naples? The most optimistic solution for any hope of unity was a federation between a north Italy ruled by the House of Savoy in equal partnership with the papacy and the Bourbons in Naples, each endowed with a reasonably democratic constitution.[14]

But as late as 1844 the chief minister of the Kingdom of Sardinia still dismissed the prospect of Italian unity as a dream of 'schoolboys, fifth-rate poets and stump orators'.[15] Italians had, in 1821 and 1830-1, not shown that they could change their own condition, partly because the liberals came from minor noble or middle-class stock, and were as fearful of the democratic daemon as was Metternich himself. High-flown sentiment was one thing, but when, in 1820, that democratic daemon popped out of the bottle into which it had been hopefully stoppered, it proved to have little more than operatic, even pantomimic powers. The Spanish revolution of July that year stirred a kingdom which had always had close Spanish links, the hidden liberals in Naples came out in strength, parading a black, red and blue tricolour, representing God, the king and the constitution, and led by a self-confessed *carbonaro*. The palace bowed its head and introduced the Spanish constitution pretty well unchanged. Gabriele Rossetti, *improvvisatore*, poet, musician and painter, and father of a murmur of singing birds, hailed it as a sign that 'in the balmy garden of Italy servitude is at an end'.

Rossettian rhetoric and the almost childish projects dreamed up in secret meetings were no match for royal perfidy and Austrian decisiveness. Metternich announced that revolution in Naples could not be allowed to succeed and, when the constitutional army met the Austrian, assembled from its various Italian garrisons, it was routed at Rieti on 7 March 1821. Two weeks later the white-coats marched into Naples. Gabriele Rossetti, whose friends included the wife of the admiral of the British squadron stationed in the bay, went aboard its flagship dressed as a British naval officer and into exile in England.[16] He was the lucky one. Very soon the prisons were full of those who had supported the constitution, kept in conditions of barbarous inhumanity – the only mercy being that Ferdinand II, who had actually sworn to uphold it, did not resort massively to the death penalty.

The Spanish constitution also inspired similar excitement in Turin. There an assembly of aristocrats and officers hoped that the heir to the throne, Carlo Alberto, dubbed by Mazzini as 'the Italian Hamlet', would put himself at the head of a constitution. But, despite a long nurtured hatred of Austria, the prince's sobriquet proved only too well deserved and, unable to put himself at the head of rebellion, he accepted exile instead, and the constitutionalists were crushed by Austrian troops who had crossed the Ticino into the kingdom. A mother and son at Genoa watched their tattered remnants trying to board ship for Spain, where the constitution was still in existence. When one of them begged for money for the exiles of Italy from the son, Giuseppe Mazzini, 'for the first time ... there was vaguely presented to my mind, I will not say the thought of country and of liberty, but the thought that it was possible, and therefore a duty, to fight for the freedom of one's country'.[17] Dickens records a story of one who did fight. An English friend of his visited one of the defeated, a condemned galley-slave, imprisoned near Genoa. Disgusted at the conditions in which he was held, he determined to secure his release. 'If the prisoner had been a brigand and a murderer, if he had committed every non-political crime in the Newgate calendar and out of it, nothing would have been easier than for a man of any court or priestly influence to obtain his release.'[18] But he succeeded only at the cost of £150. Dickens called on him in either 1845 or 1853 to deliver a message from his benefactor. The gratitude of the released man was a demijohn of wine, which Dickens carried home with him to England without losing or spilling a drop, his adventures with which were the subject of his tale.

For a time the Italian dream of unity still flickered on in England. Unlike the continental powers, she welcomed Italian exiles, and was ready to allow Mazzini, as a refugee, to operate freely from her shores in support of republican but abortive insurrections all over the peninsula. The Paris rising of 1830 that hustled out the last of the Bourbons had sparked risings in Parma, Modena, Bologna and the Marches, but they had all fizzled out, more examples of failure to combine and plan. For the next sixteen years, Mazzini flitted from one safe haven to the next, promoting his *Giovane Italia*, and writing the textbooks of liberation from the safety of a schoolroom in Eastbourne. When in 1844 it was revealed that Prince Metternich had successfully requested the British government to put Mazzini under surveillance and to relay information to Vienna, public outrage at such an abuse of hospitality to a refugee gave the Italian question a new and factitious importance. Mazzini, of whose existence the British home secretary had until that moment been in ignorance, became a national figure. Questions were asked why Austria tyrannised over lands south of the Alps, when her national interests lay so patently in *mitteleurop* and in the Balkans, and why Italy should not be united and free?

It was only with the accession of 'the liberal pope', Pius IX, in 1846 that hope suddenly blazed into life. At his invitation, Lord John Russell despatched his son-in-law, Lord Minto, to advise the pope on reform; the mission was not productive of any good but, as the son of a former governor-general of India, he advised His Holiness to encourage an Italian customs union, which had worked to unite India, otherwise as much a patchwork of independent states as Italy. Pius allowed elected politicians to form a government in Rome, and two years later constitutions were promulgated once more in the kingdoms of Naples and Sardinia and for the first time in the Habsburg-ruled Grand Duchy of Tuscany The grand duke, partly persuaded by Lord Minto's Italian mission, freed the press and authorised the formation of that constitutional prerequisite, a civic guard. To discourage counter-democratic action, which might lead to a conflagration, the ubiquitous British Royal Navy was licensed to cruise off Italian shores. Yet, when the citizens of Milan rose against the Austrians and Carlo Alberto of Sardinia and Savoy, back on the throne and a constitutional monarch of a few months' standing, invaded the Milanese, the British government, with the principal exception of Lord Palmerston, disapproved. This was armed intervention, which it was British policy to discourage. When, in July, Carlo Alberto was trounced at Custozza and the Austrians reoccupied Milan, even ministers sympathetic to Italian freedom were relieved that the Sardinian action had failed. Consent, not force, was expected to be the basis of Italian unity.

There was one English poet who was not in agreement with this polite fiction, looking out on her new world through the windows of her Florentine apartment, from which she heard a child singing '*O bella libertà*', words then on everybody's lips.[19] Elizabeth Barrett and Robert Browning moved into Casa Guidi in August 1847, just in time to witness the public enthusiasm that greeted the creation of the civic guard.[20] Was this the first fruit outside Rome of the election of a liberal pope, the dawn of a new hope? Elizabeth Barrett could not find it in her to think so, partly because she disliked the Roman Catholic Church, partly because she could not believe in the professed liberalism of an Italian pontiff – 'a bondman shivering at a Jesuit's foot' was not likely 'to stand a freedman at a despot's, and dispute / His titles by the balance in his hand / Weighing them "suo jure"' – she dismissed this hope as a phantom.[21] How could a man in his position dismantle the edifice upon which his authority was built? What Italy needed was a Reformation, a dissolution, not a strengthening of the demands of this

> ... popedom – the despair
> Of free men, good men, wise men, the dread shows
> Of women's faces, by the faggots flash
> Tossed out, to the minutest stir and throb
> O'er the white lips, the least tremble of a lash,
> To glut the red stare of a licensed mob.[22]

Constitutional government, to Elizabeth Barrett's open satisfaction, turned to ashes in Rome when the pope fled, unable to lead an Italian crusade against a power so Roman Catholic as Austria, and a short-lived Roman Republic was declared by Mazzini. The republican forces, under Giuseppe Garibaldi, conducted a brilliant but forlorn defence against armies sent by France, Austria and Naples to restore Pius to his throne. The sympathy of England, even of *The Times*, was all with his gallant little band of defenders, but the revolutions across Europe had badly frightened governments that, only with difficulty, re-established control. Even the British felt it necessary to imprison the Chartist leaders before the movement got out of hand and London imitated Milan, Paris, Rome, Vienna, Budapest, Naples and Berlin. Authoritarian rule was brutally restored throughout Italy, and a free Italian state seemed as far away as ever. Through the Casa Guidi windows the Brownings watched the despair of the Florentines as the grand duke, having fled the whirlwind his benevolence seemed to have released, rode back behind Austrian troops.[23]

Elizabeth Barrett did not lose hope. Though the cry was up in England for an end to risings and commissions, and for the pursuit of peace, what was that but

> ... a treason, stiff with doom,
> 'Tis gagged despair and inarticulate wrong,
> Annihilated Poland, stifled Rome,
> Dazed Naples, Hungary fainting 'neath the thong.[24]

She might as well shut the windows of Casa Guidi, if they opened on nothing that brought any comfort. It was necessary to find a new myth to keep Italian aspirations alive. Despite the scepticism of Arthur Hugh Clough, who was in Rome for the latter days of the republic and saw only 'ashes and dirt and ill odor' in the epic battle for an Italian nationhood,[25] the defence of the Roman Republic seemed to have re-enacted the defence by Horatius Cocles of the Tiber Bridge, the echoes of which had resounded round British drawing rooms since Macaulay had published his *Lays of Ancient Rome* in 1842. Distantly, through the still-open window, Elizabeth Barrett could see two causes of hope, one a gaunt, bereaved warrior who had lost his wife in the joint cause of *bella libertà*, the other a king, the heir to Carlo Amletico, of a state where the constitution had survived the years of revolution. 'Poets are soothsayers still, like those of old' and the sooth she was saying in her last strophe was to the infant Pen Browning, asleep in his cot. A child had sung at the beginning of her poem. Two years later a child slept. He it was who, grown to man's estate, might see that *bella libertà* finally won.[26]

However, before the myth of the heroic monarch could be created, there had to be the myth of the heroic sufferer for liberty. Revolutions in 1821, 1830 and 1848 had provided a ready supply of political prisoners, nowhere more so than in Naples, where they lay, double-chained to common felons in dungeons where the air was so noxious that doctors refused to minister to those who were sick, unless they were brought up for treatment. In 1850, one tourist, eschewing the amusements, volcanoes and excavated cities he had visited twelve years before, visited instead the local prisons. William Gladstone had come to Naples in the hope that his daughter's eyesight might be improved by clear air and sunshine; he had enough Italian to talk late into the nights with the British embassy's legal adviser who persuaded him to sit in on the trial of Carlo Poerio (1803–67), the brother of a famous patriot who had died in the defence of the Venetian Republic in 1848. In the brief constitutional interlude of 1848, Carlo Poerio had served as Neapolitan minister of education, but resigned when he realised that the king had no intention of carrying out any resolution passed by the assembly. When this was dissolved in 1849, Poerio was arrested. Gladstone listened to the crown witness pile perjury on perjury until a 'prostitute' court sentenced the ex-minister to 24 years in chains. Disturbed by what he heard about the conditions in which respectable middle-class liberals were being held, Gladstone sought and obtained permission to visit some of them. The horrors he encountered disturbed him greatly, but not as much as the 'illegality which seems to be the foundation of the Neapolitan system'.[27]

Back in London in 1851, Gladstone proposed to stir up international outrage. Palmerston had already warned Vienna that the excesses of Neapolitan reaction could only encourage good men to support any means of redressing its evils, and now he seemed, to anxious Conservatives, ready to countenance revolution. At the Foreign Office, Lord Aberdeen, sensing that he had no more chance of stopping Gladstone from publishing his criticisms of the 'negation of God erected into a system of government', than he had of putting out the fires of Vesuvius and Etna, decided to try Gladstone's critique on the Austrian chancellor.[28] Prince Schwarzenberg replied with a *tu quoque* list of British infringements of personal liberty in the Ionian islands, Ceylon, Ireland and, even nearer home, in England.[29] Disgusted with his 'idle dissertations and recriminations', Gladstone launched his thunderbolt. He published his letter to Aberdeen on the state of oppression in Naples, following it up with further evidence two weeks later.

Its effect was instantaneous. The Society of Friends of Italy invited him to become a member; letters from Italian exiles all over Europe breathed renewed hope, women composed odes to the *generoso Britanno*, and *difensore d'un popolo gemente* (generous Briton, defender of a groaning people). The British liberal press took up his cause, fuelled by the contemporary hatred of the papacy that had not only compounded an act of aggression against England in 1850 by nominating Cardinal Wiseman to a new Roman Catholic see of Westminster, but was also patron of the wicked Neapolitan king. Palmerston ordered copies of Gladstone's letter to be sent to all British embassies in Europe and refused to accompany it by the official Neapolitan refutation, consisting of 'a flimsy tissue of bare assertions and reckless denials, mixed up with coarse ribaldry and commonplace abuse'.[30]

The immediate effect was not helpful to the prisoners themselves. King Ferdinand may or may not have known what was being done in his name for, when Antonio Panizzi, Chief Librarian at the British Museum – who throughout his career there had kept up a constant correspondence with Italian exiles, and who had influential friends in Lord Brougham and Macaulay – told him, he could not bear to listen. '*Addio, terribile Panizzi*', he screeched.[31] Only when Poerio looked like dying in prison was he released with 66 other politicals into exile in America. He was put ashore, however, by the American captain at Queenstown in Ireland to join the other free Mazzinians on British soil. In 1860 Poerio returned to Italy to become a deputy in the Turin parliament and later its speaker. Yet for all his active sympathies, Gladstone was no convert to the concept of a free and united Italy. Who, after all, was to unite it? The most he hoped for was that the Kingdom of the Two Sicilies might be shamed into reform, a forlorn hope until its liberation by Garibaldi ten years after Gladstone's visit.

The revelation that the British government had spied upon a guest in their midst and Gladstone's letter to Lord Aberdeen were the catalysts that transformed a literary and cultural sympathy for the woes of Italy into a resolve to achieve their improvement by some direct action. But such action was to fall very short of war, and the antics of Cavour at the peace congress which followed the Crimean War seriously alarmed Whitehall. Suspicion of the ambitions of Napoleon III reined in any enthusiasm for direct action to liberate the Italian provinces from Austrian rule. When, in 1859, the French did go to war with Austria in Italy, even Italophiles argued over what would be the best possible result: the limited accession of the Milanese to Sardinia, so that a powerful, constitutional Piedmont ruled from the Alps to the Adriatic, or a federation of north, central and south Italy under their historic rulers. Events, however, were not to be controlled. Cavour had taken France as his protector, secretly ceding Nice and Savoy to the French in return for military intervention. Furious at the proposed amputation of his birthplace from a resurgent Italy, Garibaldi defied Cavour and led his last and greatest filibuster to liberate the people of Sicily. Suddenly, unification of the whole country became a possibility, when 'the Thousand', the '*Mille*', now expanded to a sizeable national army under Garibaldi, crossed over to the mainland and met the Sardinian army of Vittorio Emmanuele II on the banks of the Volturno in October 1860, and proclaimed the two kingdoms one. A kingdom in thrall neither to France nor to Austria, a new make-weight in the power struggles of Europe, was born.

The British had provided all support short of actual help to Garibaldi's expedition. The French nation shed blood for Italy but no Briton sailed with the *Mille* to fight for Garibaldi in Sicily. No British ship was actually engaged in defence of the Garibaldian landing, but Britain managed to scoop the tribute of history as the natural friend and ally of the new kingdom. Garibaldi's regard for the English was ambivalent.

> Being egotists and conquerors ... their history overflows with crimes. Many are the peoples whom they have enclosed in their iron coils in order to satisfy their insatiable thirst for gold and domination; but I cannot deny that they have contributed enormously to human progress and to laying the foundations of individual dignity, and they present a picture of a man standing upright, inflexible and majestic in the face of all the compelling exigencies that govern the human race.

The speaker is Clelia, in Garibaldi's anti-clerical novel of that name who, in resisting the amorous attentions of a cardinal, teams up with Julia, a young English aristocrat studying in Rome and in love with an Italian. The novel ends with the 'martyrdom' of their two lovers in Rome after the failure of Garibaldian liberation in 1867 and the departure of the two girls to England where they will wait for Rome to be freed from the priestly plague.[32]

Private English money poured into the Garibaldian cause; the landing at Marsala was indirectly assisted by the presence of a British naval detachment ashore, which might have been harmed had the Neapolitan warships opened fire; British naval officers barely concealed their support for the land attack on Palermo, protesting at the bombardment of the city by the Neapolitan squadron; volunteers flocked to the standards once they were ashore. The British refused to join an international coalition to prevent the invasion of Calabria, and an Englishman served to confuse the enemy by impersonating Garibaldi as his double. The final collapse of the Bourbon Kingdom of the Two Sicilies was seen as historical justice, and the fact that it had been achieved, not by the slippery Cavour, with a state army and his own political agenda, but by a force of volunteers dedicated to the simple idea of Italy's resurrection (*risorgimento*) made it all the more acceptable to Liberal and Tory alike. The

Italians had done what no one believed them capable of doing, and had unified most of their country. Great Britain's was the first government to recognise the new kingdom of Italy, proclaimed from Florence in 1861. She had done little positive to bring about this result but remained benevolently neutral and, when the Royal Navy had cast, as it were, a protective mantle upon the new nation, it ensured a special relationship between the two nations until the Fascist period. The glorification of Garibaldi in England, not at all welcome to Cavour, and his subsequent beatification by George Macaulay Trevelyan, completed the acceptance of Italy as an equal partner, conceived as an unlikely ideal by those second generation romantic poets. The English establishment on the occasion of Garibaldi's triumphal visit to London was, despite public excitation, less than wholly enthusiastic about a man most of whose life had been spent in acts of rebellion. His anti-clericalism worried the queen, the fact that he had brought into the Italian nation a rogue state like the Two Sicilies upset Disraeli and caused even the fervent Palmerston some anxiety. But such reservations were drowned in the applause.

12

Finale

Tempus Abire Tibi Est

O thou newcomer who seek'st Rome in Rome
And find'st in Rome no thing thou canst call Roman;
Arches worn old and palaces made common,
Rome's name alone within these walls keeps home

Ezra Pound, *Rome*, from the French of Joachim du Bellay.

Vivere si recte nescis, decede peritis
Lusisti satis, edisti satis atque bibisti,
Tempus abire tibi est.

[If you don't know how to live properly, learn from those who do.
You have played, eaten and drunk enough
And it is time for you to go.]

Quintus Horatius Flaccus, *Epistles*,
Book 2, no 2, ll. 212–14.

The Garibaldian epic had finally convinced the British that Italy could produce real heroes, not just Machiavellian tyrants, or Renaissance despots, or cynical conspirators like the real *carbonaro*, Count Orsini, who tried to kill Napoleon III, or the fictional Count Fosco from Wilkie Collins's *The Woman in White*, or even fustian creatures of poetic fantasy like Tancred, Rinaldo, Orlando and Rodomonte. There was enough romanticism left in the English literary establishment for this fact to be celebrated by the one indisputable heir to the Romantic tradition, George Meredith. Meredith, Thomas Love Peacock's son-in-law, wrote his Risorgimento novel nearly 20 years later than the event it recorded, after he found himself a war correspondent for the *Morning Post* on the Italian front, covering the Austro-Prussian war of 1866. Italy had joined the enemy of Austria, but the speed of what became known as the Seven Weeks War gave him little opportunity to report on much action, at the end of which the new kingdom was rewarded by Bismarck with possession of Venice. Meredith was to regard Italian unification as 'the main historical fact of the nineteenth century', during which 'he had constantly preached the cause of Anglo-Italian cooperation'. He was one of the principal inspirations of Trevelyan's *chef d'oeuvre* on the Risorgimento.[1] In 1864 he produced *Sandra Belloni* under the title of *Emilia in England*. Emilia, later to become Sandra and then Vittoria, is a young Italian with a voice to rival the nightingale's.[2] An unscrupulous Greek tycoon, Antonio Pericles, who is also a voice fancier, designs to keep her like a songbird in a gilded cage, releasing her on the public when he believes it is worthy of her. Sandra Belloni (Emilia), while living in England, boasts a lover, Wilfred Pole, and is adopted by his sisters as their special protégé. The novel ends with Sandra/Emilia on her way, with Pericles's money, to undergo formal voice-training at the Milan conservatory. Wilfred, because of his residual love for the young singer is unable to go through with a rich marriage to an heiress, which would re-establish the fortunes of the Pole family, but offends Sandra/Emilia grievously by deciding to make his career in the Austrian army and to take the name of his uncle, General Pierson, who wore the white uniform of the oppressor.

Meredith had promised two sequels, in which the recent events in Italy would continue the fortunes of Sandra/Emilia, and he was engaged on *Vittoria*, the only sequel to appear, when he went to Italy to cover the war. In this novel, Meredith achieves a pace, as it develops into a search and pursuit thriller that is almost breathless, his rhapsodic prose finding plenty to delight it in the Milanese countryside where the action takes place, reflecting the quickening pulse of English sympathy with the drama of Italy: witness Garibaldi's rapturous reception in London and Eton in 1864. *Vittoria* is set in 1848. Emilia, now called Vittoria, is the *prima cantatrice* at La Scala. The theatre is a hotbed of nationalist sympathisers, and when an Austrian officer is less than rapturous about her singing, Antonio Pericles, a born collaborator, is heard to mutter, 'What wonder she does not care to open her throat to these swine'.[3] A new opera (*Camilla*) is about to be performed, during which Vittoria, in a final aria, will repeat the refrain 'Italia, Italia shall be free'. This is to be the signal for an uprising, orchestrated by Mazzini ('the Chief'), and supported by the Sardinian king, Carlo Alberto.[4] Patriots from Milan, Bergamo and Brescia will rise, fully armed, in a kind of Milanese Vespers, to overthrow the hated Austrians. Unfortunately, by misadventure and the carelessness of Vittoria herself, who insists on warning her English friends, then visiting Milan, the plot miscarries, the rising is called off, and everyone, friend and foe alike, tries to prevent her from singing her inflammatory song, which was not in the version of the opera passed by the censors.

But she refuses to accept the change of plan, sings the aria, causes a riot in the theatre from which she is rescued by the intervention of Lieutenant Pierson (a.k.a Wilfred Pole) and the search and pursuit of the suspected ringleaders begins. Meredith takes great trouble with his locale and atmosphere, seeking a kind of romantic realism, but the opera he invents, as described, is so prolix and long winded that it would have rivalled *Parsifal* in length and *Il Trovatore* in complexity. It also appears to be desperately unrehearsed, considering the way the singers are abducted and rescued before the curtain ever goes up, and it is as well that Meredith did not turn his hand to being a librettist. The abbreviatory skills of such an office would have sat uneasily with his torrential prose. Despite his Italian partisanship, Meredith is not unsympathetic to the Austrians, who 'may claim at least as good a reputation for forbearance in a conquered land as our officers in India'.[5] (This only a few years after 1857, when British soldiers in India had shown very little forbearance in the suppression of revolt.) His Austrian officers rival Rupert of Hentzau in swordsmanship and excel him in gentlemanly feeling. Any rough-handed villains are Croatian mercenaries.

Vittoria's carelessness starts in La Scala where 'she has talked of a country called Italy'.[6] 'Dismembered and jealous, and corrupt, with an organisation promoted by passion chiefly, Italy was preparing to rise'. The Austrian reaction was to declare that Italians were like women 'and wanted – yes wanted – (their instinct called for it) a beating, a real beating … a thundering thrashing once a month'.[7] Thus the two sides are evenly pitched, yet even so sympathetic a partisan as Meredith cannot resist the Romantic fantasy of the stiletto. He knew very well that, as a weapon of daily work, as well as of self-defence and offence in a badly policed society, the knife was no more reprehensible than the Gurkha *kukri*, but the reputation of the Italians for dastardly murder was too strong. Berlioz, receiving hate-mail in 1838 after the performance of *Benvenuto Cellini*, told

Liszt that if he had been at Rome he would have been assassinated; now, in *Vittoria* in 1848, Mazzini's chief of staff, the conspirator Barto Rizzo, boasts a scar in his shoulder knot which he owed to a knife blow from a rival while he slept. His wife also attempts to kill Vittoria, though a heart seizure prevents her from striking home with her dagger.[8] The duel between Vittoria's pursuer, the elegant and courtly Lieutenant Weisspriess and her protector, an Italian aristocrat on the run for killing (murdering) an Austrian in a matter of honour, is fought between a man with a sword and his rival with a dagger. The flustered Austrian, finding his opponent too agile to be caught on the sword point, complains that he is blundering, because 'I have never engaged a saltimbanque before'.[9]

The ensuing plot begins to unravel from a bewildering tapestry of tableaux representing the complicated tension between time-serving Italian aristocratic patriots and the long-suffering but ultimately ruthless Austro-Hungarian military establishment. In a confused narrative worthy of both Stendhal and Tolstoy, Meredith explores the irrationality and injustice of war, in which figure Vittoria's two disappointed lovers, Merthyr Powers, a Welshman fighting in Rome under Garibaldi (never mentioned by name), and Wilfred Pole, whose treachery to the Austrians is handled with remarkable leniency. Vittoria's aristocratic Milanese husband is killed in a mêlée in the last pages, thus leaving the characters in place for the third volume Meredith never wrote.

Vittoria's last public appearance is in the Milan duomo when an emperor (Napoleon III) and a king (Victor Emmanuel II) stand beneath the vaults, after the two bloody battles of Magenta and Solferino have brought the Austro-Hungarians to a truce. Meredith may have decided by then not to write the sequel. He was clearly out of his depth in Italy and the sordid aftermath of all liberation movements would have been a sad burden to his romantic pen, which loved to linger over quixotry and intelligence like a genii. The corruption of that same class that had taken up Vittoria was best left to the pen of Henry James. It was enough for Meredith that the refrain to Vittoria's inflammatory aria had come to pass; Italy was free.

Meredith, despite his lack of qualifications for writing a libretto, had instinctively understood how opera was for Italians a means to express their national spirit. The oppressor loved it as much as they, and where the written word or poem was susceptible to censorship, the opera could hide dangerous sentiments within the art of composition. Both Rossini and Bellini, neither of whom was political in the sense that Verdi became, were both judged to be subversive. *William Tell* (1829), to Rossini's surprise, was considered to be full of revolutionary music, especially when the Swiss hail the sun as it rises above their mountains 'with that august and terrible name [of liberty] upon their lips, from the deep voices of the chorus and from the bass chords of the orchestra there seemed to proceed a menacing and formidable presage and call to deeds of prowess and self sacrifice'. Bellini, too, roused the pit with the cry of the Puritans in the opera of that name (1834) 'like a stirring shout of war and victory'.[10] Verdi (whose name formed an acrostic for *Vittorio Emmanule, Re d'Italia*), defied Elizabeth Barrett Browning's dismissive opinion of *libertà* being sung to bravos and became an icon of the freedom movement; the slave's chorus in *Nabucco* (1842), the lament of *I Lombardi* (1843) for their native land, and Ezio's plea to *Attila* (1846) to be left his homeland to rule, were canticles of liberty which could not be purged from the lips of the man and woman in the street.

With *Vittoria* scarcely three years old, Garibaldi became an object of interest to the author of *Contarini Fleming*. Disraeli had just resigned from the minority Conservative government and to employ his time embarked on what he later claimed to be his most widely read novel. Like Contarini Fleming, the eponymous hero of *Lothair* (1870) was another fantasy figure, expressing what Disraeli thought he thought as a young man. Lothair, Lord Muriel, is titled, orphaned, half educated – he has sent himself down before taking a degree from Oxford – and immensely rich. Disraeli, as besotted with the aristocratic life as Oscar Wilde or Evelyn Waugh were to be, begins by tossing Lothair into the world of duchesses, eligible daughters, country-house weekends, culminating in a coming-of-age party of opulent and bizarre extravagance. Socially naive, Lothair really wants to disassociate himself from society's triviality and to contribute to the unification of the Christian Churches by building a massive, inter-communal cathedral. One of his guardians, an unmistakable portrait of Manning,[11] is a former Church of England priest, now a cardinal; the other a Calvinist peer, whose daughters are showing Romish tendencies. Manning did not in fact become a cardinal until five years after the publication of *Lothair*, but he had been Archbishop of Westminster since 1865. A strong ultramontanist and supporter of papal infallibility, he was to Disraeli, who was an instinctive syncretist, always an agent of division. (Disraeli also harboured the quaint notion that Pope Leo X, the subject of Roscoe's second biography, had proposed to the conclave the abandonment of Christianity and the return 'to the ancient faith for which their temples had been originally erected'. His distrust of Roman Catholicism was innately fantastical.) In his novel, the tussle for Lothair's allegiance – though his soul seemed too elevated for any church to claim – is disturbed by the appearance in his life of an American gentleman who has lost his southern estates in the Civil War, and whose wife, Theodora, is a brilliantly endowed Corinne from Italy. Colonel Campian had fought and been wounded at Aspromonte, the encounter in August 1862, when Garibaldi's fili-buster, whose object was Rome, was attacked by troops sent from Genoa to prevent it. Garibaldi, while refusing to fire on Italians, was wounded and taken into custody. Theodora Campian, who can hold her own with Oxford intelligentsia and high society, in impeccable English, and who can deliver an impromptu passionate rendering of Alfieri in her native tongue, is an Italian patriot. She is also a con-summate politician of the conspiratorial ilk and in 1867, in which year the novel is set, she is Garibaldi's emissary to the Madre Nat-ura, a Mazzinian society of plotters, and to the Mary-Anne, a Disraelian invention worthy of Ian Fleming, a caucus of French secret societies powerful enough to determine the foreign policy of Napoleon III. By promising that they will restrain industrial and social unrest in France, they allow Napoleon to go to war to unify Italy in 1859.

Lothair, naturally, is bewitched by Theodora and joins the camp of Italian volunteers gathering in the foothills of the Umbrian Apen-nines for an attempt on Rome, where he instantly assumes his aristocratic due, the rank of captain. Garibaldi is still detained in Caprera, so the volunteers are uncertain what to do. Theodora has returned from Paris, having secured the assurance of 'Mary-Anne' that France will not interfere to protect the *Papalini*. At this point Disraeli switches from the novel of socio-religious manners to a novel of suspense, on the kind of quasi-mystical level that always fascinated him. As Theodora describes the forthcoming events: 'It is a mighty struggle ... between the Church and the secret societies; and it is a death struggle'.[12]

At this point Garibaldi evades his custodians and sets out to join his volunteers but, despite Theodora's negotiations with 'Mary-Anne', French troops return to defend Rome.[13] Because of this a republican rising is deferred until the volunteers arrive. They never do. In storming Viterbo, Theodora is mortally wounded and, before dying, binds Lothair solemnly never to turn papist. Garibaldi then joins his volunteers but on the road to Rome is decisively worsted at Mentana, where Lothair is seriously wounded and, in the mistaken conviction that he could only have been fighting for His Holiness, is carted into Rome among the *Papalini* wounded. By what is believed to be the miraculous intervention of Our Lady, he is found by the daughter of an aristocratic English Roman Catholic family who happen to be wintering in Rome, and is nursed back to health, closely guarded by Jesuits, who believe that this rich and elegant scion of the English noblesse is destined to 'go over', constituting a valuable prize for popery.

Disraeli's politics may have led him to distrust Garibaldi and prefer an Italian federation presided over by Pius IX, but his church allegiance was firmly English, and while he luxuriated in describing the courtly manners of Roman priests, their gorgeous churches and seductive music, he believed that Theodora was right to warn Lothair against joining the Roman Catholic Church. True to national prejudice his Jesuits glide in and out of rooms, conspiring and scheming *ad maiorem dei gloriam*: Disraeli genuinely believed that 'the great order had recognised that the views of primitive and mediaeval Christianity, founded on the humility of man, were not in accordance with the age of confidence in human energy, in which they were determined to rise, and which they were determined to direct'.[14] The battle is not between the Church and the secret societies, but the Church and the free soul of man. When Lothair learns the pious mistake of his benefactors, he recoils, remembering Theodora's dying injunction, and contrives to escape his clerical minders in order to breathe the pure air of Protestantism.

He does so in typical Disraelian style, having himself rowed to Malta overnight from Sicily and joining a yachting party for the Holy Land. The Italian saga was quietly abandoned, Lothair encounters his former Garibaldian commanding officer, now a mercenary in the service of the sultan, at an oasis near Galilee. In Palestine he meets good sound Protestant friends, and suitably sceptical philosophers who pursue spirituality without religion; and he returns eventually to marry a nice Church of England girl. (To his disgust, the Catholic girl for whom, after Theodora, he felt the nearest thing to love, has expressed her determination to join a convent.)

Disraeli never quite made up his mind whether he was writing an Italian epic, a religious novel, or a comedy of aristocratic manners. It was hardly surprising, given his opinion of Garibaldi, that the epic degenerated into a tale of mercenary adventurism. This was his real assessment of the Risorgimento. His exchanges with Archbishop Manning annoyed him – the future cardinal had no business to be changing sides; accordingly *Lothair*'s Cardinal Grandison is a sinister and ultimately foolish figure (his warm espousal of the world-shattering effects that will follow the declaration of papal infallibility are exaggerated to the point of caricature). The final message of the novel seems to be that the Rock of Peter was located in Canterbury. *Lothair* was published shortly before Victor Emmanuel marched into Rome and Pio Nono became a prisoner in the Vatican.

Garibaldi's apotheosis in English letters had to wait until the twentieth century. George Meredith had gone out to cover the Italian front during the 1866 Seven Weeks War with another newspaper correspondent, George Henty. As a novelist, Henty was as prolific a scribbler on historical themes as was Felicia Hemans as a poet. The difference between them was that he had covered conflicts, as a war correspondent, in India, Spain, Africa and Italy and, though he wrote most of his 80 or so schoolboy novels from his study, he had usually trodden the terrain of his heroes. In dashing prose he fought the good fight with Alfred the Great, Drake, Clive, Wolfe, Sir John Moore, Wellington and Cochrane; he took on Sikhs, Burmese, Ashantis, American 'rebels', Carlists and 'Fuzzywuzzies'; he defended Rhodes with the Knights of St John; he went into exile in Tsarist Siberia, and traversed middle Europe with Gustavus Adolphus. It was hardly surprising that, after his experiences with George Meredith, he produced in 1901 *Out with Garibaldi: A Story of the Liberation of Italy*. By the time he came to write it he could safely put the correct heroic sentiments into the mouths of his characters. Faced with almost certain defeat by the French, who have landed to recover Rome for the pope in 1849, Garibaldi promises that 'the stand we shall make against tyranny will touch every heart throughout Italy. … Ground down as the people have been for centuries, the old fire of the Romans is not extinct.' Henty's hero, the seventeen-year-old Leonard Percival, has left Eton early to join the leader in order to find his father who had fought with Garibaldi in South America and been with him in the siege of Rome. But his father has disappeared mysteriously after attempting a Gladstonian inspection of Neapolitan prisons and was reported killed by bandits. The young Percival covers himself in glory, becomes Garibaldi's aide-de-camp and finds his father. Henty moves his story along at the perfect pace for a schoolboy. He prided himself on getting his facts right. Written in 1901, just before he died, *Out with Garibaldi* is a not unworthy curtain raiser for Trevelyan's epic *Garibaldi and the Thousand* which appeared eight years later.

With that work the English apotheosis of Garibaldi was complete. The Italian epic had been successfully fought and won, though with little more than the sympathy of Great Britain. Italy was a great power, if still a shaky one. Her citizens had confounded their critics, the shade of Byron was appeased and poetic prejudice confounded. A Latinist as good as Shelley could have pronounced *finem lauda*. And, though England had in the event done little to bring to a conclusion what all Romantics had believed to be the only just future for *Italia*, the English had helped to nurture that intellectual sympathy which enabled it to be accepted as historical justice and Italy as a great power. Poets were soothsayers, after all.

As the nineteenth century merged into the twentieth, Italy remained a popular destination for British writers, either as temporary visitors or as exiled residents, but their interests suffered a sea change. They ceased to be commentators on the new nation. Their interest in her art remained a principal attraction; but now a new genre of writing emerged. One might call it literary holiday-making. Partly autobiographical and topographical, the new genre examined, in a curiously solipsistic way, the influence of an ancient civilisation on a new kind of visitor. In the days of the Grand Tour, the Italians were merely the custodians of the treasures which the Grand Tourists had come to see. Fate and history had given them no other role. Despite the papacy's ultramontane and ecumenical tasks, which attracted generally hostile attention (if not mockery), the popes throughout the eighteenth and early nineteenth centuries had earned high praise as custodians of the most visited cultural centre. The Napoleonic whirlwind had awakened Italians to the possibility of nationhood, and thus of national custodianship, only for it to be betrayed by Napoleon himself and then to be rejected by the restored custodians. The Romantic poets, fired by Bonapartist rhetoric, came to Italy after 1814, in order to see whether the Italians were worthy of the new status to which some of them aspired. They concluded that, worthy though the cause might be, they were personally unworthy of their great past. In that belief they wrote and died. In that belief, too, their readers largely concurred. They learned the Italian language but only so that they might read the poets and dramatists in the original, even to translate them, but not to fraternise with native speakers. Italian was for the intercourse between traveller and *valet de voyage*, master and servant, shopper and shopkeeper, when French could not be used.

The Brownings were unwittingly to be the source of this self-centered interest in the land. When they reached Florence they threw themselves into a study not of Italy but of *Italia*, ransacking the bookstalls for 'copy', like the *Old Yellow Book*, which Robert bought for a lira off a stall in Piazza San Lorenzo one June afternoon in 1860. It became the source of *The Ring and the Book*, the longest creative oeuvre on Italy ever written by a Briton. Though the work of this prolific couple did more than that of anyone else to interest the mid-Victorians in Italy, Robert's Italy was still peopled largely by characters from her historic past. Both husband and wife led a very sheltered social life in Florence and met few Italians. Their common distrust of Roman Catholicism allowed them to dally exquisitely with its quaintness and customs but not to approve of its influence on the human soul. Robert showed less interest than Elizabeth Barrett in the Risorgimento: he had met Mazzini and did not warm to him or his cause. Perhaps it was the influence of the claustrophobic and small-town society of Florence that caused him to write his best 'Italian' work after he returned to London on the death of his wife in 1861. He was to be the last Anglophone poet to find any inspiration in Italy until the American Ezra Pound came to reside in Rapallo in 1924.

Pound's first book of poems appeared in 1908, after his first visit to Italy. The first three *Cantos* appeared nine years later but it was not until he decided to settle in Italy that he continued them, until in 1948 he produced *The Pisan Cantos*, considered by some to be his greatest achievement. T. S. Eliot drew on Pound, not on Italy, and Pound drew on a range of Italian reading probably only equalled by the Shelleys. He could be as obscure as Browning and as lyrical, and his translations of and allusions to the poets who were the contemporaries of Dante sparked a whole new interest in the culture of medieval Italy. Pound was the last heir to the Grand Tour and Romantic interest in *Italia*.[15] His support for an aggressive, Fascist new Italy can be understood as an inevitable post-unification climax to that interest which attracted writers, from Horace Walpole to Robert Browning, in the cruel and wayward Middle Ages and Renaissance.

Apart from Meredith and Henty, the British novelists who wrote about Italy found the Risorgimento too exciting as well as too confusing. Where had all these Italian heroes come from? They did not trouble to find out; that old Italy of the Middle Ages and Renaissance, which reached its apotheosis in the work of Robert Browning, was too seductive. Unification once achieved, that interest slipped into sentimental romanticism, characterised, so often, as the occupation of a country villa, served by an idiosyncratic gardener, an excellent home-cook and sundry other ornaments of the obsequious Italian serving class. Here was the modern Arcadia, with cypresses fanned by mild breezes, under which selected interesting personages, all non-Italian, fuelled their conversations with estate-produced wine, with the scent of roses and orange in the air: Peacock transmogrified into Aldous Huxley. At its best it was the holiday paradise created by Elizabeth Russell in *The Enchanted April*; at its least worst it was the Italian world of Ouida, who liked her heroes handsome, strong, and brave, which on the whole she did not think Italians were. But, for one of her biographers, her best selling novels, *Pacarel* (1873) and *Signa* (1875), 'as appreciation of the people and countryside of Tuscany ... stand unrivalled to the present day'.[16] They continued to portray the old Italy that had disgusted the Shelleys when they first arrived, a raffish, degenerate influence which Victorian and Edwardian ladies did better to avoid, unless they had more effective chaperones than Charlotte Bartlett in E. M. Forster's *A Room with a View*. And even over that book the shadow of the stiletto still lay, when Lucy Honeychurch witnessed a fatal stabbing in the Piazza Signoria.[17]

When the vision was not of Arcadia, it was of a more sinister kind, the legacy of the Romantic distrust of Italians which continued to lurk in the British subconscious. Within Italy's museum-like surroundings, expatriate Britons (and Americans) tried not to succumb to Italy's persistent and fatal corruption. Within the embrace of an ancient and weary civilisation, which had corrupted so many before them, the innocence of Daisy Miller, Isabel Archer, Millie Theale and Maggie Verver was exposed to attack. Henry James's Rome, Florence and Venice are the uncaring agents of a corruption that tempts the soul. Ironically, the corrupters are not, for the most part, Italians but the English or Americans, who themselves have been corrupted by the spirit of the place.[18] The only Italian to play a part in this quartet of stories is Prince Amerigo, Maggie Verver's husband, whose treacherous ambivalence is not so much ill-natured as ill-judged. Italy provided the *mis-en-scène* but not the dramatis personae in these depictions of innocence abroad. Italy had become a nation, yet, in the British, post-Romantic imagination, Italians were either Count Fosco (1860) or Prince Amerigo (1904).

The shadows of the past lingered round both English views of Italy. To the riffraff nobility described by Lady Blessington in Naples and Charles Dickens in Genoa, always looking for a rich tenant to fleece for their palazzo, was now added the impecunious prince seeking a rich wife. Henry James saw the danger of it, E. M. Forster the folly. When the widowed Lilia Herriton proposes to marry an Italian, her brother-in-law is sent out to try to stop her or, if not stop her, at least to satisfy himself that she is being prudent. She is not, for her *innamorato* knows not a word of English, is none too clean, none too polished, and neither a *conte* nor a *marchese*. He is the son of a dentist living, to her brother-in-law's disgust, in a place 'which knew the Etruscan league, and the Pax Romana, and Alaric himself, and the Countess Matilda, and the Middle Ages, all fighting and holiness, and the Renaissance, all fighting and beauty'.[19] He was handsome enough, but his was the kind of Italian face the Italophile Philip Herriton thought he knew and loved, but 'did not want to see it opposite him at dinner'. Italy had become an environment in which the English might be tempted to do something foolish, if not shameful.

Such as becoming pope. Frederick Rolfe, Baron Corvo, was neither *conte* nor *marchese*, not even a baron, not even Father Rolfe as he styled himself, but a homosexual spoiled priest never able to break out of self-inflicted poverty. Italy was his adopted home, for if he were poor, those around him were poorer. Society owed a man of his gifts and vocation some sort of sustenance, and poverty could be alleviated by the greater poverty of those around him. *Hadrian VII* (1904) is Rolfe's wish-fulfilment novel – elected pope, Frederick Rolfe reforms the curia (which has so far defied every twentieth- and twenty-first-century pope) and brokers a world peace conference as well as astounding the world with the saints he creates (they include Mary Queen of Scots), and with his asceticism among the splendour of his surroundings. *The Desire and the Pursuit of the Whole* (1909, published in 1934), his confessional novel, is set in the slums of Venice where Rolfe is no longer pope but a homosexual predator seeking his prey among the equally poor *gondolieri*, driven to such extremes by his betrayal by the men he thought his benefactors.

Venice and Rome were where Rolfe happened to be when he wrote, and Venetians and Romans were only, like Pippa, passers-by, when they were not catamites. The master of vituperation, as he was dubbed, did write some charming stories in the *Yellow Book* tradition, as well as an eccentric defence of the virtues of Pope Alexander VI in *Chronicles of the House of Borgia* (1901), which out-Roscoed Roscoe in its erudition, both pretended and real. The *Yellow Book* itself, which produced his *Stories Toto Told Me* (1898), epitomised that vision of Italy which was antiquarian and precious, still acting as custodian of natural beauty, artistic achievement and absurd convention, which was parodied by W. S. Gilbert in *The Gondoliers* (1889). When Mary Shelley wrote *Valperga* she used the Middle Ages to remind her readers that Italy should have a future as well as a past; for 'Yellow Bookers' and popular historical novelists like Maurice Hewlett (who published his *Little Novels of Italy* in 1902), the past was back in vogue, not because the future had happened, but because aestheticism had canonised the medieval and quattrocento generally.

The only major English writer to walk out of that stained-glass attitude was D. H. Lawrence but, even for Lawrence, Italy was just one of many locales he used for for his novels. In search of physical warmth for his human condition, he was constantly searching for that human warmth that would release the humanity in everyone trapped in their own inhibitions (and, ironically, mostly in himself). He tried Italy, Mexico, Australia, and in this he was very close to repeating the wish-fulfilment novels that constituted, at their worst, literary holiday-making. Lawrence could never be so trite, but he hoped to find in Italians, as well as Mexicans, the warm-blooded spiritual life that defied convention. Italians, however, are no more unconventional or warm-blooded than any other nation. It was a polite English fiction that they were. From the impatient despair of the Romantics, English writing about Italy descended into romantic fictions that celebrated the eccentricities of themselves when they changed their address.

For with the late Victorian passion for adventuring into unusual, even dangerous places, the British began to move away from the hothouses of Rome, Florence and Venice, to the Italian Riviera and to the Capri of that sinister lecher and sadist, the Emperor Tiberius. Maddened by the sirocco, they were seeking not Arcadia and its high-minded pleasures but the sort of hedonistic delights that Tiberius was said to have cultivated.[20] Nepenthe, as it became in the one novel of Norman Douglas, *South Wind* (1917), was a bizarre resort which drove most of its denizens demented. Douglas, otherwise a literary traveller who had unveiled the deep south of Italy in

Siren Land (1912), and *Old Calabria* (1915), both travel and topographical works in which his perverse and mocking imagination made the deep south of Italy permanently suspect, was both corrupted and corrupter.[21] Capri, too, was the centre of a work of fiction passing as autobiography, *The Story of San Michele* (1924), written by fashionable 'seaside' doctor, Axel Munthe, who had, for some time, lived in No 26 Piazza di Spagna, the house in which Keats died, and whence he witnessed Gabriele d'Annunzio's tempestuous wooing of Eleanora Duse on the Spanish Steps. Capri became, more fashionably than Florence, the fly-bottle in which an expatriate community was not always lovingly examined.[22]

Douglas and Munthe rendered popular the kind of book that Landor, Fanny Trollope (*A Visit to Italy*, 1842) and Dickens had initiated, a personalised account of a trip to Italy. Like the guide books that proliferated in the 1820s, this genre is still lively and active today. Hardly a year goes by but there is another account of growing up in rural Tuscany, adventures with the dream house in which the writer chooses to expatriate himself, or more often, herself. Here is almost the apotheosis of that literary rediscovery of Italy that began in the post-bellum years following the end of the Napoleonic adventure and of the Grand Tour. Its salient characteristics are the charm of the past and the eccentricities of the present, in which Italians have walk-on parts, and the subject is autobiographical. The English, a self-regarding race, have always liked to pretend to a certain social and intellectual superiority abroad, and Italy still provides that environment. For about a quarter of a century, from the arrival of Byron and Shelley to the departure of Browning, the subject of Italy was treated with a degree of seriousness and noble intention. Today, when it is not another novelistic foray into Italy's past it is mostly a frivolous search for sun, wine and a Tuscan Arcadia without the benefit of good writing. At least the Romantics paid that tribute to the Italy that they knew.

NOTES

Introduction: *The Land of Departed Fame*

1 Jones, *Letters*, ii, p 177: P. B. Shelley to T. L. Peacock, Pisa, c. 10 March 1820.

2 Sella, p 160. Goethe found more freedom of expression in Rome than in Paris, though his attitude to French arrogance may have influenced his judgement, Bowron and Rishell, p 20.

3 Eaton, i, preface, p xv.

4 Morgan, *Italy*, i, p 438.

5 *Mémoires, documents, etc, de Metternich, publiés par son fils* (Vienna 1883), Vol. vii, p 415.

6 Boswell, *Life of Johnson*, 11 April 1776.

7 Wordsworth, *Letters, The Middle Years*, i, p 438; ii, p 650.

8 Eustace, i, p 24.

9 Springer, pp 6–7. She epitomises this in Füssli's sketch of *The Artist's Despair Before the Grandeur of Ancient Rome*, now in the Zurich Kunsthaus.

10 M. Trevelyan, *Englishmen and Italians*, Proceedings of the British Academy (London 1919–20), p 104.

11 *Contarini Fleming* (1832) and *Lothair* (1870), see below, Chapters 5 and 12. I do not include *Venetia* (1837). Though the model for the hero was Byron himself, it is not Byronic.

12 Blennerhassett, p 166.

13 Jones, *Letters*, ii, p 180: P. B. Shelley to Leigh Hunt, Pisa, 5 April 1820.

14 P. B. Shelley, 'Ode to Liberty' (1820), xiv. This idea is elaborated in Maria Schoina, 'The Poetry of Politics in Shelley's and Byron's Italian Works', *Gramma: Trajectories: New Greek Scholarship in Anglo-American Studies*, 9 (Aristotle University).

15 Byron, *Letters and Journals*, viii, p 46: Ravenna Journal, 18 February 1821.

16 Author's italics.

17 Byron, 'When a man hath no freedom to fight for at home', November 1820, *Occasional Pieces* (1804–24).

18 In the preface to *Hellas*.

19 Butler, p 123, discusses the Italianate fashion that flowered among English writers at the end of the Napoleonic wars.

20 Morgan, *Italy*, ii, p 482: Appendix III by Sir C. T. Morgan on 'Literary Disputes in Italy', quoting from No 25 of the Milan-based literary journal, *Conciliatore*.

1 'This Wilderness of a Place for an Invalid'

1 Colvin, p 98.
2 Cubberley and Hermann, pp 192–4; and Deakin.
3 Sharp, p 82.
4 Stendhal, *A Roman Journal*, 30 May 1828.
5 Byron, *Childe Harold*, iv, cxxviii.
6 Hinde, p. 54: 17 December 1819.
7 Morgan, *Italy*, ii, p 427.
8 Smollett, letter 29: 20 February 1765.
9 Boswell, *Grand Tour*, p 87: 12 May 1765. Maes, part 1, p 145.
10 Dickens, *Pictures from Italy*, 'Rome'.
11 Eaton, iii, p 288.
12 Morgan, *Italy*, ii, p 362.
13 Dickens, *Pictures from Italy*, 'To Rome by Pisa and Siena'. Lamartine also called Rome 'une terre des morts'.
14 Jones, *Letters*, ii, p 59: December 1819.
15 Eaton, ii, p 303.
16 Piozzi, *Observations*, pp 12–13.
17 de Brosses, letters 36 and 37.
18 Piozzi, *Observations*, p 218.
19 de Brosses, letter 40.
20 Boswell, *Grand Tour*, p 8: Boswell to J.-J. Rousseau, 3 October 1765.
21 Morgan, *Italy*, iii, p 50.
22 Smollett, letter 17: 2 July 1764.
23 Hinde, pp 59–64: 17 January 1820.
24 Sharp, p 269.
25 Stendhal, *Rossini*, p 173. Blessington, *The Magic Lantern*, p 59. For audience-listening generally, Gay, pp 11–35.
26 Byron, *Letters and Journals*, vi, p 132: to John Cam Hobhouse, 17 May 1819.
27 Stendhal, *Rossini*, p 171.
28 Peacock, *Crotchet Castle*, chapter 7.
29 Morgan, *Italy*, ii, p 340.
30 Ibid., p 429.
31 Powell, pp 52–3.
32 Eaton, i, p 144, arriving late in Rome early in 1817 found all the hotels and lodging houses crowded out with them, and only secured rooms with great difficulty. Jones, *Letters*, ii, p 184: to Thomas Medwin, Pisa, 16 April 1820. 'Kennst du das land, wo die Zitronen blühn', Goethe, *Wilhelm Meisters Lehrjahre* (1795–6) book 3, chapter 1.
33 Forsyth, 1816 edition, p 398.
34 Chateaubriand, iii, p 228. He wrote these words in the 1840s but could have used something like them during his embassies to London (1822) and to Rome (1827).

35 Eaton, i, 66, expressed the common view that 'the Italians seem to neglect the most obvious means of making money honestly, but spare no trouble to get at it by begging and cheating'.

36 Maes, part 1, p 29.

37 Morgan, *Italy*, ii, p 403 fn.

38 Radcliffe, *The Italian*, 1978 edition, pp 2–3. Smollett, letter 17.

39 Byron, *Letters and Journals*, vii, p 123: to John Cam Hobhouse, 6 July; 'trash about Italy', p 172: to John Murray, 7 September; 'wild justice', p 184: to Murray, 28 September 1820; 'liability to assault', vi, pp 1, 88: to Hobhouse, 30 July 1819.

40 Matthews, pp 56–7. A huge chasm had appeared in the Forum, and the oracle said it would not close until the Romans threw into it something or someone it prized. Marcus Curtius obliged, and leaped on his horse and rode into the hole, which immediately closed. For the promotion of Roman archaeology, see Springer, pp 74–90.

41 Lees-Milne, p. 45. Lady Elizabeth Faster was the mistress, wife and widow of the fifth Duke of Devonshire and, while in Rome, nourished a romantic passion for Cardinal Consalvi, which may have helped her in securing permits to dig. Foreman, p 398.

42 Morgan, *Italy*, ii, pp 353–4. Also Bowron and Rishell, pp 20–1, on papal guardianship of the Roman legacy.

43 Martineau, p 141. Las Cases quotes him as calling Pius VII, '*vraiment un agneau, tout a ... fait un bon homme, un véritable homme de bien que "estime, que aime beaucoup"*'. Marguerite Blessington, *Idler*, pp 237–8: 12 July 1823, called him 'the personification of the *beau idéal* of the Father of the Church'.

44 Peacock, *Crotchet Castle*, chapter vi.

45 Moens, i, p 16.

46 Sharp, p 82. According to Charlotte Eaton , iii, p 47, however, the prince in 1819 kept the statue safely locked away and allowed no one to see it, not even Canova himself.

47 Hinde, p 65.

48 Bate, pp 676–7.

49 Ibid., p 683.

50 Stendhal, *A Roman Journal*, p 71: 11 December 1827.

51 Birkenhead, *Illustrious Friends*: Severn to William Haslam, 15 January 1821. Morgan, *Italy*, iii, p 50.

52 Morgan, *Italy*, ii, pp 407–8 fn.

53 Martineau, p 159.

54 Ibid., p 152.

55 Sharp, p 64; Bate, p 671. Edward Williams, *Journal*, 8 November 1821, who witnessed a lark slaughter thus contrived. Jones, *Maria Gisborne and Edward E. Williams*, p 110.

56 Anthony Burgess, in *Abba, Abba* invents such an encounter, to accompany his translations of Belli's sonnets.

57 I am indebted for this information to Susan L. Davis, whose medical researches have led her to this conclusion.

58 P. B. Shelley, *Adonais*, xlix, ll. 439–41.

59 Sharp, pp 95–6, Birkenhead, *Illustrious Friends*, p 58: Severn to Mrs Brawne, 11 January 1821.
60 Brand, p 148.
61 Sharp, p 65.
62 W. C. Monkhouse, entry for 'John Gibson', *Dictionary of National Biography* (Oxford 1975 edition).
63 Eastlake, p 15.
64 Sharp, p 113.
65 Ibid., p 105.
66 Charlotte Eaton, iii, p 106, urged such an institution on her nation in 1820 but with no hope that 'the pitiful penurious spirit of our government' in anything to do with the arts would allow it. But unless artists could study Italy's art, they could never become great artists.
67 Birkenhead, *Illustrious Friends*, pp 212–13.
68 P. B. Shelley, *Julian and Maddalo* (1818), l. 449; Jones, *Letters*, ii, 170: 17 January 1820. Though always meaning that he was the exile, Shelley added 'the retreat of Pariahs' in a letter from Florence persuading his cousin in Geneva, Thomas Medwin, that Italy was the place for him.
69 Rogers, *Journal*, p 206.

2 'The Niobe of Nations'

1 Frayling, p 110.
2 The organisers of the Grand Tour exhibition at the Tate Gallery, between October 1996 and January 1997, chose this as the cut-off date.
3 Frank Salmon, 'The Impact of the Archaeology of Rome on British Architects and their Work', c 1750–1840', in Hornsby, pp 220–1, argues that the majority of visitors continued for some time thereafter to be younger sons completing their education.
4 Haskell and Penny, pp 46, 132. Rogers, *Journal*, p 134: 24 August 1814.
5 Springer, p 109, quoting Gioacchino Belli's satire, in which an English tourist is sold a rusty spade for a scudo: '*E accusì a Roma se pela la quaja*' ('that's how you get on in Rome').
6 Brand, p 143.
7 Rosselli, pp 176–7.
8 Byron, *Letters and Journals*, v, p 187: Byron to Thomas Moore, 25 March 1817. Rogers, *Journal*, p 60.
9 M. Shelley, *Letters*, i, p 74: Mary Shelley to Maria Gibson, 2 July 1818.
10 Trevelyan, *Lord Macaulay*, i, p 466.
11 M. Shelley, *Letters*, i, p 180: Mary Shelley to Claire Clairmont, 21 January 1821. The naval officer was Captain Bowen.
12 Rogers, *Journal*, p 73. The play was Rossi's *Il Calzolaio [Cobbler] Inglese in Roma*. It was possibly the source of Stendhal's story of the Englishman riding through the Colosseum, remarking that it would be a fine building when finished. (See above, p 12).
13 In 1851, when reasonable records began, sufferers of pulmonary tuberculosis in England nunbered 2,579 per million lives. The onset of the

Industrial Revolution began to create conditions out of which those, who could, chose to spend the winter.

14 Brand, p 11.
15 Though the Blessington-d'Orsay caravan, which occupied one of the finest palazzi in Vomera, Naples, found it cost more than if it had been in London. Blessington, *Idler*, pp 245–6: 20 July 1823.
16 Addison, *A Letter from Italy, to the Rt Hon. Lord Halifax*, (London 1703), p 51.
17 Smollett, letter 31: 4 March 1765.
18 Mavor, p 7: 10 September 1780.
19 Rogers, *Journal*, pp 169, 171: 14 and 15 October 1814.
20 Blessington, *Idler*, p 295: December 1823
21 Ibid., p 273: 13 August 1823.
22 Rogers, *Journal*, p 163: 7 October 1814.
23 Jones, *Letters*, ii, p 9: to T. L. Peacock, Milan, 20 April 1818; ii, p 22: to William Godwin, 25 July 1818, Bagni di Lucca.
24 Clay, p 48: 4 August 1823. Johann Goethe, *Reise in Italien*: 16 March 1787. Jones, *Maria Gisborne and Edward E. Williams*, pp 21, 28.
25 M. Shelley, *Letters*, i, pp 317–18: to Thomas Jefferson Hogg, Albano near Genoa, 28 February 1823.
26 Ibid., p 85: to Maria Gisborne, Naples, 22 January 1819.
27 Ibid., pp 244, 249: to Maria Gisborne, Pisa, 15 August 1822.
28 Smollett, letter 20: 22 October 1764; letter 35: 20 March 1765.
29 M. Shelley, *Collected Tales and Stories*, pp 33, 75–6, 354, 361.
30 Blessington, *Idler*, p 250: 23 July 1823.
31 Brand, p 10.
32 Clairmont, p 103: 27 March 1819.
33 Eaton, i, p 78 fn, and preface, p xvi; 'The Italian noblemen for the most part are ill-educated, ignorant and illiterate', iii, p 221.
34 Brand, pp 189–90.
35 G. M. Mathews, 'A New Text of Shelley's Scene for Tasso', *Keats–Shelley Memorial Association Bulletin*, XI (1960), pp 39–46. See also Chapter 4, p 70 below.
36 Sydney Morgan, in calling him 'one of the greatest captains and greatest geniuses of the age' in 1821, anticipated Mary Shelley in presenting him to an English reading public. *Italy*, iii, p 31.
37 Byron, *Childe Harold*, preface to Canto IV.
38 *Hansard Parliamentary Debates*, XXIX, p 728, quoted by Brand, p 197.
39 October 1818, quoted by Brand, p 200.
40 Byron, 'Ode to Naples' (1820), strophe II.
41 Letter to Lord Holland on foreign policy, 1819, quoted by Brand, p 201.
42 Morgan, *Italy*, iii, p 259.
43 Letter to Lord Lansdowne in Trevelyan, i, p 466.
44 Morgan, *Italy*, i, p 29.
45 'Valerius, the Reanimated Roman', unpublished but possibly written in 1819, after her first visit to Rome. M. Shelley, *Collected Tales*, p 333.
46 Jones, *Letters*, ii, p 67: to Leigh Hunt, Naples, ?20 December 1818. T. Webb, 'City of the Soul: English Romantic Travellers in Rome', in Liversidge and Edwards, p 27.

47 M. Shelley, *Rambles in Germany and Italy*, ii, pp 260–1. Also Pemble, *Mediterranean Passion*, p 135. Mary Shelley had, however, revised her poor opinion of Italian manners during this return visit after 20 years, *Rambles*, ii, p 106

48 Meredith, *Sandra Belloni*, chapter 28.

49 D'Azeglio, author's preface, p XV.

50 Hunt, *Autobiography*, pp 448–9.

51 Pemble, *Mediterranean Passion*, p 229, quoting from *The Letters of E. B. Browning*, ed. F. G. Kenyon (London 1897), i, p 310.

52 Eleazar of Worms, 1165–1238, Jewish mystic and pietist, born at Mainz, who exposed the Kabbalah, the esoteric manner of theosophical contemplation, to non-Jewish readers. G. Scholem, *Ursprung und Anfange der Kabbalah* (Cologne 1962), pp 448–9.

53 Smith, pp 3, 25.

54 *Monthly Review*, vi (1837), p 132, quoted by Brand, p 132.

55 Hunt, *Selected Essays*, p 474.

56 Ridley, p 45.

3 'Behind the Black Veil'

1 *The Critical Review*, August 1794. Crabb Robinson, i, p 304.

2 Tompkins, p 250.

3 Jane Austen, *Northanger Abbey*, chapter 25.

4 Smollett, letter 20: 22 October 1764.

5 Charlotte Smith (1748–1806), a prolific writer admired by Leigh Hunt and Walter Scott. Her most Gothic novel, *Emmeline*, appeared in 1788.

6 Tompkins, p 377.

7 Byron, *Letters and Journals*, v, p 145: 19 December 1821.

8 Medwin, p 321.

9 Jones, *Letters*, ii, p 324: Shelley to Mary Shelley, Ravenna, 8 August 1821.

10 Byron, *Childe Harold*, preface.

11 Churchill, p 6.

12 Radcliffe, *A Sicilian Romance*, ii, chapter 3.

13 Lady Sydney Morgan, *The O'Briens and the O'Flahertys* (3 vols, 1827), iii, chapter 6, 'The Confraternity'.

14 Robert Southey, *The History of Brazil* (London 1810, 1813, 1819), i, chapter 8.

15 Scott, *Rob Roy*, chapter x.

16 George Eliot, 'Janet's Repentance', *Scenes of Clerical Life* (1857), chapter iv.

17 Dickens, *Pictures from Italy*, 'Genoa and its Neighbourhood'.

18 Evelyn Waugh, *Vile Bodies* (1930).

19 Morgan, *Italy*, iii, p 392.

20 George Eliot, 'Mr Gilfil's Love-Story', *Scenes of Clerical Life*, chapter iii.

21 Sultana, p 88

22 *S. T. Coleridge's Notebooks*, ed. K. Coburn (New York 1957), N 2261.

23 Ibid., N 2547.

24 Eustace, iv, pp 293–4. See Churchill, pp 19–21 for details of convent horror stories set in Italy.
25 Byron, *Letters and Journals*, v , p 180: to John Murray, 23 September 1820.
26 Morgan, *Salvator Rosa*, pp 120–1.
27 Kitson, p 8.
28 Ibid., p 74.
29 Morgan, *Salvator Rosa*, pp 44–8.
30 Moens, i, p 151.
31 Lytton, *Zanoni*, 1874 edition, p 125.
32 Ruskin, *Modern Painters*, v, p 228.
33 Gamer, p 167, quoting Walter Scott, *Miscellaneous Prose Works* (Edinburgh 1834–6), iii, p 314–15.
34 E. Johnson, *Scott*, ii; p 972. Scott, *Journal*, 1826, pp 87–8.
35 Colvin, pp 83, 221.
36 Byron, *English Bards and Scotch Reviewers* (1809), ll. 339–40, 355–6.

4 'The Silence of the Living'

1 Colvin, p 95. Colvin's footnote left the last part of the anatomy to the imagination.
2 Hilton, p 93.
3 Butler, p 119.
4 M. Shelley, *Journals, 1814–1844*, i, pp 266, 347.
5 Muriel Spark among them. Spark, p 150.
6 M. Shelley, *Valperga*, i. p 30.
7 Ibid., i, p 119.
8 Byron, *Childe Harold*, Canto IV, stanza 42.
9 'Italy, Italy. whom the gods have given the fatal gift of beauty'. Vincenzo da Filicaja (1647–1707).
10 De Staël, *Corinne*, pp 110–11.
11 Ibid., p 114.
12 Forsyth, 1816 edition, p 18.
13 Landor, *High and Low Life in Italy:* Mr Stivers to Lady C., quoted in van Thal, p 276.
14 Ibid., p 116.
15 Peacock, for example, read Boiardo's *Orlando Innamorato* in the original seven times, and Ariosto's *Orlando Furioso* 'for the I-know-not-how-manieth-time'. Peacock, *Letters*, ii, p 355: Peacock to John Cam Hobhouse, 10 September 1856.
16 Dante Alighieri, *Inferno*, xxxxiii.
17 V. Tinkler-Villani, 'Translation as a Metaphor for Salvation: 18th Century Versions of Dante's Commedia', *Journal of Anglo-Italian Studies*, 1 (1991), pp 95–6, 98.
18 Medwin, pp. 376–7.
19 Butler, p 119.
20 Jones, *Letters*, ii, p 276: to T. L. Peacock, Pisa, 21 March 1821. Also Brand, pp 66–7.

21 P. B. Shelley, 'A Defence of Poetry' (1821, first published 1840).
22 See the epigraph at the head of this chapter, p 60.
23 Crabb Robinson, ii, p 28: 17 December 1825.
24 Brand, p 79.
25 Carlyle, pp 102, 111, 113, 127.
26 Hunt, *Autobiography*, p 135.
27 Ibid., p 492.
28 Jones, *Letters*, ii. p 345: to Leigh Hunt, Pisa, 26 August 1821.
29 Torquato Tasso, *La Gerusalemme Liberata*, Canto VII, ll. 1–4. Hunt, *Seletect Essays*, 'The Italian Girl'.
30 Piozzi, *Observations*, p 90. De Staël, *Corinne*, Book 15, chapter 9.
31 Gotch, p 269.
32 P. B. Shelley, *A Defence of Poetry*.
33 An edition was published in 1972, edited by Robert McNulty.
34 Boswell, *Johnson*, ii, p 338: October? 1780.
35 Praz, p 524.
36 Boswell, *Johnson*, ii, p 472.
37 Ibid., ii, 526.
38 Ibid., ii, 397: 6 April 1781.
39 S. Johnson, *English Poets*, i, p 176. The passage he quotes are stanzas 1–18 of Canto VII, the opening stanza of which Leigh Hunt tried to quote to the Italian girl. (See pp 69–70 above).
40 Lamb, i, pp 72, 11–12: to Coleridge, 5 February 1797; 10 June 1796. Southey 'knew no poem which can claim a place between it [his epic poem *Thalaba*, 1801], and the Orlando ... I should not dread a trial with Ariosto'. Southey, *Letters*, p 42: letter to C. W. W. Wynn, 21 February 1801. A modern Italian critic, Praz, p 524, called Hoole's verses pedestrian.
41 Brand, pp 74–5.
42 Jones, *Letters*, ii, p 20: to John and Maria Gisborne, Bagni di Lucca, 10 July 1818.
43 See Chapter 5, p 88 below.
44 Sharp, p 68.
45 Colvin, p 23: 10 September 1817.
46 Ibid., p 313: 22 September 1819.
47 Ibid., p 284: 5 September 1819.
48 Ibid., p 33: to John Taylor, 17 November 1819.
49 Tasso, *La Gerusalemme Liberata*, Canto IV, stanzas 31–2:

> *Mostra il bel petto le sue nevi ignude,*
> *Onde il foco d'amor si nutre e desta:*
> *Parte appar de le mamme acerbe e crude,*
> *Parte altrui ne ricopre invida vesta;*
> *Invida, ma, s'agli occhi il varco chiude,*
> *L'amoroso pensier già non arresta,*
> *Che, non ben pago di bellezza esterna*
> *Ne gli occulti segreti anco s'interna.*

Come per acqua o per cristallo intero
Trapassa il raggio, e nol divide o parte;
Per entro il chiuso manto osa il pensiero
Si penetrar ne la vietata parte:
Ivi si spazia, ivi contempla il vero
Di tante meraviglie a parte a parte;
Poscia al desio le narra e le descrive,
E ne fa le sue fiamme in lui più vive.

50 Sharp, p 83.
51 Quoted by Bate, p 313.
52 Colvin, p 113: letter to Bailey, 10 June 1818.
53 John Keats, 'A Dream after Reading Dante's Episode of Paolo and Francesca'.
54 Medwin, pp 199–202. Cf. Weinberg, passim. The review of this book by the poet, Charles Tomlinson, a long-time resident in Italy, in the *Keats–Shelley Review*, 6 (Autunm 1992), pp 168–74, is an essential key to an otherwise heavily detailed work, which explores with exhaustive thoroughness what debt Shelley owed to both Italy and the Italian books that he read while there.
55 It was not Keats's last poem; indeed it was probably written in 1818 and was in Fanny's hands by 1819.

5 'A Full-Grown Oak'

1 Thackeray, *The Newcomes*, chapter 2, 'Colonel Newcome's Wild Oats'. Cavaliero, p 103.
2 Morgan, *Italy*, iii, pp 251–2. Marguerite Blessington, who also heard him, wondered 'how a similar recitation would have been received by the lower classes in the streets in London'. *Idler*, p 249: 23 July 1823.
3 Vassallo, p 4. Füssli's *Ezzelin and the Repentant Meduna*, now in the Zurich Kunsthaus, was drawn in 1817.
4 Byron, *Letters and Journals*, iii, pp 253–4: Journal, 20 March 1814.
5 Perceval i, p 193.
6 Oscar Wilde, *The Picture af Dorian Gray*, chapter 11.
7 Sismondi, pp 62–3, 80–2.
8 Byron quotes the French from Sismondi, Vol. 3 (of the 16-volume edition), p 219.
9 Byron, *The Corsair*, Canto I, stanza xi, ll. 31–4.
10 Ibid., ll. 23–4
11 Ibid., ll. 19–20, 23–4.
12 John Milton, *Paradise Lost*, Book I, ll. 106–8, 263.
13 Mozart, *Don Giovanni*, Act 2, scenes 1 and 17.
14 Jane Austen, *Persuasion*, chapter xi: Anne Elliott to Captain Benwick.
15 Byron, *Manfred*, Act 1, scene 2.
16 Ibid., Act 3, scene 4.
17 Byron, *Letters and Journals*, v, p 180: to John Murray, 23 September 1820.

18 Byron, *Beppo*, stanzas 41 and 42.
19 Maurois, p 314.
20 Byron, *Don Juan*, Canto IX, stanza 1.
21 De Staël, *Corinne*, Book 3, chapter 1.
22 Byron, *Don Juan*, Canto XIII, stanza 110.
23 Tasso, *La Gerusalemme Liberata*, opening lines.
24 Forsyth, 1816 edition, p 22, dubbed Casti 'the profligate of genius', but he reckoned without Mozart.
25 Da Ponte, pp 115-28.
26 Ibid., pp 296-7. In the 1976 Milan edition of the *Memoirs*, introduced by Giuseppe Armani, the correspondence between da Ponte and Casti in November/December 1802 is introduced on pp 252-8.
27 Scott, *Journal*, i, p 277: 19 October 1826.
28 Byron, *Letters and Journals*, vii, p 202: Byron to John Murray, 12 October 1820.
29 Marchand, p 340.
30 Vassallo, pp 94-5.
31 Medwin, pp 336-9.
32 Byron, *Don Juan*, Canto I, stanza i.
33 On the intricacies of undressing a woman of the French Second Empire see Isak Dinesen, *Seven Gothic Tales* (London 1934), 'The Old Chevalier', p 88. I am grateful for this reference to Glen Cavaliero. Italo Svevo, in *La Coscienza di Zeno* (Milan 1983 edition), p 462, musing on da Ponte's *Memoirs*, exclaimed: '*Dio mio! Corne facevano quelle donne ad arrendersi cosi presto e tanto frequente essendo diffese da tutti quegli stracci*'. ('My God, how did women surrender themselves so quickly and so often, protected as they were by all those garments'.)
34 Donelan, p 43.
35 *The Blue Lagoon* (1908) by Henry de Vere Stacpoole (1863-1951).
36 Butler, p 140.
37 Blessington, *Idler*, p 188: 1 May 1822
38 Byron, *Letters and Journals*, vii, p 237: Byron to R. B. Hoppner, 20 October 1819.
39 Benjamin Disraeli *Contarini Fleming* (1832), Part the Fourth, chapter viii.
40 Ibid., Part The Third, chapter iv.
41 Ibid., Part the Fourth, chapter v.
42 Quoted by Bradford, p 254.
43 Disraeli, *Contarini Fleming*, Part the Second, chapter x.
44 Ibid., Part the Seventh, chapter ii.

6 'Yet Fallen Italy, Rejoice Again'

1 Angelo Poliziano, *Stanze per la Giostra del Magnifico Giuliano* (*Stanzas on the Jousting of the Magnificent Giuliano* [de Medici, Lorenzo's brother]). P. F. Tyler, *The Life of the Admirable Crichton* (Edinburgh 1823), p 24.
2 Macnaughton, p 17.
3 The 1806 Parliament was dissolved a year later and Roscoe did not stand again. His dislike of travelling - he never set foot outside

England – extended to having to stay in London for his parliamentary duties. Other great histories had been written without the author's ever setting foot in the country that was their subject: Robertson on Charles V's Spain, Grote on Greece, Southey on Brazil and James Mill on India.

4 *Dance Songs* and *Carnal Cantos,* which use sexual innuendo and double entendre and sometime straight pornography. Corinne Lanergan, '"With a Wild Surmise": on Translating Lorenzo de' Medici's Ambra Two Hundred Years after William Roscoe', *Journal of Anglo-Italian Studies,* 6 (2001), pp 1–5. Also Roscoe, pp 56–64.

5 S. Johnson, *English Poets,* i, 313. It is not certain whether a line was ever written but Roscoe certainly knew about the project.

6 Walter Scott, 'Memoir of his Early Years Written by Himself, 26 April 1808', forming chapter 1 of Lockhart, p 35.

7 Scott, *Rob Roy,* chapter 16.

8 Walter Scott, *Waverley* (1814), chapter 48.

9 Forsyth, 1816 edition, p 401.

10 Piozzi, *Observations,* p 218.

11 M. Shelley, *Valperga,* i, p 86.

12 Scott, 'The Two Drovers', Oxford World Classic edition, 1934, p 155.

13 Eliot, 'Mr Gilfil's Love-Story', *Scenes from Clerical Life,* chapter xiii.

14 Morgan, *Italy,* i, p 98.

15 Jones, *Maria Gisbourne and Edward E. Williams,* p 104: 22 October 1821.

16 Gell, p 20.

17 Ibid., 9.

18 Ibid., 9.

19 E. Johnson, *Scott,* ii, pp 1232, 1270.

20 Gell, p 30.

21 E. Johnson, *Scott,* ii, p 1245.

22 Abraham Borg, 'Ivanhoe – dal Romanzo al Pasticcio, *The Journal of Anglo-Italian Studies,* 5 (1997), pp 108–9.

23 Borg, 'Ivanhoe', pp 114–24.

24 E. Johnson, *Scott,* ii, p 1246.

25 Jones, *Letters,* ii, pp 239, 245: Shelley to Marianne Hunt, Bagni di Pisa, 29 October 1820; Peacock, *Letters,* i, p 175: Peacock to Shelley, 4 December 1820.

26 Medwin, p 59.

27 From the memoir by William Michael Rossetti in *The Poetical Works of Mrs Hemans* (London 1906), pp v–ix.

28 From the 'Sketch of the Life of Mrs Felicia Hemans' (unsigned) in *The Poetical Works of Mrs Hemans.*

29 Felicia Hemans, 'The Restoration of the Works of Art to Italy' (1816), ll. 280–5, 301, 307. The works of art had not exactly been pillaged but ceded to France by the unequal Treaty of Tolentino, which the papacy had been obliged to sign in 1797.

30 *The Poetical Works of Mrs Hemans*: letter to the Rev. Henry Milman, 16 December 1823, pp 123–4.

31 Runciman, pp 214–15.

32 Verdi to Louis Crosnier, intendant of the Paris Opera, quoted by Budden, p 69. Nothing Verdi could say or do could persuade Scribe to change it.
33 Lampedusa, p 24.
34 Moens, ii, 164.
35 Hemans, *The Vespers of Palermo* (1821), Act 1, scene 3, ll. 245–50.
36 Ibid., Act 2, scene 3, ll. 36–42, 51–8.
37 Gary Kelly, 'Last Men: Hemans and Mary Shelley in the 1820s', *Romanticism* (February 1997), pp 203.
38 William Wordsworth, *The Prelude* (1798–1805), Book v, ll. 677–80. Brand, p 25.
39 Quoted in Moorman, pp 526–7.
40 Wordsworth, *The Prelude*, Book viii, ll. 180–5.
41 C. L. and A. C. Shaver, *Wordsworth's Library: a Catalogue*, (New York and London 1979), Alan G. Hill, 'Wordsworth and Italy', *The Journal of Anglo-Italian Studies*, 1 (1991), p 122, in a footnote.
42 Wordsworth, *The Prelude*, Book ix, ll. 453–5.
43 William Wordsworth, 'After Leaving Italy', *Memorials of a Tour in Italy*, ii, ll. 1–3.
44 Wordsworth, 'At Bologna', *Memorials of a Tour in Italy*, i, ll. 18–19; iii, ll. 10–14.
45 Wordsworth, *Memorials of a Tour in Italy*, xxv, ll. 7–10.
46 Ibid., ix, ll. 5–8.
47 Ibid., xxiv. ll. 1–4.
48 M. Shelley, *Collected Tales*, p 30.
49 Wordsworth, *Memorials of a Tour in Italy*, i, ll. 39–40.
50 Ibid., xxv, ll. 13–14.
51 Ibid., xxvi, ll. 12–14.
52 Ibid., xiv, ll. 52, 61, 68.
53 Moorman, p 526. Forsyth, 1816 edition, p 91, acknowledged St Francis 'a genuine hero original; independent, magnanimous, incorruptible. His powers seemed designed to generate society but, taking a wrong direction, they sank men into beggars.' He was not claiming him for the spirit of true Protestantism.
54 Forster, *Landor*, i, pp 443–5.
55 Ibid., ii, p 220.
56 Crabb Robinson, i, p 380. It was August 1830. In the July revolution the French had replaced the reactionary Charles X by the Orleanist 'citizen king', Louis Philippe.
57 Forster, *Landor*, ii, p 255.
58 Van Thal, p 361: Landor to Emerson, 1856.
59 Peacock, *Letters*, ii, p 355: Peacock to John Cam Hobhouse (Lord Broughton), 10 September 1856.
60 Ibid., i, p 165: Peacock to Shelley, 13 January 1819.
61 Ibid., i, p 145: Peacock to Shelley, 19 July 1818.
62 Ibid., i, p 183, Peacock to Shelley, 11 or 16 October 1821
63 Thomas Love Peacock, *Melincourt* (1817), chapter 19, though *venericoribantentusiasmo* could be the Italian for that night clubber's new fad, lap

or pole dancing. Peacock, *Letters*, i, p 75: letter 40, to Thomas Foster 27, 27 January 1812.
64 This is not a wholly singular fancy. Professor Marilyn Butler, in her essay on 'Druids, Bards and Twice-Born Bacchus', *Keats-Shelley Memorial Association Bulletin*, xxxvi (1985), p 63, avers that '*Maid Marian* is a stylish, witty performance, much influenced by the newly fashionable operettas [sic] of Rossini and Bellini.' Peacock himself wrote an essay on Bellini, doom-laden for an early death by his 'pathetic musical composition'. Cf. Mozart, Weber, Keats, Pushkin? The notice appeared in *The London Review* in January 1836.
65 Both words coined by Melinzini.
66 Peacock, *Letters*, ii, p 381: Peacock to Lord Broughton, 9 September 1859.

7 'What Elysium Have Ye Known?'

1 Morgan, *Italy*, ii, p 81.
2 Andrea Battisttini, 'Vittorio Alfieri, le "mosche" francesi e le "api" inglesi', in *La Rivoluzione Francese in Inghilterra*, ed. L. M. Crisafulli (Naples 1990), pp 403–4.
3 Vittorio Alfieri, *Vita*, Part i, epoca terza, 'Giovinezza', cap 6; Part ii, epoca quarta, 'Virilità', cap 21.
4 Segré, p 124.
5 Byron, *Letters and Journals*, v, p 206: to John Murray, 12 August 1819. The tale is in Book 10 of Ovid's *Metamorphoses*.
6 Blessington, *Conversations of Lord Byron*, p 96.
7 Alfieri, *Vita*, Part i, epoca terza, 'Giovinezza', cap 1.
8 Alfieri, *L'Italia Futuro*, ll. 9–11.
9 Morgan, *Italy*, i, p 92.
10 Giacomo Leopardi, 'All'Italia', ll. 1–6.
11 Carsaniga, p 47. Carsaniga quotes from *Il Zibaldone*, p 799.
12 Crabb Robinson, ii, p 154. Alan G. Hill, 'Wordsworth and Italy', *The Journal of Anglo-Italian Studies*, 1, (1991), p 118.
13 Origo, p 170.
14 Colvin, p 201.
15 Carsaniga, p 19.
16 Keats, *Endymion*, Book 1, ll. 22–4.
17 John Keats, from *Poems Published in 1817*.
18 Carsaniga, p 6.
19 Richard Garnett, 'Leopardi', in *Encyclopedia Britannica* (1911), p 457.
20 Origo, p 251.
21 G. Leopardi, 'Dialogo di Timandro e di Eleandro', *Operette Morali* (1824), in *Opere, a cura di F Flora* (2 vols, Milan 1962), i, p 984.
22 G. Leopardi, *Epistolario*, vi: 6 April 1836.
23 John Keats, 'When I have Fears that I May Cease to Be', ll. 2, 6.
24 G. Leopardi, 'Consalvo', ll. 99–100.
25 G. Leopardi, 'Coro dei Morti', ll. 1–5.
26 G. Leopardi, 'Il Tramonto delta Luna', ll. 63–5.

27 G. Leopardi, 'Zibaldone', i, 8662; ii, 1333.
28 G. Leopardi, *Epistolario*, ii, 15 February 1823.
29 G. Leopardi, 'Zibaldone', ii, 1087–8.
30 Ibid., ii, 3175.
31 Keats, 'On the Story of Rimini', ll. 1–2, 11–12.
32 Keats, 'Sleep and Poetry', ll. 389–91.
33 G. Leopardi, 'A Silvia', ll. 7–14.
34 Carsaniga, p 24: letter to Giuseppe Montani, 21 May 1819.
35 Morgan, *Italy*, ii, p 485: Sydney Morgan admitted to her book on Italy various appendices by her husband who, in 1821, wrote on the present state of Italian literature: Appendix III, 'Notes on Literary Disputes in Italy by Sir T. C. Morgan'.
36 Brand, p 34.
37 John Milton, *Paradise Regained*, Book 3, ll. 338–40.
38 Hunt, 'The Italian Girl', *Selected Essays*, p 69.

8 'Metropolis of a Ruined Paradise'

1 M. Shelley, *Collected Tales*, p 335.
2 Forster, *Dickens*, i, pp 359–60 (The year referred to is 1845).
3 Johann Goethe, *Reise in Italien*: Naples, 25 February 1787.
4 John Fleming, 'Robert Adam: the Grand Tourist', *The Cornhill*, 1004 (Summer 1955), pp 132–3.
5 Piozzi, *Observations*, p 114.
6 Addison, p 16 (1701).
7 Forsyth, 1816 edition, pp 254–5.
8 Eaton, i, p 286.
9 Rogers, *Journal*, p 62.
10 Byron, *The Two Foscari*, Act 1, scene 1.
11 Foster, p 156.
12 Byron, *Marino Faliero*, preface.
13 Byron, *Letters and Journals*, vii, p 182: to John Murray, 28 September 1820. It was, however, put on in a stage version at Drury Lane, four days after its publication in April 1821. For the dedication to Goethe, see ibid.: to Murray, 17 October 1820. In the event, though, he changed his mind, and dedicated *Faliero* to Douglas Kinnaird and *Sardanapalus* to Goethe but, through Murray's error, not until 1829, when Byron was dead.
14 Ibid.: 3 November 1820.
15 *Marino Faliero*, Act 2, scene 2, Philip Calendaro speaking.
16 Ibid., Act 5, scene 3, Faliero's final soliloquy.
17 In the sense that the setting of it was Venice. Byron referred to his three Venetian dramas as *Faliero, Sardanapalus* and *Foscari* as they were written in Venice.
18 Byron, *Letters and Journals*, viii, p 218: to John Murray, 20 September 1821.
19 *Marino Faliero*, Act 2, scene 1: Francesco Foscari to Marina Foscari.
20 Byron, 'Ode on Venice' (1818), stanza 1.

21 Blessington, *Idler*, p 182: 27 April 1822, thought the story of Andrea Doria would have made a better drama for the stage.
22 Budden, p 179.
23 P. B. Shelley, *Julian and Maddalo*, ll. 91-2.
24 Ruskin, *Stones of Venice*, ii (1853), chapter iv, 'St Mark's', sub-para 14.
25 Cubberley and Hermann, p 14.
26 Wilton, *The Great Age of British Watercolours*, pp 13-14.
27 Byron, *Childe Harold*, Canto IV, stanza lxix; Cubberley and Hermann, p 32, plate 7, pp 170-1.
28 Liversidge and Edwards, pp 73-4.
29 Ibid., p 77, quoting from D. Blaney Brown, *Turner and Byron* (London 1992), pp 128-9.
30 *Arnold's Magazine*, quoted by Wilton, *Turner*, p 151.
31 William Finden, *Landscape Illustrations to the Life and Works of Lord Byron* (1832-3), and Thomas Moore, *The Works of Lord Byron: illustrated with his Letters and Journal, and his Life* (London 1832-4).
32 A contemporary (1839) critic, quoted in M. Butlin and E. Joll, *The Paintings of J. M. W. Turner* (London 1984) pp 210-11.
33 Evelyn, 8 February 1645. The diary was not, in fact, published until 1818 but most other Grand Tourists appear to have been told the same thing.
34 Rogers, *Journal*, p. 248.
35 Quoted in Seymour, p 221: Mary Shelley to Sophia Stacey, 7 March 1820. Mary was quoting Forsyth, 1816 edition, p 112, who was persuaded that the devils in Naples were merry devils.
36 Ruskin, *Praeterita*, p 262.
37 De Staël, *Corinne*, Book II, chapter 2.
38 Forster, *Dickens*, i, p 360.
39 This catalogue of wonders had all been explored by John Evelyn in 1645.
40 Forster, *Dickens*, i, p 360. Forsyth, 1816 edition, p 409, was convinced 'that the most noted sharper or the lowest buffoon shall, three to one, be a nobleman'.
41 Cairns, i, p 64: Berlioz to his family 2 October 1831. Jones, *Letters*, ii, p 56: Shelley to T. L. Peacock, Rome, 20 November 1818.
42 Goethe, *Reise in Italien*: 3 March 1787. Jones, *Letters*, ii, p 159: Shelley to Amelia Curran, Florence, 18 November 1819.
43 Morgan, *Italy*, iii, p 172.
44 Guiton and Crook, p 111, quoting William Lawrence, *A Treatise on Venereal Diseases of the Eye* (1830), p 55.
45 Morgan. *Italy*, iii, p 182 fn.
46 Ibid., iii, pp 274-8.
47 Rogers, *Journal*, p 252. 'Still the poor', wrote Walter Landor in a poetic epistle to Charles Dickens,

> Flock round Taranto's palace door,
> And find no other to replace
> The noblest of a noble race.

> Amid our converse you would see
> Each with white cat upon his knee,
> And flattering that grand company:
> For Persian kings might proudly own
> Such glorious cats to share the throne.
>
> Van Thal, p 293.

48 Jenkins and Sloan, p 15.
49 Goethe, *Reise in Italien*, pp 305-6: 13 March 1787.
50 See Chapter 10, pp 175-6.
51 Piozzi, *Observations*, pp 229-31; Godwin, p 168; Seymour, p 28.
52 Daniel Charles Solander (1736-82) was a pupil of Linnaeus, who travelled as a botanist in Captain Cook's *Endeavour* with Joseph Banks, and gave his name to one of New Zealand's islands.
53 Piozzi, *Observations*, p 250.
54 H. Trevor-Roper, 'Pietro Giannone and Great Britain', *The Historical Journal*, 39: 3 (1996), pp 657-75.
55 Crocco, pp 15-16.
56 Piozzi, *Thraliana*, i, pp 64-5: 3 July 1786. Also Piozzi, *Observations*, pp 234-5.
57 Piozzi, *Thraliana*: 12 March 1787.
58 Piozzi, *Observations*, p 165.
59 Ibid., p 222.
60 Michael Liversidge, 'William Marlow's Grand Tour Landscapes', in Hornsby, p 95.
61 'Warwick' Smith, *Select Views of Italy*, (London 1798), plate 60.
62 Cairns, i, 465: 5 October 1831.
63 An engraving of this event in 1771 by Pietro Fabris formed one of the plates (no xxxviii) of Campi Phlegrei, commissioned by William Hamilton in 1776, Jenkins and Sloan, pp 26-7.
64 Masaniello's story was known from Sydney Morgan's *Salvator Rosa*, pp 148-54.
65 Rogers, *Journal*, pp 253-4: 20 February 1815.
66 Byron, *Letters and Journals*, i, p 238. In. 1832, four years before his death in Naples, Gell published his *Pompeiana*, in two volumes, completing an earlier work which appeared in 1819. This, and a later *Topography of Rome and its Vicinity* (1834), helped to establish a British strength in classical topography which continues to this day. A. Wallace-Hadrill, *The British School at Rome, One Hundred Years* (Rome 2001), pp 14-15.
67 Rogers, *Journal*, p 263: 5 March 1815.
68 M. Shelley, *Collected Tales*, pp 327-8.
69 Brydone, i. p 137.
70 Ibid., pp 183-4.
71 Ibid., pp 194-5: letter x, 29 May 1770.
72 Cairns, i, p 465. De Staël, *Corinne*, Book II, chapter 4. Piozzi, *Observations*, p 253. Morgan, *Italy*, iii, p 166.
73 Moens, passim. He was kidnapped on an expedition to Paestum. In 1823 a young husband and wife were killed in gruesome circumstances by armed robbers. Blessington, *Idler*, pp 343-4.

9 'The Kings of Apulia'

1 Byron, *Childe Harold*, Canto I, stanza xxi.
2 Morgan, *Rosa*, pp 44–5.
3 See Chapter 11, pp 194–5 below.
4 Macfarlane, p 9.
5 Moens, i, p 242.
6 Macfarlane, p 13.
7 Moens, i, p 276.
8 Ibid., p 30. David Hannay, 'Brigandage', *Encyclopedia Britannica* (11th edition, 1910), says it was Benedetto Mangone.
9 Moens, ii, 224.
10 Acton, *Bourbons of Naples*, p 381.
11 Morgan, *Italy*, iii pp 43–4.
12 'The Sisters of Albano', Mary Shelley's first story for *The Keepsake* in 1828. M. Shelley, *Collected Tales*, pp. 51–64.
13 Bargellini, p 54.
14 Ruskin, *Praeterita*, pp 163–4.
15 See Chapter 8, pp 147–9.
16 Moens, i, p 244.
17 Moore, p 41: 12 November 1819; Hinde, pp 67–8: 21 March 1820.
18 Gotch, p 175.
19 Maria Graham, *Three Months in the Mountains near Rome* (1820).
20 Eaton, iii, p 398: letter of 19 November 1818.
21 Morgan, *Italy*, ii, p 422 fn; iii, p 136 fn.
22 Ibid., iii, p 138.
23 Moens, i, pp 157–8.
24 Morgan, *Italy*, iii, p 136 fn.
25 Eaton, iii, pp 401–2: letter of 4 February 1818.
26 Keates, p 350.
27 Dickens, *Pictures from Italy*, 'Through Bologna and Ferrara'.
28 Birkenhead, *Against Oblivion*, p 226, quoting a letter of 10 July.
29 Eaton, i, pp 92–3, found her *vetturino* (carriage driver) as they approached Rome in 1817, 'quaking with fear of robbers', while she and her companion 'might have fancied ourselves heroines betrayed to banditi [sic] and made most glorious efforts to escape out of their hands'.
30 Cairns, i, p 455.
31 Blennerhassett, pp 138–9. See also Hobsbawm, pp 24–33.
32 Henty, *Garibaldi*, chapter 3, 'Troubles'.
33 Don Gaetano Vardarelli as reported by General Sir Richard Church in Church, p 44.
34 Ibid., p 142.
35 Ibid., p 54.
36 Ibid., p 254.
37 Ibid., p 29.
38 Macfarlane, pp 117–47. Acton, *The Bourbons of Naples*, p 698.
39 Ibid., pp 54–5.

40 Ibid., pp, 26–7, 108.
41 Moens, ii, p 122.
42 Strutt, pp 56–65. Strutt (1819–1883) was a landscape- and animal-painter who resided and died in Rome.
43 Moens, i, p 314.
44 Ibid., ii, pp 300–9.
45 Morgan, *Salvator Rosa*, preface, p iv.
46 Ibid., p 47.
47 Helen Langdon, in an unpublished talk to the British Academy on 14 March 2001.

10 'The Mingled Beauties of Exalting Greece'

1   Boswell, *Grand Tour*, p. 30: 10 January 1765.
2   Hinde, p 35: 23 October 1819.
3   Jones, *Letters*, ii, p 58: to T. L. Peacock, Naples, 17 or 18 December 1818; ii, p 92: to T. L. Peacock, Rome, 6 April 1819.
4   M. Shelley, *Collected Tales*, p 30.
5   James Thomson, 'Summer', *The Seasons*.
6   Rogers, *Italy*, p 105.
7   Jameson, p 98.
8   Smollett: letter xxviii, 5 February 1765.
9   Morgan, *Italy*, ii, pp 173–4.
10 Haskell and Penny, pp 485–91. Also Brand, p 130.
11 Hinde, p 45: 17 November 1819. Blessington, *Idler*, p 221: 28 June 1823, found her 'immeasurably inferior'.
12 Helène Demoriane, 'Canova: Napoléon l'admirait', *Connaissance des Arts*, 209 (July 1969), p 27.
13 See Chapter 8, above, p. 142.
14 Young, p 207.
15 Quoted by Chloe Chard, 'Emma Hamilton and Corinne', in Hornsby, pp 164–5.
16 Lori-Ann Touchette, 'Emma Hamilton and Her Attitudes', ibid., pp 123–46.
17 Jane Stabler, 'Figuring Disorder: Women Travellers in Italy, *Journal of Anglo-Italian Studies*, 6 (2001), p 56, picks up on a thesis by E. A. Bohls, *Women Travel Writers and the Language of Aesthetics, 1716–1818* (London 1991).
18 Letter to Wortley Montagu, Rome, 13 January 1841. For the Duchess see Chapter 1, pp 21–2 above.
19 Morgan, *Italy*, i, 405 fn.
20 P. M. S. Dawson, 'Shelley and the Improvvisatore: an unpublished Review', *The Keats–Shelley Bulletin*, 32 (1981), pp 19–29. Shelley never finished the review, which he must have been writing for a local journal.
21 Eaton, iii, pp 259–60.
22 Medwin, *Conversations with Lord Byron*, p 137. The style was declamatory in loose or rhyming verse, lending itself to the rhythms of the Italian language, and usually accompanied by music. Eaton, iii, p 262.

23 Byron, *Letters and Journals*, vii, pp 51–2: to John Cam Hobhouse, 3 March 1820.
24 M. Shelley, *Letters*, i, p 171: to Leigh Hunt, 29 December 1820; p 182: to Claire Clairmont, 21 January 1821. Forsyth, 1816 edition, pp 49–5.
25 Eaton, iii, pp 266–7.
26 Morgan, *Italy*, ii, pp 248–9 fn.
27 Hinde; p 43: 12 November 1819; Eustace, ii, p 141.
28 Dolan, pp 286–8. His subjects were Lady Anna Miller (1741–81), *Letters from Italy* (3 vols, 1776–7), and Mariana Starke (1762?–1838), *Letters from Italy between the Years 1792 and 1798* (2 vols, 1800).
29 Piozzi, *Observations*, p 33.
30 Piozzi, *Thraliana*, ii, p 636: 1 March 1785.
31 Ibid., p 52.
32 Eaton, iii, p 219; Morgan, *Italy*, ii, p 231.
33 Quoted in Morgan, *Italy*, i, p 91.
34 Jones, *Maria Gisbourne, and Edward E. Williams*, p 128: 19 December 1821.
35 Morgan, *Italy*, i, p 445.
36 M. Shelley, *Collected Tales*, p 243.
37 Morgan, *Italy*, ii, p 160.
38 Ibid., ii, 49.
39 Morgan, *Rosa*, pp 9–10.
40 Byron, footnote to *The Two Foscari*, Act 3, scene 1, claiming that they had both spontaneously and independently dubbed Venice 'an ocean Rome'.
41 Morgan, *Italy*, i, pp 85, 87 and 98.
42 Ibid., iii, p 26 and ii, p 15
43 Ibid., iii. pp 5 and 25.
44 Ibid., iii, p 194.
45 Ibid., ii, p 9.
46 Ibid., i, p 112.
47 Ibid., iii, pp 42–3 fn.
48 Ibid., i, p 116 fn
49 Ibid., ii, p 59.
50 Ibid., iii, p 406, writing particularly of Venice.
51 Ibid., ii, pp 345–9.
52 J. Stabler, 'Figuring Disorder, Women Travellers in Italy', *Journal of Anglo-Italian Studies*, 6 (2001), pp 113–22, 116. See Chapter 3, pp 48–50 above.
53 Eaton, i, p 232 and pp 126–7. Charlotte Eaton was almost a professional residentialist. An earlier sojourn in Belgium had produced its *Narrative*, with a graphic account of the Battle of Waterloo, used by Thackeray for *Vanity Fair*.
54 Brand, p 24.
55 Gibbon, chapter lxx, para 1.
56 Ugo Foscolo, *Essay on Petrarch* (1823), quoted by Brand, p 101.
57 Byron, *Letters and Journals*, iii, p 240: Journal, 17–18 December 1814.
58 Elizabeth Barrett Browning, 'Casa Guidi Windows', 1, strophes 20–6.

11 'Thou Crimson Herald of the Dawn'

1 *Oxford Book of Italian Verse*, (1952), p 364.
2 Morgan, *Italy*, i, pp 453–4, 464.
3 Ibid., i, p 491.
4 Ibid., i, p 293.
5 Dickens, *Pictures of Italy*, 'Through Bologna and Ferrara'.
6 Jones, *Letters*, ii, p 112: to Leigh Hunt, Leghorn, 20 (?) August 1819.
7 Morgan, *Italy*, i, p 295; Dickens, *Pictures of Italy*, 'Genoa and its Neighbourhood'.
8 Ibid., 'To Parma, Modena and Bologna'.
9 Ibid., 'Through Bologna and Ferrara' and 'Rome'.
10 Hunt, *Autobiography*, p 451. Forsyth, 1816 edition, pp 70–1, described its farmers as 'more industrious, intelligent and liberal than their neighbours born to the same sun and soil'.
11 Byron, *Letters and Journals*, v, pp 217–18: to John Murray, 20 April 1817.
12 Byron, *Childe Harold*, Canto IV, stanza liii.
13 Dickens, *Little Dorrit*, chapter 1.
14 It is interesting and disturbing that political forces in Italy today, especially in Milan, believe that this would have been the best solution for modern Italy, towards which they think the unified state should be dissolved by a return to regionalism. The author recalls a conversation with a *custode* of the Corsini gallery in Rome as they shared the view of Garibaldi's statue on the Janiculum: 'Ecco l'uomo chi ha rovinato Italia', by bringing Naples and Sicily into the union.
15 D. Mack Smith, 'Britain and the Italian Risorgimento', *Journal of Anglo-Italian Studies*, 5 (1997), p 84, quoting Cesare Balbo, *Delle Speranze d'Italia* (Capolago 1844), p 21.
16 J. Woodhouse, 'The Rossetti Siblings in the Correspondence of their Father', *The Journal of Anglo-Italian Studies*, 6 (2001), p 203.
17 Segré, p 117.
18 Charles Dickens, *The Uncommercial Traveller* (1868), 'The Italian Prisoner', p 171. The prisoner's name was Carlovero, an improbable Italian name, which could well have been Cavaliero.
19 Barrett Browning, 'Casa Guidi Windows', part I, strophe 1.
20 Ibid., part I, 13.
21 Ibid., part I, 13.
22 Phelan, pp 143–4; Barrett Browning, 'Casa Guidi Windows', part I, 15.
23 Ibid., part II, 5–6, 10–12.
24 Ibid., part II, strophe 17.
25 Phelan, p 149.
26 Barrett Browning, 'Casa Guidi Windows', part II, 21.
27 Morley, I, p 291.
28 This well-known quotation originated with one of Gladstone's Italian interlocutors.
29 Ernest Jones, the Chartist leader, was sentenced in 1848 to two years in solitary confinement, during which he wrote an epic, *The Revolt of Hindustan*, modelled on Shelley's *Revolt of Islam*.

30 Ashley, *Palmerston*, ii, p 179.
31 Fagan, ii, pp 102–3.
32 *Clelia*, by Giuseppe Garibaldi, a novel subtitled *The Rule of the Monk (Rome in the Nineteenth Century)*, was published in 1868. Ridley, pp 592–4.

12 Finale

1 Carradine, p 32 The trilogy consists of *Garibaldi and the Defence of the Roman Republic*, (1907), *Garibaldi and the Thousand* (1909) and *Garibaldi and the Making of Italy* (1911).
2 Emilia actually joins a night-time chorus of nightingales one English summer evening. George Meredith, *Sandra Belloni*, chapter lviii, 'Frost on the May Night', pp 594–5.
3 George Meredith, *Vittoria*, chapter xx, 'The Opera of Camilla', p 230.
4 Was Meredith consciously remembering Elizabeth Barrett Browning's sardonic jest in 'Casa Guidi Windows', part II, 7, that liberty was more than the 'trilling on an opera stage / of "libertà" to bravos'?
5 Meredith, *Vittoria*, chapter ix, 'In Verona', p 82.
6 Ibid., chapter iv, 'Ammiani's Intercession', p 31.
7 Ibid., chapter ix, 'In Verona', pp 86–7.
8 Ibid., chapter xxvii, 'A New Ordeal', p 324. Cairns, ii, p 173.
9 Ibid., chapter xxvi, 'A Duel in the Pass', p 315.
10 Segré, p 129.
11 Bemjamin Disraeli, *Lothair*, chapter liv.
12 Ibid., chapter lii.
13 The French in fact never left Rome until the outbreak of the Franco-Prussian War in 1870, when they were recalled to defend France. The Vatican Council declared the pope infallible on 18 July, three day after the war broke out. The withdrawal of the French garrison began on 4 August and the 'Sardinians' (as Augustus Hare persisted in calling the Italian government) marched into Rome on 20 September
14 Disraeli, *Lothair*, chapter lxi.
15 I do not include Hilaire Belloc who, despite his old-fashioned Roman Catholicism, was not really interested in Italy at all. In his *Path to Rome* (1907) Rome hardly figures. Belloc gets there in the end but with no sense of triumphalism, as if Rome, now accessible to everyone and capital of a free Italy had no particular resonance for the English. Pemble, 'Rome and Cenrality', in Hopkins and Stamp, pp 37–8.
16 Eileen Bigland, *Ouida, the Passionate Victorian* (London 1915), p 115.
17 E. M. Forster only suggests a stabbing, though the blow was fatal. He was concerned with the effect of the incident on Lucy, rather than with making any reflection on the Italian character. The passage, however, suggests that such a scene was not to be unexpected, even in so civilised a city as Florence.
18 Henry James, *Daisy Miller* (1879), *Portrait of a Lady* (1881), *The Wings of the Dove* (1902), *The Golden Bowl* (1904).
19 E. M. Forster, *Where Angels Fear to Tread*, chapter 2.

20 Tiberius, about whom legends abound, was believed to be, in reality, a retiring, rather dull, imperial administrator, not a hedonist at all.
21 For an example of this dual role see Artemis Cooper, *Writing at the Kitchen Table: the Biography of Elizabeth David*, (London 1999), pp 64–9.
22 Compton Mackenzie's *Vestal Fire* (1927) was a kinder satire than that of Douglas, but expatriates had by then become odd, odder indeed than the natives.

PICTURE CREDITS

1 Courtesy *Ente Provinciale di Turismo di Roma*
2 Courtesy Galleria Borghese
3, 5, 7, 8 Courtesy The Keats–Shelley Memorial House
6 National Gallery, London
10 Mary Evans Picture Library
12 Capella San Severo, Naples
13 Courtesy Teatro San Carlo
16 Musée de Beaux Arts, Besançon

BIBLIOGRAPHY

Where there are several editions of the nineteenth-century texts, I have included in parentheses the edition that I have used.

Acton, Harold, *The Bourbons of Naples*, London 1956

— —, *The Last Bourbons of Naples, 1825–1861*, London 1961

Addison, Joseph, *Letters from Italy*, London 1726

Ashley, E., *Life of Lord Palmerston*, London 1879

Azeglio, Massimo d', *I Mei Ricordi* (trans. as *Things I Remember*, E. R. Vincent), Oxford 1966

Bargellini, Piero, *Fra Diavolo*, Milan 1931, 1975

Bate, W. J., *John Keats*, London 1979

Birkenhead, Sheila, *Illustrious Friends*, London 1965

— —, *Against Oblivion, a Life of Joseph Severn*, London 1943

Blennerhassett, Lady, *The Papacy and the Catholic Church*, Cambridge Modern History, Volume X, 1907

Blessington, Marguerite, *The Idler in Italy*, Paris 1839

— —, *The Magic Lantern*, London 1822–3

— —, *Conversations of Lord Byron*, London 1834

Boswell, James, *Boswell on the Grand Tour: Italy, Corsica and France, 1765–66,* (ed. F. Brady and F. A. Pottle), London 1955

— —, *The Life of Samuel Johnson*, 2 vols, Oxford, 1933

Bowron, E. P., and Rishell, J. R., *Art in Rome in the Eighteenth Century*, Philadelphia 2000

Bradford, Sarah, *Disraeli*, London 1982

Brand, C. P., *Italy and the English Romantics, The Italianate Fashion in Early Nineteenth Century England,* London 1957

Brosses, Charles de, *Lettres familières écrites d'Italie en 1739 et 1740*, Paris 1799

Brydone, Patrick, *A Tour through Sicily and Malta*, 2 vols, London 1775

Budden, Julian, *Verdi*, London 1985

Burgess, Anthony, *Abba, Abba*, London 1977

Butler, Marilyn, *Romantics, Rebels and Reactionaries, English Literature and its Background 1760–1830,* Oxford 1981

Byron, Lord, *Letters and Journals* (ed. L. Marchand), vols 1–9, London 1974–90

Cairns, David, *Berlioz, Volume I, The Making of an Artist*, London 1989

— —, *Berlioz, Volume II, Servitude and Greatness*, London 1999

Carlyle, Thomas, *On Heroes, Hero-worship and the Hero in History*, London 1893

Carradine, David, *G. M. Trevelyan: A Life in History*, London 1992

Carsaniga, Giovanni, *Leopardi*, Edinburgh 1977

Cavaliero, Roderick, *Strangers in the Land; the Rise and Fall of the British Indian Empire*, London 2002

Chateaubriand, René de, *Mémoires d'Outre Tombe* (ed. E. Biré), 6 vols, Paris 1880

Church, E. M., *Sir Richard Church in Italy and Greece*, London 1895

Churchill, Kenneth, *Italy and English Literature, 1764–1930*, London 1980

Clairmont, Claire, *Journals* (ed. M. K. Stocking), Cambridge, MA, 1968

Clay, Edith, ed., *Lady Blessington at Naples*, London 1979

Colvin, Sidney, *Letters of John Keats to his Family and Friends*, London 1928

Crabb Robinson, Henry, *Diary, Reminiscences and Correspondence* (ed. T. Sadler), 2 vols, Boston 1869

Crocco, Augusto, *Breve Nota di quel che si vede in casa del Principe di Sansevero*, Naples n. d.

Cubberley, T., and Hermann, L., *The Twilight of the Grand Tour, a Catalogue of the Drawing by James Hakewill in the British School at Rome Library*, Rome 1995

Deakin, R., *Flora of the Colosseum in Rome*, London 1873

Dickens, Charles, *Pictures from Italy*, 1844

– –, *Little Dorrit*, 1855–7

– –, *The Uncommercial Traveller*, 1868

Dolan, Brian, *Ladies of the Grand Tour*, London 2001

Donelan, Charles, *Romanticism and Male Fantasy in Byron's Don Juan: a Marketable Vice*, Basingstoke 2000

Eastlake, Elizabeth, *The Life of John Gibson RA*, London 1870

Eaton, Charlotte, *Rome in the Nineteenth Century … in a series of letters written during a residence at Rome in the years 1817 and 1818*, 3 vols, London and Edinburgh 1820

Eustace, J. C., *A Classical Tour of Italy*, 4 vols, London 1821

Evelyn, John, *Diary*, 2 vols, Everyman edition, London

Fagan, L., *Life of Sir Anthony Panizzi*, 2 vols, London 1880

Foreman, A., *Georgiana, Duchess of Devonshire*, London 1998

Forster, John, *The Life of Charles Dickens*, 2 vols, Everyman edition, London 1927

– –, *Walter Savage Landor*, 2 vols, London 1869

Forsyth, Joseph, *Remarks on Antiquities, Arts and Letters During an Excursion in Italy, in the Years 1802 and 1803*, London 1813; 1816 (ed. Keith Crook, London 2001)

Foster, Roy, *Mr Paddy and Mr Punch*, London 1993

Frayling, Christopher, *Vampyres*, London 1991

Gamer, Michael, *Romanticism and the Gothic*, Cambridge, 2000

Gay, Peter, *The Naked Heart*, London 1995

Gell, Sir William, *Sir Walter Scott in Italy* (ed. J. Coran), Edinburgh 1957

Gibbon, Edward, *The Decline and Fall of the Roman Empire*, 6 vols, London 1776–88

Godwin, William, *Memoirs of the Author of a Vindication of the Rights of Women*, Harmondsworth 1987

Gotch, Rosamund Brunel, *Maria, Lady Callcot*, London 1937

Graham, Maria, *Three Months in the Mountains East of Rome*, London 1820

Guiton, D., and Crook, N., *Shelley's Venomed Melody*, Cambridge 1986

Haskell, F., and Penny, N., *L'Antico nella Storia del Gusto*, Turin 1984

Henty, George, *Out with Garibaldi*, London 1901

Hilton, Tim, *John Ruskin, the Early Years*, Newhaven and London 1985

Hinde, Mrs C. A., *Journal of a Tour Made in Italy in the Winter of 1819 and 1820* (ed. M. Merlini), Geneva 1982

Hobsbawm, E. J., *Bandits*, London 1962

Hornsby, Claire, (ed.), *The Impact of Italy; the Grand Tour and Beyond*, London 2000

Hunt, James Leigh, *Autobiography*, Oxford 1928

– –, *Selected Essays*, Everyman edition, London 1949

Jameson, Anna, *Diary of an Ennuyée*, London 1826

Jenkins, I., and Sloan, K., *Vases and Volcanoes*, London 1996

Johnson, Edgar, *Sir Walter Scott, The Great Unknown*, 2 vols, London 1970

Johnson, Samuel, *The Lives of the Poets, 1779–1781*, 3 vols, Everyman edition, London 1953

Jones, Frederick L., (ed.), *The Letters of Percy Bysshe Shelley, Volume 2: Shelley in Italy*, Oxford 1964

– –, *Maria Gisborne and Edward E. Williams: their Journals and Letters*, Norman, OK, 1951

Keates, J., *Stendhal*, London 1984

Kitson, Michael, *Salvator Rosa*, London 1973

Lamb, Charles, *Letters*, 2 vols, Everyman edition, London n. d.

Lampedusa, G. T. de, *Il Gattopardo (The Leopard)*, Milan 1960

Las Cases, *Souvenirs de Napoléon 1er*, Paris 1935

Lees-Milne, James, *The Bachelor Duke: William Spencer Cavendish, 6th Duke of Devonshire, 1790–1858*, London 1991

Leopardi, Giacomo, *Operette Morali*, Milan 1976, 1994

– –, *Poesie*, Florence 1976

– –, *Epistolario* (ed. F. Moroncini), 7 vols, Florence 1934–41

– –, 'Zibaldone', in *Pensieri di Varia Filosofia e di Bella Letteratura di, Giacomo Leopardi*, 7 vols, Florence, 1898–1900

Leopardi, Monaldo, *Autobiografia* (ed. Anna Leopardi), Bologna 1993

Lewis, Matthew, *The Monk*, 1796 (Oxford 1989)

Lockhart, J. G., *The Life of Sir Walter Scott*, Everyman edition, London n. d.

Liversidge, M., and Edwards, C., *Imagining Rome: British Artists and Rome in the 19th Century*, London and Bristol 1996

Lonergan, Corinna, *Lorenzo de' Medici: Selected Writings*, Dublin 1992

Lytton, Edward Bulwer, *Rienzi*, 1835 (Everyman edition, London 1911)

– –, *Zanoni*, 1842 (Knebworth edition, London 1874)

Macfarlane, C., *The Lives and Exploits of Bandits and Robbers*, London 1939

Macnaughton, Donald A., *Roscoe of Liverpool*, Birkenhead 1996

Maes, Constantine, *Curiosità Romane*, Rome 1885

Marchand, L. A., *Byron, a Portrait*, London 1970

Martineau, G., *Madame Mère, Napoleon's Mother* (trans. Frances Partridge), London 1978

Matthews, Henry, *The Diary of an Invalid, being the Journal of a Tour in Pursuit of Health in Portugal, Italy, Switzerland and France in the Years 1817, 1818 and 1819*, London 1820

Maurois, André, *Byron* (trans. H. Miles), London 1930

Mavor, Elizabeth, *The Grand Tour of William Beckford*, Harmondsworth 1986

Medwin, Thomas, *The Life of Percy Bysshe Shelley* (ed. H. B. Forman), Oxford 1913

Meredith, George, *Sandra Belloni*, 1864 (Mickelham edition, London 1924)

— —, *Vittoria*, 1864 (Mickelham edition, London 1924)

Moens, W. J. C., *English Travellers and Italian Bandits*, 2 vols, London 1866

Moore, Thomas, *Journal* (ed. P. Quennel), London 1964

Moorman, Mary, *William Wordsworth, The Later Years, 1805–1850*, Oxford 1965

Morgan, Lady Sydney, *Italy*, 3 vols, London 1821

— —, *Life and Times of Salvator Rosa*, London 1823 (1855)

Morley, J., *The Life of William Ewart Gladstone*, 2 vols, London 1908

Origo, Iris, *Leopardi, A Study in Solitude*, London 1953

Peacock, Thomas Love, *Crotchet Castle*, 1831

— —, *Letters* (ed. N. Joukovsky), 2 vols, Oxford 2001

Pemble, John, *The Mediterranean Passion: Victorians and Edwardians in the South*, Oxford 1987

— —, 'Rome and Centrality from Shelley to Lutyens', in A. Hopkins and G. Stamp (eds), *Lutyens Abroad*, London 2002

Perceval, George, *A History of Italy*, 2 vols, London 1825

Phelan, Joe, 'Elizabeth Barret Browning's "Casa Guidi Windows" and the Italian National Uprising of 1847–9', *Journal of Anglo-Italian Studies*, 3 (1993)

Piozzi, Hester Lynch (Mrs Thrale) *Observations and Reflections Made in the Course of a Journey through France, Italy and Germany*, Michigan 1967

— —, *Thraliana, the Diary of Hester Lynch Piozzi, 1776–1809* (ed. K. C. Balderstone), 2 vols, Oxford 1951

da Ponte, Lorenzo, *Memoirs*, (trans. and ed. A. Shephard), London 1929

Powell, Cecilia, *Italy in the Age of Turner: the Garden of the World*, London 1998

Praz, Mario, 'Ludovico Ariosto', *Atti del Convegno su L. A.*, Accademia dei Lincei, Rome 1975

Radcliffe, Ann, *A Sicilian Romance*, 1790 (Folio edition, London 1987)

— —, *The Mysteries of Udolpho*, 1794 (Oxford 1966)

— —, *The Italian*, 1797 (Oxford 1978)

Ridley, Jasper, *Garibaldi*, London 1994

Rogers, Samuel, *The Italian Journal* (ed. J. R. Hale), London 1956

— —, *Italy: a Poem*, London 1836

Roscoe, William, *The Life of Lorenzo de' Medici*, 9th edition, London 1847

Rosselli, John, *Lord William Bentinck: the Making of a Liberal Imperialist, 1774–1839*, Brighton 1974

Runciman, Steven, *The Sicilian Vespers*, Cambridge 1958

Ruskin, John, *Praeterita*, Oxford 1978

— —, *Modern Painters*, Volume V, London 1856

Scott, Walter, *Journal*, Volume I, London, 1890

— —, *Rob Roy*, 1817

— —, 'The Two Drovers', *Chronicles of the Canongate* 1827

Segré, Carlo, *Italy, Cambridge Modern History, Volume X*, Cambridge 1907

Sella, Domenico, *Italy in the Seventeenth Century*, London and New York 1997

Seymour, Miranda, *Mary Shelley*, London 2000

Sharp, W., *The Life and Letters of Joseph Severn*, London 1892

Shelley, Mary Wollstonecraft, *Journals, 1814–1844* (eds P. R. Feldmann and D. Scott-Kilvert), 2 vols, Oxford 1987

— —, *Letters* (ed. B. Bennett), 3 vols, Baltimore 1980

— —, *Collected Tales and Stories* (ed. Charles E. Robinson), Baltimore 1976

— —, *Rambles in Germany and Italy in 1840, 1842 and 1843*, 2 vols, London 1844

— —, *Valperga*, 3 vols, London 1823

Sismondi, J. C. L., *The History of the Italian Republics*, Everyman edition, London 1907

Smith, Denis Mack, *Mazzini*, Newhaven, CT, 1994

Smollett, Tobias, *Travels through France and Italy*, 1766

Southey, Robert, *Letters* (ed. M. Fitzgerald), Oxford 1912

Spark, Muriel, *Mary Shelley*, London, 1993

Springer, Carolyn, *The Marble Wilderness: Ruins and Representation in Italian Romanticism, 1775–1850*, Cambridge 1987

Staël, Germaine de, *Corinne* (trans. S. Raphael), Oxford 1998

Stendhal, (Henri Beyle), *Promenades dans Rome, Paris 1829* (trans. as *A Roman Journal*, Haakon Chevalier), London 1959

— —, *Life of Rossini* (trans R. N. Coe), London 1956

Sultana, Donald, *Samuel Taylor Coleridge in Malta and Sicily*, Oxford 1969

Strutt, A. J., *A Pedestrian Tour through Calabria and Sicily, London 1844* (ed. Guido Pucci), Catanzaro 1961

Thackeray, W. M., *The Newcomes*, 1853–5

Tompkins, J. M. S., *The Popular Novel in England, 1770–1800*, London 1932

Trevelyan, George Otto, *The Life and Letters of Lord Macaulay*, 2 vols, Oxford 1932

van Thal, Herbert, *Landor, a Biographical Anthology*, London 1973

Vassallo, Peter, *Byron: the Italian Literary Experience*, London 1884

Weinberg, A. M., *Shelley's Italian Experience*, Basingstoke and London 1992

Wilton, Andrew, *The Great Age of British Watercolours, 1750–1880*, London 1993

— —, *Turner*, London 1974

Wordsworth, William, *Letters, The Middle Years*, 2 vols, London 1937

Young, Desmond, *The Fountain of the Elephants*, London 1959

INDEX